D0403135

GREAT PROMO PIECES

OTHER WILEY BOOKS BY HERMAN HOLTZ

GREAT PROMO PIECES

Create Your Own Brochures, Broadsides, Ads, Flyers, and Newsletters That Get Results

Herman Holtz

WILEY

John Wiley & Sons, Inc.

New York • Chichester • Brisbane • Toronto • Singapore

Publisher: Stephen Kippur
Editor: Katherine Schowalter
Managing Editor: Ruth Greif
Editing, Design, and Production: Publication Services, Inc.

This publication is designed to provide accurate and authoritative information in regard to the subject matter covered. It is sold with the understanding that the publisher is not engaged in rendering legal, accounting, or other professional service. If legal advice or other expert assistance is required, the services of a competent professional person should be sought. FROM A DECLARATION OF PRINCIPLES JOINTLY ADOPTED BY A COMMITTEE OF THE AMERICAN BAR ASSOCIATION AND A COMMITTEE OF PUBLISHERS.

Library of Congress Cataloging-in-Publication Data

Holtz, Herman.
   Great promo pieces : create your own brochures, broadsides, ads,
   flyers, and newsletters that get results / Herman Holtz.
     p. cm.
   ISBN 0-471-63224-4. ISBN 0-471-63227-9 (pbk.)
   1. Sales promotion. 2. Advertising layout and typography.
  3. Business writing. 4. Broadsides. 5. Advertising fliers.
  6. Newsletters. I. Title
  HF5438.5.H65 1988
  659.13'2--dc19   88-14253
                                       CIP

Printed in the United States of America
 89 10 9 8 7 6 5 4 3 2

Preface

Probably no society on this planet works at marketing—advertising and selling—more energetically or enthusiastically than does ours in the United States. We are a nation of hucksters. Apparently, it is almost instinctive with us.

There is virtually no new development that is not immediately considered a potential advertising medium. Radio and TV grew immediately and almost automatically from their cradles into commercial life as major marketing media. Book matches, given away freely by many businesses, as well as sold in stores, almost invariably (and inevitably) carry advertising messages, as do many other items given away precisely for that reason, i.e., to deliver a sales message. The manufacture and marketing of pens, key chains, notebooks, calendars, desk pads, memo pads, and an almost endless variety of other items as "advertising specialties"— items inscribed with sales messages—is itself a large industry or subindustry of advertising and marketing. Buses and taxicabs are plastered with signs, and subway station platforms exhibit billboards to waiting passengers, while New York's Times Square is as well known for its millions of candlepower of illuminated and flashing electrical billboards as for anything else. (It is, perhaps, the only thing about Times Square and New York City that has not changed.)

Today, if you travel the back roads in rural areas you can still find a few rusting Burma Shave signs and red barns painted with chewing-tobacco advertisements, relics of an earlier era. And for a time, even early aircraft —wood-and-canvas biplanes and blimps—became advertising media, with skywriting, illuminated signs, and trailing banners. (There is still a bit of this airborne advertising via trailing banners to be seen at such seaside resorts as Atlantic City, New Jersey, and Ocean City, Maryland.) And only legislation resulting from public protest has prevented the new superhighways from becoming an almost endless procession of billboards.

Today, there are three major advertising media: broadcast—radio and TV, especially the latter; print—newspapers and magazines; and direct mail. Newspapers have been very much on the decline in recent decades, under the onslaught of radio and, especially, TV. Even the magazine industry is vastly different from what it was a few years ago, with numerous new periodicals flashing brilliantly for a time and vanishing after brief life, to be replaced by even newer candidates. Nevertheless, print advertising remains a major force in marketing and a mainstay of the advertising industry.

In the meanwhile, mail-order and direct mail have grown rapidly as advertising and marketing media. (Although many think of the two terms as synonymous, mail-order and direct mail are not truly identical, as examination will show presently.) Mail-order is alive and well, but it is direct mail, that marketing methodology that creates the load of "junk mail" most of us see in our mailboxes every day, that is burgeoning. Among other things, it supports, as the journals of the direct-mail trade, a thick biweekly tabloid, a monthly smooth-paper magazine, and a number of newsletters, as well as more than a few books, while it also contributes to many other marketing and advertising trade journals.

This small book, then, represents a most ambitious effort, an effort to provide a guide to developing all the myriad written materials of advertising and marketing—the "sell copy" of all kinds for the entire vast advertising and marketing world, that is. The focus is therefore necessarily not on the details of each medium, nor even on the many kinds of special devices available to support and reinforce the sales effort, but on the central factors that make the difference in all sell copy: the effective means and methods available to a copy writer for capturing attention, arousing and sustaining interest, generating desire to buy, and moving the prospect to action. For in the end, that is the true objective of this book—a guide to *writing* sell copy that works—copy that persuades prospects to become buyers.

Therefore, in terms of this book and its purpose, the differences between print advertising, mail-order, direct mail, TV and radio commercials, and the many other media and avenues of marketing are superficial. There are verities of advertising and marketing that do not change, regardless of the medium, the product or service being sold, and the many other variables involved: for example, selling—all selling, in every situation—requires proper motivation. These principles are immutable; the differences are entirely in scale, in adaptation to each need, and in method of presentation, not differences in kind or in principle.

It is therefore the strategy here to first identify the basic principles, types of motivation, and basic structure of the essential sales presentation, and then proceed to demonstrate the various applications and adaptations. In so doing, I have tried earnestly to address the practical problems of producing the physical product—e.g., the editorial processes and the production processes. And in addressing that aspect of the work, I have tried to introduce a guide to the latest relevant technologies, which are based on the already ubiquitous desktop computer and the new desktop publishing hardware and software.

A word of reassurance is in order here: although such terms as "user friendly" and "computer literate" have vanished from the popular press coverage and everyday language of the modern computer revolution, many lay people have as much apprehension as ever toward confronting or being confronted by the desktop computer. This is at least partly due (although I think personally that it is largely due) to the murky, ponderous, and heavily technical prose of many computer professionals and even computer aficionados writing what purport to be discussions in lay language. Far too often these treatises prove to be minefields of technical jargon and journeys into dark, arcane areas of computer technology. But have no fear of that here: I have no desire to exhibit a sophisticated knowledge of computer technology, nor do I even possess such knowledge. I am a reasonably experienced user of computers, and I am compelled to explain what I know and what I recommend to others in the simplest of lay language, lest I reveal the depth of my ignorance! You will therefore have no trouble learning what little I know of the subject and becoming at least as "computer literate" as I am.

That said, and, I hope, your fears allayed, let us proceed.

Herman Holtz
Wheaton, MD

Contents

GREAT PROMO PIECES

CHAPTER ONE

Everyone Markets

We are all marketers, some of us consciously and full-time, others of us unconsciously and only occasionally. But humans cannot live together in any society—not even two humans in marriage—without marketing to each other.

■ Establishing a Few Ground Rules

Marketing is almost as popular a subject in the business world as is management. There are also probably as many opinions on what marketing is and how it ought to be conducted as there are on what management is and how it ought to be conducted. That means that most of the terms used— *marketing, sales, advertising,* and *promotion,* for example—are less than precise and unequivocal. These and many related terms encountered in the business world tend often to mean what the individual wants them to mean. That makes it necessary to discuss these terms briefly and understand what they mean, at least as used in these pages. Here, we will deal in general concepts and principles. Later, in discussing specific practices and products, we will have to introduce new terms, including jargon such as "response device" and "broadside." In such cases, it will often be necessary to explain others' definitions of those jargon terms, for even within the world of frequent advertisers and advertising professionals, definitions are far from being uniform or standardized, and those definitions make an important difference in whether we do or do not understand each other.

This first chapter is thus intended to serve the purpose expressed: whatever these terms mean elsewhere, even to other advertising specialists, and whatever are the concepts and principles expressed elsewhere for carrying out the functions referred to, let us agree on our own set of ground rules as introduced in this opening chapter. (I will introduce and define for our purposes many other terms as we proceed through other chapters.)

■ What Is Marketing? Is the Definition Important?

Even professional marketers often use the word *marketing* interchangeably with the word *selling*, although the two terms are not truly identical in meaning. The confusion is easy to understand because the end-goal is the same in each case. The goal is to persuade others to do something. In the majority of cases—in those cases that match the images which the very word *marketing* conjures up—the goal is to persuade others to *buy* something—to surrender money for goods or services. But marketing is actually far broader than that, and it is not always money that the marketer wants from the prospect. For example, military organizations engaged in recruiting new enlistees and persuading incumbents to reenlist are marketing; they want recruits, not money. So are all other membership organizations pursuing new members and renewals of existing memberships; they want both new members and money—membership fees. That is, recruiting is marketing. People in pursuit of *gifts* of money (donations)—political parties and candidates, charities, nonprofit groups, and others conducting fund drives—are marketing. Candidates soliciting votes are marketing. Organizations recruiting volunteer workers are marketing. Publishers of periodicals soliciting articles from writers are marketing. Individuals seeking jobs—you, too—are marketing. Anyone trying to sell anything to another person—even a husband trying to sell his wife on buying a new car and the wife trying to sell the husband on mowing the lawn this Sunday—are marketing. Make no mistake about it. Selling is the effort to persuade specifically, to get the money, agreement, the name on the dotted line, the pledge, or some other objective; marketing is the planning, the strategy formulation, the conceiving of sales arguments, the design of the sales campaign, and many other elements that make up and support—underpin—the sales effort.

But do all these other kinds of marketing really result in selling per se? Of course they do; persuading others is always selling, whether it is a political idea, a vacuum cleaner, or a donation to a charity. And making sales, even those that do not include the trading of goods and services for money, is the *objective* of marketing. But the generic term *sales* refers to the actual program and efforts to persuade prospects to order, surrender money, sign up, or otherwise agree to the sale; it is, in fact, a *part* of marketing, the final act. But there are many acts that go before that final one, acts that are necessary preliminaries to the sales effort. They include advance planning and the development of many kinds of sales materials and special promotions. Special promotions may include participation in trade shows, sponsoring contests, and launching broad publicity campaigns, among other things.

All of these special promotions require the development of many kinds of material in addition to the classic need for media advertising copy. Among the many other kinds of sales materials used for these programs are the usual advertising copy for print media, sales letters, brochures, flyers, posters, newsletters, releases, and scripts for broadcast commercials.

■ Sales versus Advertising

If there is a tendency to consider sales and marketing identical functions and synonymous terms, the problem does not exist with regard to sales and advertising. They are generally accepted as distinctively different from each other, both as terms and as functions. Still, the functions are obviously closely related to each other. Advertising is itself an element of marketing, and its direct objective is sales or at least the support of sales efforts. And yet, when you begin to dissect and analyze sales and advertising functions, you discover that the principles are almost exactly the same, except for the obvious limitations that are inherent in each case. Too, if sales activities are constrained, shaped, and guided by circumstances and conditions, so is advertising so constrained, shaped, and guided by surrounding circumstances.

In short, it soon becomes apparent that advertising is, in effect, an alternative form of sales activity, as well as a sales-support service. There is, in fact, no principle of selling that does not apply equally to advertising. The reverse is also true. This leads me to the opinion that advertising is written salesmanship. I find this a most convenient and useful view, as I think you will too.

■ Promotion

We use the term *promotion* or *sales promotion* in a dual sense. The terms are used to refer to general marketing and advertising campaigns, but it is also used to refer to PR and publicity activity. For the sake of clarity in communication, conventional marketing, advertising, and sales activity will be referred to in these pages by those names, and the term *promotion*, with or without adjectives, will be used to refer to other kinds of marketing and sales effort, those that I will describe as among the functions of PR or public relations.

■ PR

PR—public relations—is another term about which there seems to be much confusion. Despite what the initials PR stand for, it is directed to generating favorable publicity at least as much as it is to other activities that might be described as public relations. In fact, many people think of PR only in terms of efforts to gain what amounts to free advertising— publicity—through the news media. And to be honest, in many cases the major emphasis and bulk of PR effort is so directed, even justifiably so, in some cases. However, literally defined, PR includes all activity that affects the image of the principals and all efforts to create and sustain a favorable image. Among those activities are the publishing of free newsletters; sponsoring sports teams, community activities, awards, contests, and other activities; and being active in trade associations and professional societies.

■ Media

Media is not a precise term. It is a collective term, and it has multiple denotations and connotations. It can be defined broadly as the channels of sending forth sales messages. But when we consider the options available to us in classifying or sort-ordering media, we begin to see the problems.

One term we encounter immediately, for example, is *print media*. Taken literally, that term would include all direct mail and even much of PR, since they depend heavily on printed materials. However, the term is used generally and most commonly to refer to all kinds of periodicals that accept advertising, and we shall use it here in that meaning only.

Today, for reasons that ought to be obvious to everyone, the other major medium is *broadcast media*, and that refers much more to TV than to radio. Cable TV backers have made a determined effort to make cable TV a major advertising medium, and have made significant advances in that direction. However, at the time of this writing it is commercial TV broadcasting that attracts the bulk of broadcast advertising dollars. There is, of course, an uncomplicated explanation for this: commercial TV reaches a much greater audience than does cable TV at present. This fact is not likely to change, as long as viewers must subscribe and pay monthly fees for cable TV in contrast and in competition with free TV. Cost is always a major factor, and cable TV is expensive. Many people will always find that the additional programming on cable TV is not worth the cost.

The broad classification of media into only two categories, print and broadcast, is suitable for our purposes only as "openers"—as generalizations. These definitions soon prove to be much too all-encompassing to serve the practical needs of planning and executing sales and advertising campaigns. We find it necessary to seek more specific definitions of media. Almost everything we must plan and do in sales and advertising drives this lesson home. In fact, a brief look at media costs alone, for example, illustrates why this is true.

Media Costs

Costs for space and time in print and broadcast media are in proportion to the size of the audience reached. Newspapers and magazines claim specific circulation figures. These are usually the number of copies sold, although the publishers also claim additional readership or circulation, under the theory that more than one individual reads each copy of the periodical. They often tend to claim, for purposes of setting advertising space rates, as many as three or four readers per copy paid for, thereby tripling and even quadrupling their claimed circulation.

Calculating audience size—"circulation"—for radio and TV is a totally different and far more difficult thing to do. For one thing, radio and TV broadcasters do not have the convenient evidence of paid circulation upon which to base a claimed audience size. So they are forced to resort to certain surveying methods to estimate audience sizes. These methods sample the general population according to a plan that is supposed to reflect listeners and /or viewers proportionately and so reflect an accurate percentage of the total number of listeners or viewers. Of course, these estimates must be made individually for each program, for audience size varies with different programs, and each tries to maximize its audience size because that is accepted as a mark of its success.

Circulation or Audience Size: Basis for Rates

The premise upon which publishers and broadcasters base their charges for space and air time is, of course, that all readers/listeners/viewers are prospects for whatever the advertiser is offering. Of course, that is simply not the case—it *can not* be true when advertising in some mass medium, such as a daily newspaper or on prime time broadcasting slots that attract a large, general audience. And so before opting for advertising to that general audience, advertisers must consider how popular the interest is likely to be in what is being offered. If it is a food product and one that is not specialized to any great degree—butter or bread, for example—presumably a large enough portion of that mass audience will be good prospects to justify the cost. But if items are being sold that are likely to interest only a small fraction of that audience—a sophisticated item of electronic test equipment, for example—most of the advertising dollar is wasted by spending it on coverage in a mass medium. That is, the advertisers will be paying for a great deal of circulation or audience that is of no use to them. A more suitable medium than a daily newspaper or general-interest magazine is needed so that a reasonably large portion of the audience for which advertisers pay are truly prospects for what they are selling.

Selecting Media

In choosing print media, you can select specialized periodicals— magazines, tabloids, and newsletters that are normally circulated only within given trades or professions and are not normally found on newsstands and other magazine racks reaching the general public. But even periodicals that are found on newsstands, often appeal to special interests. These are periodicals that appeal to some special interest that a great many people share, such as investments, sports, and health care. If you are selling investment services of some sort, for example, you will almost surely find better prospects among readers of *Money* magazine than among those who read *Mad* magazine. And it is likely that there is among the readers of *Business Week* or *Forbes* a larger proportion of executives, managers, and entrepreneurs than is the case among the readers of the more popular *Newsweek* or *U.S. News & World Report* magazines. (That is, the latter news periodicals are *slanted* to the average consumer, while the others are slanted to executives and entrepreneurs.)

By their very nature, trade journals almost always have much more modest circulation figures than do general-interest periodicals, and so their advertising rates are much lower. Advertising in them, you reach a much smaller readership, but your cost per true prospect is normally far smaller. In fact, you may actually reach a greater number of true prospects.

In the case of broadcast media, you have similar options. It is not by chance that commercials aired during sports events are skewed towards those products and services more likely to appeal to men than to women, nor that products advertised during daytime "soaps" are the reverse—more likely to be of interest to women than to men. These are measures of the audience, the kinds of viewers—prospects—the advertisers want to reach and believe they will reach by advertising during these programs. (But I admit to being surprised to find commercials for fingernail polish and false nails during breaks on professional wrestling programs. This suggests a much larger audience of women than I suspected.)

Newspapers are mass media publications. They are designed for the average consumer, Mr. & Mrs. John Q. Citizen. And yet it is possible to reach specialized audiences with newspaper advertising because large newspapers have "departments" or "sections" for specialized subjects. I read the news section of the *Washington Post*, and I always review the Business and Style sections, in pursuit of material of interest. I rarely read most other special sections included in the daily editions. But if you want to advertise golf clubs or tennis rackets, or even reach men in general, the sports section of any newspaper is probably a good bet. And if you want to reach executives, managers, and business owners, the business or financial pages of the newspaper are a good medium.

What you must not do in making such decisions is use your personal preferences and biases as a guide. I do not normally read the Sports section of any newspaper, but I am atypical in this. It would be a serious mistake for me to assume that most men do not read sports news; many—probably most—do. However, I am surprised to find Lee Nails advertising offered to viewers of professional wrestling, but since the advertising is rather consistent and since I must assume that neither the advertiser nor the agency involved are fools, I must believe that enough women who watch wrestling also use cosmetics enough to justify the cost of the commercials.

Determining such things as the identities—generic identities, that is— of readers, listeners, and viewers is usually not difficult. Those who own the media and set the rates do studies and can usually furnish detailed information on who/what these people are. This is a special kind of demographics, about which subject we will say more later. However, this is a subject of great interest to anyone who advertises, since copy must reach a given prospect who has been clearly identified, if the advertiser has planned with any care.

Which Comes First, the Copy or the Media?

It is easily possible to get into a chicken-egg problem: shall you first select the media/medium and then write copy that is best suited to the advertising media/medium you have selected or shall you write the copy first and then seek the media/medium most appropriate for the copy? There is no standard or pat answer; each case must be decided on its own merits. Still, there is a logical approach possible, and one approach that makes a great deal of sense is to first decide just who are your best prospects, for that is really the important first question to answer. Then you must decide what is the most effective or efficient means for reaching those prospects. As a result of those decisions you can then select the media and begin planning the appropriate copy. In broad outline form, considering only the most basic possibilities, such initial analysis and planning would follow this general line:

I: PROFILE BEST PROSPECT
    A. Male/female/both
    B. Occupation
    C. Economic status
    D. Age
    E. Other characteristics
II: WHERE/HOW TO REACH
    A. Radio (automobile?)
    B. TV, daytime

    C.   TV, prime time

    D.   TV, late night

    E.   Print media

    F.   Direct mail

    G.   Other

This is a greatly simplified explanation. In the actual case, each of these items would have to be analyzed, but this explains the basic principle of first determining just who you wish to reach with your sales message. Other questions are irrelevant until you have settled this one. For example, suppose you wish to sell correspondence courses. Occasionally a senior citizen decides to take up a correspondence course, and sometimes a quite junior citizen—a teen-ager—enters into such a course. But those are exceptions; usually it is young men and women stuck in unskilled and semi-skilled jobs who undertake correspondence courses in the hope of bettering their economic position. Are there exceptions to this? Certainly there are. Today, many people retire early enough in life to pursue a second career, and they are good prospects for correspondence courses. But how do you reach such rather special prospects? That is an important question, one of many that we will address in later chapters.

Of course, these will usually not be the only set of prospects you can define. In many cases you can define several different kinds of prospects for a given product or service. But what makes them different? The difference that is significant to you is only that which makes a difference in how/when/where you approach them with your offer. All prospects that can be approached with the same copy and via the same media—in the same campaign, that is—are not different from each other, as far as you are concerned.

■ A Few Conceptual Considerations

I have already confessed to being something of a maverick. I think differently than do others in advertising and direct mail, because I embrace different concepts and I use different terminology, among other things. But these are not merely differences in nomenclature or terminology; they are true differences in basic concepts about sales and advertising, and so deserve at least brief explanations here.

What Is an *Offer*?

Most advertising and direct-mail professionals apparently use the word *offer* to mean something quite different from what I mean by it in these pages.

Most advertisers apparently use it to refer to what I prefer to think of as the *proposition* or the *terms* of the offer. That is, most think of the offer as encompassing what they promise to deliver and what the respondent is asked to pay for it. In that definition, bonuses, discounts, rebates, free merchandise, credit terms, and other inducements represent "the offer." On the other hand, what the advertiser promises will result from the purchase are "the benefits."

I find it useful to define the offer as what I promise the respondent will occur as a benefit of the purchase—i.e., if I sell a diet plan, my *offer* is to help the client lose weight; if I sell a correspondence course, my offer is to help the respondent better his or her position in life; etc. But the conditions under which I will sell my product or services—cost, terms, bonuses, discounts, refund policy, and/or other conditions—is the *proposition*, and I think of it in that light and context. I hope that later, when we discuss sales and advertising strategies, you will agree that these are helpful concepts, for then you will see how they link with other concepts I wish to impart.

■ AIDA versus Proof and Promise

One of the traditional presentations purporting to explain advertising and sales techniques is known as AIDA, charted as follows:

A - attention
I - interest
D - desire
A - action

I strongly suspect that while there are kernels of truth buried here, some of the words were devised to support the acronym, as they so often are when someone thinks up an oh-so-clever acronym. (I confess to a growing revulsion for acronyms generally, and cutsie-clever ones especially.) In any case, these words are supposed to explain the cumulative and progressive process of selling in this manner:

A - [get the] *attention* [of the reader/listener/viewer]
I - [arouse the] *interest* [of the reader/listener/viewer]
D - [generate the] *desire* [of the reader/listener/viewer to buy]
A - [ask for] *action* [meaning ask for the order]

You can see that some of the terms were contrived, despite the fact that AIDA does list valid objectives. However, my quarrel goes beyond the superficial fault of finding and force-fitting words to the acronym. My problem with the AIDA concept is that it is too much like the ironic advice of Bernard Baruch for success in the stock market: "Buy low and sell high." It describes desired results, but gives no hint of how to achieve them. It does not begin to answer the logical questions that it, in fact, raises: how does one get attention? Arouse interest? Generate desire to buy? Ask for the order? This is a good place to introduce these basics, although we will examine them in greater depth in later pages.

Getting Attention

Doing something deliberate to get attention is usually necessary in this world, when so many things are competing for your prospect's attention. It is especially relevant to all selling via advertising—in print advertising, in direct mail, and radio and TV commercials. But it is also relevant in many face-to-face sales situations, such as in the case of casual browsers in department stores, automobile showrooms, and many other places and occasions. One problem is that it is too often achieved through a device that is totally unrelated to the product or service the seller offers. Or, as an almost equally ill-advised device, something that is so subtle that a reader or viewer cannot make the connection without reading the body copy of the advertisement (or listening to/watching the rest of the commercial). That defeats the very purpose of the headline, illustration, or other device, of course, so that, in effect, there simply is no attention-getting device.

There are two basic means for capturing attention in print advertising. The most common is via a headline, a caption in bold type (usually, although not always) to dominate the advertisement as the first thing the reader's eye is directed to. But many advertisements use illustrations as their most prominent feature—cartoons, photographs, or drawings—above, below, or beside the headline.

A full-page commercial for the Braun electric shaver uses the headline, which is a centered block of rather small type (about 14-point), "4 minutes a day. 28 minutes a week. 2 hours a month. 1,344 hours in a lifetime. Make the best of it." Beneath that modest block of type is a black and white photograph of the shaver, and at the bottom of the page is a final message, the body copy, in small type.

The shaver is not readily recognizable as such. At least I did not find it so. I had to read the body copy to discover what it was. The "headline" was cryptic, as far as I was concerned, until I read the body copy. Nothing in this presentation is truly an attention getter. There are lost opportunities, however: there are some good sales arguments—benefits resulting from better features of design, for example—buried in the body copy. Any of these might have been made into a more useful and less cryptic headline.

TV commercials are often equally guilty of using something sensational but unrelated to capture the viewer's attention. Turning then to a sales argument that has no connection with the headline leaves the viewer rather puzzled, which is hardly what you want to accomplish. One series of TV commercials for a famous perfume opened with a shadowy male figure plunging into a pool, followed by the shadow of a swooping airplane and accompanied by some rather strange music. The connection? I haven't the faintest idea. Subtle? Obviously. Communicative or meaningful to an average viewer? Certainly not.

On the other hand, a Buick automobile is illustrated in a magazine with a photograph under a prominent headline that reads, "The car is Regal. The price is not." Despite the pun, based on the word *regal*, the headline and photo serve their purpose: they are relevant, and they are likely to draw the attention of anyone interested in cars. But why, oh why, do so many copywriters dredge up laborious puns, under the mistaken notion that it demonstrates their wit and makes effective copy? (Rarely are they as appropriate as in this exceptional case.) Many, many advertisements, especially print advertisements, miss the mark widely because the copywriter (or the client!) cannot resist being too-too clever, especially with labored puns.

Arousing Interest

Arousing interest can be helpful only if the interest is in what you are selling. You might explain in print copy that for many years oats were considered excellent food for horses but not suitable for human consumption. Many readers might find that quite interesting. However, if you are selling oatmeal, that arousal of interest alone will do little to help your sale; it is not a sales argument or a reason for buying your oatmeal. You need to go on to point out that the reader's self-interest is served by eating oatmeal because there is a growing medical opinion that oatmeal is helpful in reducing cholesterol levels in the body. That is the true approach to arousing interest: show the reader/listener/viewer why it is in his or her interest to buy and use your product or service. The initial observation about oats and horses is not relevant to the sales argument, but it may help arouse some interest and keep the reader reading, and so serve a good purpose after all. That is a matter of judgment; you must decide whether you benefit from introducing copy that is only indirectly relevant, as in this case.

In short, appeals to self-interest are the most direct and most certain way to arouse interest. But, as we will see in example after example, that is also by far the best way to get attention: nothing captures one's attention as rapidly as something of direct concern to one.

Generating Desire

Now we come to a truly throwaway element in AIDA. It is not easy to distinguish between arousing interest and generating desire, although they may be considered two stages of a process. In the case of oatmeal, pointing out that oatmeal combats cholesterol is the step that should arouse desire to buy and use the product. But, again, note that we are still talking about self-interest, but have now reached the stage of supporting our claim that oatmeal is good for one; we are offering some evidence by reporting a growing medical opinion of benefits to the user, an argument that most people will give credence to and accept.

Asking for Action

It is a well-known phenomenon of human behavior that a great many of us—perhaps most—are somewhat indecisive and procrastinate. Or, at least, many of us will not take the initiative. Professionals in sales know, for example, that even the thoroughly convinced prospect will stand mute if they wait to hear an "I'll take it" or "Write up the order." The most successful salespeople are usually those who ask for the order by a technique often referred to as "assuming the order." This is a method of prodding the customer gently by requiring the customer to say, "No, no. I am not ready to buy yet." Few do, if the salesperson has calculated correctly in deciding that the customer is now convinced and needs only a gentle shove to consummate the sale, and "asking for action" refers to that gentle shove.

In print advertising, asking for the order must be somewhat different, but it is still telling the customer what to do:

Fill out the coupon below and drop it in the mail to get a free sample or more information.

Hurry down to your drugstore today and take advantage of our special two-for-one offer.

Call this toll-free number now and reserve your own copy of _____.

Summation

It is my view that aside from the need to urge the prospect to do something specific, the other three elements of AIDA can be summed up and explained much more effectively—and certainly more definitively—in two words: promise and proof. Let's have a quick look at what this means.

■ Proof and Promise

Actually, we must reverse these two words to discuss their logical order, but the rhythm of our language is such that "proof and promise" is a more fluent and more memorable phrase than "promise and proof." Hence, my choice.

If we talk about appeals to the prospect's self-interest—and, from this point on, we will use the terms *prospect* and/or *customer*, instead of the collective phrase *reader/listener/viewer* that is used earlier—we are actually covering the first two items of the AIDA idea. The *promise* of direct benefits to the prospect, made directly and clearly—for advertising and selling is truly no place for subtlety—accomplishes those first two steps. It gets attention and arouses interest when we make a valid and strong enough appeal to the direct self-interest of the prospect. (*You* is the most important word in selling, and *I* and *me* are the least important words.)

The late Joe Karbo's now well-known headline "THE LAZY MAN'S WAY TO RICHES," is a good example. The headline was stark and plain, at the head of the page, and was followed by a full page of solid blocks of text, with little of the famed "white space." It, the headline, alone got attention and aroused enough interest to persuade millions of prospects to plod through all the small print that followed.

The promise of the headline is clear enough. It implies, quite plainly: read on, and you will learn how to get rich the easy way. And of course the copy that follows continues and expands on that theme, as it should. (The headline should always be a direct lead to the body copy, with a smooth transition, and the ideal headline will contain the clearly stated or clearly implied promise.) Consider the following headlines and decide which ones state or imply a clear promise and are likely to arouse immediate interest:

1. DO YOU MAKE THESE MISTAKES IN ENGLISH?
2. WHY GOLDEN'S IS *BETTER* MARGARINE
3. HOW TO WIN FRIENDS AND INFLUENCE PEOPLE
4. 10 REASONS...
5. HOW I IMPROVED MY MEMORY IN ONE EVENING
6. CARLSON'S RESORT HOTEL FOR YOUR NEXT MEETING
7. DO *YOU* DO ANY OF THESE TEN EMBARRASSING THINGS?
8. OUR MONEY-BACK GUARANTEE
9. WHO ELSE WANTS A SCREEN STAR FIGURE?
10. HASN'T SCRATCHED YET

All the odd-numbered items—1, 3, 5, etc.—were outstandingly successful headlines from the past. All proved themselves in practice. One of them, the first one, ran in magazines successfully and without change for 40 years!

Note that each of them states or clearly implies some promised benefit, while the others are either cryptic or talk about the advertiser and his product, not about benefits to the prospect. Consider, too, the following two headlines, and think about them for a moment before reading on:

FIVE ACRES

FIVE ACRES AND INDEPENDENCE

In fact, these were not headlines at all, but were book titles, which were (as they often are) used as headlines for advertising. *Five Acres* was the original title of a book that did not do well in the market place. When the title was changed to *Five Acres and Independence*, sales picked up sharply. The difference is apparent, of course: the first title is cryptic; the second title makes a most fundamental appeal with its promise.

Of course, the prospect may or may not accept your promise. In fact, there are relevant ratios here, for the more ambitious the promise—the greater the promised benefit—is, the more the probability of some skepticism and the greater the proof required. For you must assume that most prospects will require some proof, some evidence that you can and will make good on your promise or that what your copy states is true. In the case of the oatmeal copy, the "proof" is the report that medical authorities now believe in the salutary effects of ingesting oatmeal. In the case of Joe Karbo's copy, it was quite different, but obviously highly persuasive, since his campaign was highly successful. Inventive promoter that he was, Karbo invented a device that helped greatly to persuade prospects of the truth of his claims, a device that has been widely imitated and will be discussed in detail later. In fact, we will later discuss the nature of "proofs" in general, and with many examples of what does and does not constitute proof for practical purposes.

■ Myths and Other Unfacts Commonly Propagated

Myths, exaggerations, and plain misconceptions have sprung up about advertising and sales, as they do in all fields. One of the most pernicious is the notion that prospects will not read copy that does not have a great deal of white space and a text layout that appears to be easy to read. The fact is that many highly successful advertisements were all large bodies of text set solid, as in the case of Joe Karbo's THE LAZY MAN'S WAY TO RICHES, Sherwin Cody's DO YOU MAKE THESE MISTAKES IN ENGLISH?, and one that was headlined I WANT TO GIVE YOU THIS BEFORE IT IS TOO LATE, as well as many others that ran *for years* without change. The simple fact is that prospects will read any copy that *captures and holds their interest*. And, of course, they won't read copy that does not interest them, no matter how much white space you provide or how easy to read the copy appears to be.

In many cases, emphasis is placed on the wrong things, so that many students of sales and advertising draw the wrong conclusions. For example, because so many salespeople do not know how to close properly and fail to do so, there is great deal of emphasis placed on closing in sales training, and justifiably so. Unfortunately, this is sometimes stressed to the exclusion of other important factors, and some people have interpreted this to mean that closing skill is all that is needed to make sales. But that inference is mistaken: important although closing is, you cannot close successfully until you have done a proper selling job—offered the right persuasive promise and proved your case. Moreover, closing has another purpose, one that affects the other major factors greatly, but is rarely recognized. That, too, will be discussed later.

In many cases, far too much is made of the need to get attention. Again, it is an important consideration, but it should never be interpreted to mean that it is a major goal in itself. It is that notion that has led to many extreme efforts to get attention, and doing so in ways totally unrelated to the main issue of the advertisement or other material. Getting attention should be done within the context of the message, in some way that is part and parcel of the promise, as a minimum.

These are just a few of the many false ideas you are likely to encounter. We will come across others in our journey through the chapters to come.

■ Summary

We have focused in this first chapter on the basics of marketing, sales, and advertising—on the common factors, that is, involved in those acts of persuasion we refer to by those names. In this we established some definitions—what certain terms will mean when they are used in these pages. Most important has been establishing the basic principles of proof and promise, clearly established, as the essence of sales persuasion, along with the support of closing, as the necessary supporting act in the process.

Along the way I have tried to expose some of the mythology and other false notions that cloud our views, if we are not careful to always remember what is logical and has been demonstrated to be true and not fall prey to notions that have no basis in fact.

In the next chapter we will begin to get down directly to specific applications of these concepts and principles.

CHAPTER TWO

Writing Is the Common Denominator

The bulk of marketing activity is based on words and illustrations on paper, even when the message is delivered verbally. That is, it is based on writing—creative writing, in fact.

■ What Is "Writing"?

Almost everyone with a normal education—through high school—reads and writes, to at least some small degree. Those with higher levels of formal education—professionals, executives, and others—tend to do a certain amount of writing as necessary chores in their careers.

That tends to lead to two popular misconceptions about writing: one, that anyone with an education can write; and, two, that writing is an activity concerned entirely or nearly entirely with the correct use of language. Both are mistaken ideas or oversimplifications, at best.

Are Writers Born or Made?

Of course, in the literal sense, anyone who is literate can write—can exercise the mechanical function of stringing words together into sentences and progressions of sentences. But that is very much the same as saying that anyone can draw, for anyone can create crude sketches, especially of simple illustrations such as stick figures, diagrams, and charts. Few of us are "born artists"—able to create drawings of professional quality without directed training of some sort and a great deal of practice, through some unconscious and somewhat mysterious process or inherent ability we call *talent*. (In fact, however, we really do not know what that latter word means.) Similarly, few of us are "born writers" in that same sense of having a certain instinct or talent for writing well without special training, although there are some individuals who appear to fit that term. Both illustrating and writing are arts, but both are arts with methodologies. And methodologies can be learned.

Probably all truly skilled writers and artists *are* trained—self-trained in many cases. And perhaps no one can become an accomplished illustrator without that basic instinct or talent for the art, because a certain manual dexterity is required, in addition to special intellectual skills. But probably everyone who is completely literate and fluent in the language can learn to write with reasonable skill. But to do so, one must first recognize and accept the principle that writing is not entirely a subjective art; there is a need to learn and adopt that discipline—to learn the methodologies and practice them. Being literate is not itself qualification as a writer; communicating effectively is most definitely a special skill.

Consider the following example of a statement on a U.S. Department of Education loan-guarantee form that lenders are asked to sign:

> Should the maker of the obligation tender payments thereon to the undersigned subsequent to the filing of this application, it is hereby agreed that such moneys will be accepted for and the proceeds immediately transmitted to the U. S. Office of Education.

This is a form that lenders of guaranteed student loans are asked to sign. Simply stated—restated, that is, for it was not stated simply in this case— this says that if the named borrower makes any payments on this loan to the lender after the Department of Education has repaid the lender under the guarantee, the lender will immediately forward those payments to the Department of Education.

The original language is grammatical and technically correct, but it is "bad" writing because the meaning is masked by ponderous language. It could have been stated more simply in several ways, including this one:

> Should the borrower make payments on this loan after the government has paid my claim, I will immediately forward such payments to the U. S. Office of Education.

This simple example illustrates that it is not only better writing practice— clearer communication—to use simple language and simple sentences, but it is also easier. Why, then, do so many writers choose to write so badly when it is really so much easier to express themselves clearly? My own experience suggests that there are several reasons for this, and sometimes more than one of these apply in a given instance:

1. Some choose, consciously or unconsciously, to display their fine vocabularies (even if they have to use an unabridged dictionary to do so), in the

mistaken notion that the use of such language reflects a favorable or even prestigious image of the writer.

2. Some simply adopt phrases and terms found in source literature or other research documentation, possibly out of laziness, for it requires effort to think out such language and translate it into simple terms, and possibly out of fear of error in interpreting and translating the original language.

3. Many do not recognize the need to rewrite a first draft at least once, with simplification of language at least one objective of rewriting.

4. Many do not plan their writing, and so their writing meanders, almost aimlessly, without clear objectives. The writer, in this case, often fails to even recognize the difficulty in such expression as that of the example shown here.

The second and third items are related, for many professional writers admit that they write poor first drafts. But, being professionals, they make it a firm practice to do at least one rewrite (most do more than one), revising and polishing until they have eliminated such poor prose and replaced it with clear expression. However, it is the fourth item that frequently undermines inexperienced writers.

The answer to the question posed, why do some writers choose such ponderous language when it is actually easier to write simply, should now be apparent: writing simply is more often than not *re*writing and/or made possible only through thorough planning. The total effort to achieve simple, clear expression is not always easy. As at least one professional has put it in summation, "All good writing is rewriting."

What Is the Real Skill?

Despite all that has been said about writing and rewriting, the objective of that to which we refer as writing is communication, the exchange of ideas and information. Writing *must* communicate, to be successful. That is the real skill—the ability to communicate effectively. But even that does not explain it all: communicating effectively includes the ability to select the message and how best to convey it. It includes the recognition that words are only one of the writer's tools, and often not the most effective tool. It includes other factors, which are the subject of the remainder of this chapter.

■ Preparation and Planning

A Broadway hit musical or play is presented in its entirety in two to three hours the first evening that it runs, but months of planning and preparation have gone into that two to three hours. No one attempts to present a play without the planning, the rehearsals, and all the other preparation. Yet, many individuals will try to write a final salesletter, brochure, or advertising copy spontaneously, without planning and preparation and without considering whether the result does or does not represent their best effort.

It is a simple truth that the final quality of a written product depends quite heavily on both the amount and quality of the planning and preparation that have preceded the writing of it. James Michener, for example, is well known for the several years of intensive research that go into the writing of each of his books, most of which are then good enough to reside on the best-seller lists for a long time. That (the research, planning, and other preparation) is the usual price of quality in any writing, with only rare exceptions.

The First Step

The first step in anything, including writing, is deciding what your objective is: just what do you wish to accomplish? Obviously, since we are discussing sales and promotional materials here, your ultimate goal overall in each undertaking is to persuade prospects to become customers. But there are a number of things to be identified or defined first, even before attempting to outline the approach and content, including answering the following questions as the minimum starters:

- ☑ The readers–who/what are the readers to be (i.e., who are the suitable prospects for whatever you wish to sell)?
- ☑ What are their probable motivations; what promise is most likely to persuade them to buy what you are selling?
- ☑ How will you convince the readers—i.e., what proofs will you offer to back up your promise?
- ☑ By what means do you plan to reach them—i.e., what kind of piece are you going to write?

Where do the early answers come from?

You don't pluck the answers to these questions out of thin air. You arrive at answers by analysis and arbitrary decision. In some cases the analysis consists of exploring your own knowledge, where you are already expert in the field; in other cases you make arbitrary decisions. For example, having had a great deal of direct experience in selling to government agencies, a great deal of my basic market analysis—but not all of it—was based on my own accumulated knowledge. (Nevertheless, in this case the field is so large and complex that it was necessary to study a great deal of research material to support my own knowledge.) On the other hand, if you are selling radios or steak sandwiches your market is virtually everyone, so the job of determining who are the most suitable prospects is simplified immediately; almost anyone is a good prospect.

In creating sales literature for a book on marketing to the federal government agencies, I knew that nominally every businessperson was a potential prospect, for there is virtually no goods or service the government does not buy. But I perceived, first of all, two broad categories in which I could divide prospects: those businesspeople who already did business with the government, and those who did not. The second category then had to be divided into those who wanted to do business with the government but did not know how to begin, those who definitely were not interested in government business (there are those), those who have never thought about it but could be persuaded to become interested, and those who think they cannot qualify for government contracts and need to be educated about the subject. The first category could also be subdivided into the large companies and the small companies, and both categories could also be subdivided by the types of goods and services they sell.

Deciding who your readers are

By now it begins to become apparent that with all these different characteristics and interests, we are talking about many different prospects and markets. We are also talking about such a diversity that there is no single approach that is suitable for all. The time is at hand to make an arbitrary decision as to which of these markets—types of prospects—we will address and pursue. Here, for example, are some broad headlines, which will indicate different approaches and strategies, depending on what we choose to select as our targets:

HOW TO WIN (MORE) GOVERNMENT BUSINESS
ANYONE CAN WIN GOVERNMENT CONTRACTS
HOW TO SELL TO GOVERNMENT AGENCIES
NO BUSINESS IS TOO SMALL TO SELL TO THE GOVERNMENT
HOW TO WRITE WINNING PROPOSALS
HOW TO APPEAR TO BE THE LOW BIDDER

You can see, of course, that different kinds of prospects are being envisioned by each of the above headlines. And if you are familiar with selling to the government you can see some of the more subtle differences, such as the difference in kinds of prospects that would be addressed by the last two headlines.

The point is that it is impracticably difficult to write a single appeal that will work equally well for all prospects in this and in many—perhaps most—other cases. One major goal of advance planning and preparation is to decide which prospects you will address in the effort you are currently planning. (This does not preclude addressing all possible markets, but you may have to prepare other literature in separate efforts to pursue other classes of prospects.)

If you do not discover this fact of life at once, you will sooner or later when you try to plan an approach and discover that rarely will any approach work equally well for all classes of prospect or markets you might address. Let's put that to the test by doing some broad analysis of just a few products or services you might wish to sell. That is, let us take just a brief, sampling look at how diverse an array of prospects you might address in each case:

Product/Service	Prospects/Markets
Air travel (airline or travel bureau)	Business travelers; vacationers; weekenders; regular travelers; occasional travelers
Hotel accommodations	Business travelers; meeting planners; vacationers; party/wedding planners; seminar producers
Vitamins	Dieters; youngsters; oldsters; the health-conscious in general
Correspondence courses	High-school dropouts; young retirees seeking second careers; housewives returning to the work force; individuals wishing to change careers or advance in their careers

You can see from these few examples that you can make more than one approach and employ more than one strategy in pursuing business in each of these. The common mistake is failing to make this simple analysis and launching an unfocused campaign, trying to appeal to everyone equally. Unfortunately, it does not work well, and this should become more and more apparent as we proceed. The basic reason, however, is that most people have to be furnished some special reason for buying. That is, if they have not decided in advance to buy such a product or service, they have to be given some reason to want that product or service. On the other hand, if they have decided to buy such a product or service—a vacation package, for example—they must have some reason for buying it from you, rather than from a competitor. (Of course, those are two most basic marketing problems, in any case.) Ordinarily, you cannot furnish strong motivation to any class of prospects unless you are able to focus on some want or need, and that is tantamount to deciding who or what the prospect is.

What are your prospects' motivations?

It is difficult to separate the identity of your prospects from their motivations, as you can see; the two are closely related because you must define your prospects at least partly in terms of their motivation. When you define a traveler as one traveling on business, you have not only identified or defined the prospect but you have laid the groundwork for deciding on the appeal or motivation, for business travelers are motivated differently from vacationers—they travel for different reasons and have different needs.

For example, a vacationer generally plans travel well ahead, whereas a business traveler quite often—perhaps most of the time—must act on short notice and must sometimes make abrupt changes of plan while en route. A vacationer will often plan around the most economical time and way to travel, while the business traveler will usually want the most expeditious way to reach a destination. The vacationer is likely to have lots of luggage, while the business traveler is more likely to "travel light." For short flights, the business traveler is likely to travel during business hours, while a vacationer may travel during any hours.

But there are other considerations. The frequent traveler may be motivated to pile up "frequent flyer credits," which ultimately afford him or her some free flights. You can take advantage of this in your sales appeal. Of course, this appeal will not have much effect on the buying decision of the occasional traveler. The regular, experienced traveler is also more likely to be motivated by the promise of an expeditious check-in than is the occasional or inexperienced traveler.

What proofs will you offer?

Proofs must be conceived so as to be entirely compatible with the promise and with the reader's characteristics. Remember, first of all, what "proof" means in this case: it means *whatever the reader will accept as proof*. Consider the "proofs" offered in TV commercials, for example. Some are assurances by actors in white jackets, representing the medical profession. Some are assurances—testimonials—by well-known actors, representing themselves. (For some reason, many people will accept the assurance of a popular celebrity, where they would not accept the assurance of an unknown actor or actress.) In some cases a simple argument, one that appears to be founded in logic, is offered to substantiate the promise. Still another device used is the simple assurance of the advertiser, often as represented by a key figure of the advertiser's organization, as in the case of Chrysler Corporation and its chief executive officer, Lee Iaccoca.

Again, the proof must be in proportion to the promise—the greater the promise the heavier must be the evidence—and of a nature that is relevant to the product or service being offered, as well as appropriate to the type of prospect. For example, to illustrate these three points, consider this:

☑ If the promise appears to be too good to be true, it will require a great deal of evidence to support it for all but the most credulous prospect.

☑ A persuasive testimonial by someone who travels frequently, especially a well-known figure, would be a good way to promote a travel commercial promising comfort and timely schedules.

☑ A business executive or professional, for example, is more likely to want some logical rationale—perhaps even some quantitative data, in some cases—to back up the promise than would many other types of prospects.

How do you plan to reach your prospects?

There are several ways to reach your prospects, and there are logical, analytical methods for deciding on the most appropriate ways for each case. But for the moment, let us assume that you have made that analysis and chosen your method, so we can now consider just the relationship between how you plan to reach your prospects and how that affects what you write.

All approaches must reach the prospect via sight and/or sound—eyes and ears—of course. The most common and most popular ways to reach prospects via written materials are these:

Print advertising
Direct mail
Radio
TV

There are other ways—trade shows, in-store demonstrations, seminars, and newsletters, to name a few. We will take them up eventually, but they are all similar enough to one or more of the four media named here so that these four illustrate the points clearly enough.

☑ Print advertising usually means relatively short copy, from a few column inches to a full page, normally. (A full newspaper page can be a rather large amount of copy, but we will consider most print advertising to be confined to a few hundred words at most, in most cases.)

☑ Direct mail is usually relatively voluminous copy because it usually involves a minimum of two written pieces, a sales letter and a brochure, and often several other pieces as well.

☑ Radio commercials require scripts, and in many cases it requires great skill to write an effective script because words alone must carry the whole burden of description.

☑ TV commercials also require scripts, and even more writing skill is required, in many cases, because the medium is visual, and the script must cover that. In fact, a writing device called a *storyboard* is generally used, if there is anything more than a narrator and straight narration required—i.e., if the commercial is to involve dramatization and/or special visual effects.

The Second Step: What Action?

You now have established at least beginning premises about who you will address, how you will reach them, what you will promise, and what evidence you will offer. As a second step—and the chronology is arbitrary, for purposes of explanation; in practice the processes are usually iterative or concurrent— you must ask yourself just what it is that you want the reader to do. Hurry to the store to buy whatever you sell? Come to the showroom and see one? Write and ask for more information? Visit your booth at the trade show? Send for a sample?

What Is Your Direct Objective?

If the answer to the question is not immediately apparent, you must do some more thinking about the matter. Even the preceding brief analyses may not have covered the subject adequately, for there are other considerations. And the answer to what you want the reader to do may be revealed by the answer to another question: just what are you trying to accomplish as the direct objective of a sales piece? To get an immediate order, or something else? If, for example, you are selling some kind of "big tag" item—i.e., an item with a cost great enough so that few sales are made with a single appeal or presentation—any or all of the four approaches listed would normally be used only as door openers. That is, they would be used to generate sales leads to be followed up. A print advertisement, for example, may simply call for response by the reader. Mail order firms often advertise invitations to send for a free catalog, brochure, sample, or other item. To run such advertisements you must obviously have the brochures, letters, newsletters, and/or other literature ready to send out to inquirers. If you exhibit at a trade fair of some sort you must have literature to hand out.

The nature of what you are selling may dictate to you how you must advertise and market. Direct mail enthusiasts are fond of saying that anything can be sold by mail, but this must often be qualified. It would be rather difficult to sell an automobile or house by mail, for example, although direct mail might well be used to persuade prospects to visit showrooms and model homes. The nature of your prospects also may be a decisive factor in your choice. If what you sell would be of interest to only some certain class—perhaps truck farmers or self-employed accountants—there may be only one way to reach prospects, such as via direct mail or trade shows.

An Example

In my own case, for example, when selling books and newsletter subscriptions to one class of prospects, direct mail was the only practical means for reaching my prospects, but it proved impossible to get the mailing lists I wanted. This compelled me to turn to methods for compiling my own mailing lists, partly through inquiry advertising, as described.

The Sales Strategy

All marketing and sales efforts are based on some strategy, even when the strategy is not a deliberate choice. If there is no deliberate strategy, the sales are based on chance or pure probability that some given number of prospects will become customers spontaneously. However, the most successful sales strategies are usually those carefully designed to fit the situation.

The strategy may be dictated at least partially by such circumstances as those already described—limitations on how suitable prospects can be reached or the nature of the item being sold, for example. But beyond that, it is necessary to design a successful strategy.

Again, we have the problem of chronology. Strategy is not developed as a discrete and isolated matter, but is implemented in and to a degree dictated by the promise, the proof, the nature of the prospect, and all the other factors. All must be integrated properly to achieve a proper strategy. This makes strategy formulation at least as much an art as a science: as a writer and marketer—and to write effective sales materials you must be as much a marketer as a writer—you must think in terms of sales strategies. With a firm set of definitions, you must ask yourself such questions as these:

- ☑ What are this prospect's most acute needs and wants?
- ☑ What about this product/service would most appeal to this prospect?
- ☑ What are the appropriate or reasonable promises that can be made here?
- ☑ What would be the most persuasive proof for this prospect?
- ☑ What is the most logical and persuasive sequence of presentation?
- ☑ What is the most important or most persuasive single issue here?

That single issue

That last point, the most important single issue, is usually the most critical item in any strategy formulation. The main effort should be to identify that single item and build the strategy directly upon and around it. As in other matters we have discussed here, focus is most important.

When I pursued buyers for information and services related to government marketing, for example, my strategy was different for each group or class of prospects. For those small businesspeople who had never even thought of doing business with the government, my main strategy was to convince them that they could easily win government business, once they learned how. But with the large companies who did business regularly with government agencies, I focused on guidance in writing better proposals.

The evolution of strategy

This was not all the result of my wisdom; for the most part these strategies evolved out of experience, over a period of time, during which I made distinct and specific efforts to determine what the most effective motivating factors were for each kind of prospect.

That approach, learning steadily from accumulating experience, has its limitations. It can be highly effective in some sales. On the other hand, as you will see later, in developing proposals for custom projects you must sink or swim on the best judgment you can make in formulating sales strategies. In these cases, each sale is unique, and the experience gained is rarely directly useful for the next one, although your ability to devise successful strategies should improve with experience.

Research, Need and Reasons for

Writing even short pieces—especially short pieces, in many cases—usually requires some research. Again, this is part of the general planning and preparation process and is largely concurrent with the other "front end" activities, but must be explained as though it were a discrete and isolated activity.

Sales literature must be credible, and nothing can destroy your credibility faster than glaring error. Be careful that you do not report rumors or biased opinions as facts or get your facts wrong. And to be sure that you know what you are talking about, do adequate research.

That is only one of the several reasons for doing adequate research. "Adequate" research usually means collecting gallons of information in preparation for presenting a few teaspoons of it. That is not illogical. You cannot select the largest or whitest egg in the box without examining all the eggs in the box, and you cannot select the most useful, relevant, or cogent information without looking at all or nearly all of it. The purpose of research is to survey all the available information to select that which is most suitable for your needs, as well as to ensure accuracy. But even that is not all of it. Still another quite important purpose of research is your own education about the subject of your writing. It is quite astonishing what improvements in your writing style come about almost automatically when you improve your knowledge of the subject and you no longer have even a subconscious need to be vague or evasive about any of the details or relationships among the facts.

The data-gathering phase of research should continue as long as it turns up pertinent new facts. It may be considered to be complete when you are beginning to turn up information you have already collected. You may, however, run into a common problem of research, that of finding material that raises new questions which are not answered by what you have gathered. That may compel you to do special research, such as seeking out and interviewing some individual on the subject. However, even then, the learning phase of research—absorbing the facts and selecting those you will use— continues until you are sure that you have mastered the subject and have everything you need in the way of information. That may continue, in fact, until you have completed your planning and preparation.

Outlining

The need to outline is an accepted fact of life among writers. For the writer, outlines are what drawings are to engineers and architects: they are plans. The engineers and architects translate those drawings into physical realities—machines, bridges, and buildings—as the writer translates those outlines into brochures, books, and scripts.

There is a difference. The engineer and architect usually begin with rough sketches, develop carefully detailed conceptual drawings—known as "artist's concepts"—of the finished product, and then develop the completely detailed drawings from which others can and do build the machines, bridges, and buildings. But many writers do not develop their outlines beyond the preliminary, rough ideas, and then write their brochures, books, and scripts with only these rough ideas as guides.

There is at least one other difference. The very word *outline* has more than one interpretation for the writer. It may or may not be in what is classically regarded as the outline form—i.e.:

I: MAJOR TOPIC
    A. First Subtopic
        1. First sub-subtopic

Often, what purports to be an outline is in narrative form, as a series of paragraphs that summarize the material and describe what is to be written. Or it may be a lead only, doing not much more than setting the scene and telegraphing most generally what is to come. Or, especially for short pieces, it may exist only in the mind of the writer. All methods are used by and work for many professional writers. But they are usually counterproductive for the writer who is not an experienced professional. If you are of that latter description, you will almost surely find it best to prepare the most detailed outline possible, and use the classical outline form to ensure yourself the most complete guidance possible in translating all that planning and preparation into the final product.

Even so, too often writers prepare outlines that do not truly define the product because they are far too broad and general. Hence, they are not useful as guides in writing. The following "before"and "after" examples illustrate this in principle, albeit on a small scale. (In practice, a thorough outline would go down at least one additional level of detail.)

Before (a broad and general outline):

I.   SERVICING PRODUCTS
    A.   Where service accomplished
    B.   By whom serviced
    C.   Requirements for service
    D.   Types of service

After (detailed outline):

I.   SERVICING PRODUCTS
    A.   Where service accomplished
        1.   Factory
        2.   In field
    B.   By whom serviced
        1.   By company field engineers
        2.   By authorized service stations
        3.   By authorized dealers
    C.   Requirements for service
        1.   Service contracts
        2.   In warranty
        3.   At standard labor rates and parts
    D.   Types of service
        1.   Routine/preventive (periodic) maintenance
        2.   Troubleshooting specific malfunctions
        3.   General overhaul and repair

The difference between the two is quite obvious, of course. The "before" example might well have been written before researching the subject, perhaps even as a beginning guide to research, indicating the areas of information to be investigated. And that raises another important point about outlining: just as manuscripts are normally developed as rough drafts that must be edited, reviewed, and rewritten, so must outlines be developed in a similar manner. There is nothing wrong with developing a general, broad outline as a first step, as long as you recognize it as such. In fact, it is a good practice, for all designs are normally developed in progressive stages, starting with general or rough ideas and evolving through numerous refinements. A beginning outline is thus a guide to the questions you must ask, the information you must seek.

■ The Writer's Art

The main point of all the previous discussions of planning and preparation was that content is at least as important as writing skill *per se*, and it requires a great deal of careful planning and preparation to ensure the proper content. This is not to minimize the role or importance of the other two factors that determine the effectiveness of any given piece of writing: organization and style, factors that are undeniably essential elements of the writer's art.

Organization

One of the advantages of using the classical outline form advocated here is that it almost compels a logical organization, inasmuch as by its very structure it groups related ideas, with subordination and relationships of various items and areas clearly indicated. It also tends to reveal gaps in the chain of reasoning or events. In so doing, it directs your attention to what you need to cover to bridge the gaps properly.

There are several basic patterns of organization. Here are a few of the most common orders in which information may be organized:

- ☑ Forward chronological sequence.
- ☑ Reverse chronological sequence.
- ☑ From cause to effect.
- ☑ From effect to cause.
- ☑ In ascending order of importance.
- ☑ In descending order of importance.
- ☑ Hybrids or combinations of these.

No single organization is best for all uses, of course. The order of presentation is dictated by the nature of the material and, especially, by the point you want to make. If you want to show how some modern product you sell was developed or how the company you represent originated and grew to its present state, you may find the forward chronological sequence optimal. However, cause and effect organization is often useful, such as when you want to point out something that was seminal in the creation of a product or corporation. The corporation known today as U.S. Industries, Inc., for example, was founded as the U.S. Pressed Steel Car Co. That bit of information has little significance for most people. Explain that the corporation was founded to build railroad cars in the heyday of railroads, and it might arouse just a trifle more interest. But explain that the founder was the well-known, flamboyant Diamond Jim Brady, and you have added a strong element of romance that will get the attention and pique the interest of many readers. If you wanted to relate the story of the corporation, you might do well to start with that latter bit of information, explaining who Diamond Jim was, for those who have not heard of him. (Note once again that attention and interest are aroused by self-interest, the prospect of being amused or entertained, in this case.) However, note too that this requires a hybrid order of presentation.

Hybrid orders of presentation

Except for rather short pieces of writing, it is quite often necessary to use hybrid orders of presentation, as in the example just cited. There is, of course, nothing wrong with doing that, as long as you do not lose the reader along the way. Abrupt changes in order, shifts in chronology, breaks in a train of thought, or other such jagged edges in writing confuse the reader and make some readers fling the material aside in frustration. Making such changes in a manner that brings the reader along easily involves one element of writing—creating smooth transitions—that is more art than method, although a method can be rationalized.

Transitions or "bridges"

To illustrate the need for transitions when shifting from one thought to another, suppose that I concluded one paragraph and started a new one as shown by the following:

> The main point of all the foregoing—discussions of planning and preparation—was that content is at least as important as writing skill *per se*, and it requires a great deal of careful planning and preparation to ensure the proper content.
> One of the advantages of using the classical outline form advocated here is that it almost compels logical organization.

What we have in this example is an abrupt shift of ideas from proper content to organization, but this is without blazing the trail. If this kind of shift confuses and frustrates the reader, it is the writer's fault. The writer must pave over the gap for the reader. The method is this, in principle: the new paragraph must begin with a directly linked thought so the train of reasoning or the orderly sequence of thought is not broken. And that link must be some word or term that is common to the conclusion of one thought and the beginning of the next.

In the actual case from which this sample was taken—it was material that appeared earlier in this chapter—the first paragraph ended with an introduction to the need for organization in writing, and even included a headline identifying the subject, further strengthening the bridge. The headline is not a necessity, normally, nor should you depend on a headline to make the transition; the text itself must make the transition by providing the connecting thought whether there is or is not a headline.

Transitions are not always between paragraphs. There must be proper transitions whenever and wherever a shift in thought occurs, whether that is between sentences, paragraphs, chapters, or other discrete elements. The wise use of titles and headlines helps a great deal to ensure smooth transitions, but neither ought to be depended upon for the transition. The transition ought to be a smooth and proper one even if there is no headline or title to introduce the new subject. In fact, that is an excellent test of a transition: does the concluding text introduce the new text without the support of a title or headline? If the answer is *no*, the copy needs some more work to achieve that bridge.

Style

Style is difficult to define, for there are two levels at which it can be defined. One is the virtual *signature* of the author, the style that is peculiarly his or hers, as in the case of Ernest Hemingway or Henry James. The other is the general level or general trait that can be defined and might be characteristic of any writer, such as *simple and direct, baroque*, or *portentious*. It is that latter style that is of concern here.

Whether it is or is not embellished by fetching and distinctive personal characteristics, there is only one general style that is appropriate to the writing of sales and promotional materials. That is the simple, direct, and forceful style. It is essential in all sales copy that the reader understand your exact meanings to the maximum degree possible and totally without confusion. There are a number of points to be made in that connection. Let's look at some dos and don'ts.

NOTE: I will use the term *reader* here for convenience, but I mean reader/listener/viewer, for the lessons to be learned are common to all the media for which you may be called upon to write advertisements, commercials, sales letters, and other sales and promotional copy. I will also refer to *sales copy* and *advertising copy*, but in all cases these terms will include and the points apply to all those kinds of copy referred to here.

Klever kopy

One of the most common and most serious mistakes some copywriters make is trying to be clever. They invent puns, acronyms, and feeble humor, and in their efforts to do so they find it necessary to stretch rhetoric and facts so far that meaning is lost. If you fall prey to this temptation, you will often create subtleties that only you understand, with obvious results (or, to be more exact, the lack of results). Subtlety has no place in advertising and related copy under normal circumstances. Readers of sales copy are almost invariably reading casually; they are rarely interested enough to spend their time studying and interpreting the meaning of what you write. Remember always that they are really interested only in their own lives—their own problems, desires, daydreams, and wants. Even when they appear to show interest in other matters they are serving their own interests—curiosity, amusement, escape, achieving a feeling of satisfaction, or any of many possible motivations.

Periodicals are full of the evidence of the too-too-clever writings of many copy creators. An advertisement for gelatin, as one example, headlines "Give someone you love a ring tonight," with an illustration of a gelatin ring, the saving grace—the *only* saving grace.

"Cover your rear" is another one, done even less well than the gelatin ring. It is the headline of an advertisement for some kind of device to be attached to the rear window of your car. It is apparently a special lens that refracts—bends—light so that you can see objects that are below the normal window level. The illustration depicts a young child playing behind the vehicle, out of the direct line of sight and so hidden from normal view. Most readers will not understand the concept and will wonder what the device is, for the body copy does not really explain it, but merely states that it "bends your line of sight." (This is a truly lost opportunity to use that illustration with the strong headline "Now you can know what—or *who*—is behind you before you back up.")

Here is a case that is even worse because the writer strained so to drag in an outrageous pun by the ears and then, not content yet, added hype with the word "best. " Few will appreciate the pun without pondering it (and few readers will spend the time doing so). It is copy for a bottled tartar sauce, that is, a sauce for fish. The headline claims that it is "Best among its piers."

You need feel no shame if you need to ponder that one a bit to grasp the not-too-obvious play on words that the writer had to truly reach for.

Humor is another matter. It can be and is sometimes used quite effectively, but like cleverness, it is a double-edged tool; it is quite dangerous unless used with great skill. And achieving it is not as easy as it may appear to be; it is far more difficult to be truly humorous and to be humorous in good taste.

Again, the bad pun is the favorite weapon of writers who think they are humorists. Presumably it is because so many writers discover that writing humor is not easy that they tend to turn to puns and other weak and usually misguided attempts to be clever and humorous. Humor that does not quite come off is a disaster, and creates a negative effect. But that is only one hazard in using humor. There are others.

Humor must be in good taste, and that means, in practical terms, that it must not offend anyone. It must not be ethnic humor or at the expense of any religious, racial, or other easily visible group. It must not offend anyone's sensibility to humor that is sexually oriented. It must skirt rubbing sensitive nerves raw on matters of politics and other emotional subjects. That narrows the field considerably. In these times of instant communication everywhere, it is a tall order to even say or write anything without offending someone, much less joke about it.

There is another hazard in using humor in sales copy: in the eagerness to be humorous or clever, you always run the risk of distracting the reader's attention from the real message. Clever copywriters often win Clio awards (the advertising industry's equivalent of Hollywood's Oscars and TV's Emmys), but they also often forget to sell the product. An Alka-Seltzer advertising campaign of some years ago furnishes a good example. The campaign featured stomachs in clever and amusing pictorials—vignettes—but the campaign was abandoned when it became clear that it was not selling the product. Copy writers for Volkswagen made a similar error, as have many others. I can personally recall many clever and amusing commercials, but I often was unaware of what the commercial was selling. The "ring around the collar" commercial was one such. The concept was a good one, one we will discuss later, but it was a long time before I became conscious of the product identity because the copy seduced me into ignoring the real message by entertaining me.

Some copywriters are evidently frustrated novelists or philosophers, and turn their drive for cleverness into efforts to be "literary. " In fact, they may write quite well, but advertising and sales literature is the wrong avenue for the expression of literary ambitions.

Yet another common error in copy writing is the apparently irresistible urge on the part of some copywriters to make overly ambitious promises and use "hype"—swarms of adjectives in an effort to force-feed the reader superlatives as proof, seemingly in an effort to bludgeon the reader into submission. Or to offer long and tortuous arguments as proof, which appear to me sometimes to also be efforts to beat a weary reader into surrender.

True cleverness in copy

None of the foregoing is intended to say that there is no room in copy writing for true cleverness, cleverness that creates forceful and successful copy while still being simple, direct, and clear. A print advertisement for Pam, the spray to make cooking and baking surfaces non-stick, uses clever copy effectively. The headline is "PAM can save you an arm and a leg." Wisely, the headline is near the bottom of the page; the top two-thirds of the page is devoted to a clear and colorful photograph of a gingerbread man whose arm and leg stuck to the baking pan when the rest of the cookie was removed. Thus, the meaning is absolutely clear immediately, even before the reader sees the headline. No subtlety there; just a well-defined point made clearly and directly. In fact, this copy would probably have been equally effective had there been no headline at all, but just the illustration and the product identity.

Relevance is essential. If you are inclined to cleverness, make a rigorous analysis of the relevance of your copy to the real message—*why* the reader should read the copy and buy the product.

A writer must establish a relationship with readers, a relationship that is reflected in the writer's style and based on the writer's ability to visualize, understand, and empathize with readers. But there is even a bit more to the relationship than that. It has been said, with a great deal of justification, that the cardinal sin a writer can commit is boring readers. It is probably equally true that another way to estrange your readers swiftly is to betray them. Using tricky headlines, reaching far out for puns, and otherwise luring the reader's attention with something that is irrelevant to the body copy and the real message is a betrayal, and readers will repay such a betrayal by turning swiftly to something else. You must keep faith with the reader. A headline or lead in sales copy, is like the lead in any other copy: it is a promise of what is to come, and you must keep that promise.

Another way to lose readers rapidly is to shatter their confidence in you through carelessness or other sins. Ordinarily, the typical reader begins reading what you have written with a willingness to believe you or, at least, to give your copy a fair hearing. But if you are careless with facts, blatantly dogmatic, highly opinionated, excessive in use of hyperbole, or otherwise abusive toward the relationship of trust, the reader will go on to a less stressful and more comfortable writer-reader relationship. It is essential that in writing copy you strive for accuracy, minimize your use of superlatives and other adjectives, and deliver a clear image of objectivity and honesty. If you achieve that, at least one-half your battle is won; your copy is far more likely to do the job.

You must build trust in your writing. That's relatively hard to do in short copy, of course; you need time to develop that kind of writer-reader relationship. But it can be done even in short copy by building *credibility* rapidly. Credibility is an important asset in all writing; it is an essential one in advertising and sales copy.

■ Credibility

There are those who tend strongly to believe anything they see in print. But even they are inclined to skepticism as a reaction to what is obviously advertising matter, especially when that advertising matter is heavily hyped with grand adjectives, adverbs, and other sweeping claims of superiority in what has come to be known as "Madison Avenue" and "Hollywood" overstatement. These have traditionally depended on such adjectives as "stupendous" and "marvelous," creating formidable obstacles to believability. Bear in mind always that superlatives are merely claims; they do not have even the appearance of factual statements, and so they invite disbelief from even trusting readers.

Advertising Lightly Disguised

Some advertisers go to the extreme of creating advertisements that appear to be straight editorial matter. You may have noticed such advertisements: they are composed as though they were news stories, with captions and body copy, but they carry the word *advertisement* in small, plain type. Evidently, judging by reported results, these advertisements work well because they do not *appear* to be advertisements, although it is plain enough that they are.

It is not necessary to go to this extreme to make your copy believable. There are many ways to minimize the tendency to instantaneous skepticism and encourage reader acceptance of what your copy promises. These call for good writing practices, including the following:

- ☑ Use subdued language by minimizing adjectives and adverbs, especially superlatives; use nouns and verbs instead.
- ☑ Avoid generalization; explain in as much detail as possible.
- ☑ Quantify whenever and wherever possible, and do so with as much precision as possible.
- ☑ Use the words *you* and *your* as often as possible. (Most people's favorite word!)
- ☑ Make emotional appeals (instead of logical arguments).

Generalization versus Specificity

The problem of generalization versus specificity is closely related to that of using superlatives and similar adjectives and adverbs. To use such terms as "many years," "large numbers," and "wide approval" invites the cynical smile and raised eyebrow, almost as much as "stupendous" and "magnificent." Generalizing about a subject is something anyone can do, of course, and the reader is well aware of that, even without reasoning it out consciously.

On the other hand, the inclusion of detail has the opposite effect, and makes the material far more authoritative, hence far more credible. When you provide details you soon find that you need few adjectives or adverbs to make your point. An advertisement for a book, for example, might carry such terms as "hundreds of illustrations" and "many pages of look-up tables." That is something of an improvement over "heavily illustrated, with many tables." But it is still much more general than it ought to be. The reader may well ask, "Just how many hundreds of illustrations are there? What kinds are they? What does 'many' mean?"

Here you can further improve believability by elaborating expanding your coverage of details to "hundreds of full-page illustrations in color. " But you can go even further by being precise in your quantifying, and state that there are "327 full-page, full-color illustrations and 62 reference tables. " Those numbers, because they are precise and not rounded off or expressed by some superlatives, are entirely believable, and that ring of truth begins to rub off on the rest of your copy.

The Effect of Inaccuracy

For the same reason it pays to double-check anything you state as fact. Ten thousand accurate statements will not undo the damage to credibility that one inaccurate statement can bring. The reader expects accuracy, takes it for granted, and is shocked and even outraged to find errors.

Worse yet is ridicule. If you are guilty of an error that makes you appear foolish, even a laughable misuse of language, you risk immediate loss of the reader's confidence in you. The technical writer who wrote of the "duplicity" of the circuits when he meant to refer to circuit duplication (i.e., redundancy to increase reliability) and "assignation" of terminal numbers when he meant the assignment of terminal numbers, made himself appear somewhat ridiculous, for example. Editors normally catch such errors, but what if you do not have the advantage of getting professional editing? In any case, the responsibility is yours as the writer, and you should never depend on editors or anyone else (other than Webster!) to ensure the correctness of your usages.

■ Impact and Its Effects

Most of the writing we encounter every day is highly forgettable. In fact, much of it does not succeed in getting our full attention even when we do stop to read it; only seconds later we cannot remember what we have just read.

The lack of impact that so weakens a great deal of what is written every day may be due to any or all of several possible faults. Probably the most common fault is that of failure to make a point clearly and/or failure to get to it with reasonable directness. That alone, the lack of clarity, is probably the chief cause of the lack of impact. But it is not the only cause; there are other possible causes for the lack of impact, including one or more of the following:

☑ **Vagueness.** Copy that rambles about and never makes a point cleanly and clearly makes little impression on the reader's consciousness. You will be wise to be sure in advance that you know precisely what the main point to be made is, to frame it in the most direct language possible before writing, and to then keep that language before you to make sure that your copy does make that point, especially the main point, as clearly as you planned it and framed it.

☑ **Circumlocution.** Evasive writing, writing that suggests but never actually makes a statement, also fails to make points clearly and is therefore also "weak" writing.

☑ **Deliberate omissions.** Some writers, discovering that they are uncertain about a given item or the answer to a logical question, deliberately skirt the item, assuring himself or herself that "it's not important, and nobody will notice or miss it."

☑ **Subtlety.** Subtlety is a hazardous tool to use in sales copy. If used at all, it must be in such a way and in such places that it can not affect the reader's understanding of the main points.

☑ **Irrelevant/inappropriate themes.** In a current copy of the information-systems trade journal *INFOSYSTEMS*, VM Software, Inc. advertises what it identifies as VMCENTER II. It is not clear just what this is, and the dominant illustration is of a frosty bottle of Pepsi. The headline is "VMCENTER II," the subhead is "Smart Economics," and this is followed by a lead-in blurb that says, "For the new generation, a new choice in VM systems management." The copy then begins by saying that for a company as large as PepsiCo "it takes a lot to keep the sparkle in your data processing operations," a gratuitous and not very relevant or appropriate reference. If you find all this copy somewhat cryptic by the time you reach this point, you are not alone.

☑ **Jargon.** Some writers are so fond of showing that they are "in" and know the jargon of the subject that they forget their main mission–to communicate with a reader who may not be in a position to understand the jargon. Writing that the reader does not understand has little impact on the reader. Unless you know and are sure that you are writing to readers who are totally familiar with the jargon, be careful to write in lay language as much as possible and translate jargon when you find it necessary to use it. If there are some technical experts among your readers, they will not be offended by this. In fact, they will hardly notice it.

☑ **Weak language.** Rhetoric itself—the choice of words and sentence structure—can have little or great impact, according to how you use it. Even the most prosaic, everyday ideas can be expressed in dramatic, hard-hitting terms.

Making Important Points Clearly

The enemies of clarity enumerated—general vagueness, circumlocution, use of jargon, subtlety, and the use of irrelevant themes—are the result of failing to do at least two things every writer ought to do: be sure that you know your main point and all your subordinate points—that you *fully understand* the subject about which you are writing, in fact—and that you do edit your copy scrupulously after completing your first draft.

The first admonition requires little elaboration. The necessity for thorough research and planning in detail has come up many times already in these pages. The second injunction has been touched on less thoroughly, but it is related to the first item, as you will soon see.

Few people, even few professional writers, write "tightly"—without excess verbiage and rambling discourse—in their first drafts. That is a simple fact of writing, and most professional writers accept that (overtly, anyhow, even if many covertly embrace the notion that they are exceptions!). Most of them tend to use euphemisms, avoid issues and commitment, skip over or around items they are not sure of, and ramble a bit or more than a bit in writing first drafts. Many are even conscious of what they are doing, but scribble blithely on, reassuring themselves that "it's only a first draft" and they will "fix it" later, when they revise it. All too often, then, they forget the item and it is never "fixed" or noticed until readers ask about it.

This applies to language, too, unfortunately. Some writers use words, the meaning of which they are not quite sure of planning to "look it up later," but never doing so. Or they deliberately employ euphemisms for no better reason than that they are not sure of their facts and find that euphemisms, if they are less precise than the original terms, offer some security in the form of an escape hatch. "Sanitary engineer" is far more vague than and not as likely to give offense as "garbage collector"or "trash man" is. Unfortunately, the reader is likely to be quite unsure of what is meant by a "sanitary engineer."

This then defeats the basic purpose, which is to communicate the desired points.

In many cases the evasion is far more subtle than that, although it is no less evasive. Evasion in writing is also achieved through thoroughly rambling discourse, discourse that buries the message so deeply that there is little hope of extracting it—or resorts to hyperbole because there is no message, but only claims without proof: "Performance and reliability are up. Operator errors and administrative headaches are down. While problem resolution is faster, easier, and more accurate than ever before. " Thus one advertiser resorts to ungrammatical sentence structure in the hope that this will blind the reader to the fact that only vague claims, without evidence (much less proof), are offered here. In fact, the early general impression conveyed by the layout and copy is that the advertiser is a subsidiary of PepsiCo. Later, it appears that PepsiCo is a client of the advertiser. But nowhere is a statement made to specify the relationship, and the reader is left to draw his or her own conclusions. And the illustration of a frosty bottle of Pepsi is something of an attention-getter, but for the wrong reason—because it appears to be a complete non-sequitur, appearing in a computer information systems trade periodical, so that it is almost totally irrelevant—the relationship is quite tenuous. Overall, this is a most forgettable advertisement, despite the process color and the premium position (inside front cover).

The Impact of Drama

The line "I want you to have this while there is still time" has been used successfully by more than one marketer. The first time it appeared as a headline with a photograph of a gray-haired man, lending the clear impression that "while there is still time" meant while the man in the photograph, by implication the advertiser, remained here on Earth. It was obviously effective, for the advertisement continued to appear unchanged for some years. It has been adopted by others, most recently to advertise a diet plan. The appropriateness of the phrase in this usage is somewhat questionable, but it is apparently still effective. It is not difficult to see why: for one thing, it is dramatic, and so commands attention, while it is also somewhat mystical but with a clear enough implication that time on this sphere is limited for each of us. It also has a heavy emotional content, itself no mean consideration. (More on this subject presently.)

Again the Myth About White Space

The copy referred to here is, incidentally, a full page of solid text. It is a narrative that is identified clearly as a true story, and it is capped by a simple headline. It is presented as a first-person story of someone who identifies herself as a physician who was once overweight and frequently embarrassed by it—she relates her most embarrassing experience as a victim at the hands of college mates—until she discovered the solution in a special diet, the characteristics and virtues of which she then describes and extols in the remaining text. This is an advertiser who has used this identical technique to launch an earlier and obviously successful campaign, selling a book on how to start a small mail-order business. This proves, once again, that copy that is solid text, with no illustrations and little white space, will work and work well if it "strikes a nerve" in its appeal to the reader's interests. Make no mistake about that, for the evidence is clear that the need for white space is a myth; it has been demonstrated to be a myth again and again. In fact, it is a general truth, as direct-mail expert Richard K. Benson points out in his book, *Secrets of Successful Direct Mail* (Benson Organization, Inc., Savannah, GA), that long copy usually produces better results than does short copy. (My own experience supports this belief.)

One Minus, Several Pluses

This is an excellent advertisement, although I find the headline ("Nine girls stood giggling at me as I opened the door . . .") a poor one because it really gives no clue to the copy that follows nor does it involve the reader immediately; it is not really a good lead. A far better headline would be one that identified the copy as dealing with the problems of being over-weight, thus ensuring that every overweight reader could and probably would identify immediately with the copy. But there are good features other-wise:

- ☑ It has the dramatic opening already described.
- ☑ It is alleged to be a true story, told in first person. That makes it far more credible than a hypothetical case would be, and first-person narration adds further to credibility and impact.
- ☑ It enables every overweight reader to identify immediately and sharply with the narrator and her problem.
- ☑ The body copy appeals directly to the self-interest of every overweight reader who is distressed by his or her excess weight and the difficulty of losing some of it. (The plan is, of course, "easy, painless, without drugs, etc.")
- ☑ A money-back guarantee is offered as a clincher.
- ☑ The writing is simple, direct, easy to understand, expressing one thought at a time.

Here are a few examples of that "simple, direct, easy to understand" writing that expresses one thought at a time:

☑ My grades were good. Everything was great. Except that I was 74 pounds overweight. A real porker.

☑ There are no drugs. No appetite suppressants. No artificial foods. All the food comes right from your supermarket.

Grammar versus Impact

The grammarian would complain that some of these are non-sentences, "sentence fragments," in grammarian's jargon. They are correct, of course, as far as the technicalities of usage are concerned. They were also correct in that same sense when they complained that the now well-known slogan, "Winston tastes good like a cigarette should," was grammatically incorrect. (The correct form would have been "*as* a cigarette should.") But from the advertiser's viewpoint the grammatical conventions are irrelevant; the impact of the language is important, and the staccato effect and rhythm of the choices made were therefore more important. That is, the language was right for advertising purposes, even if wrong grammatically.

◼ Other Techniques

The marketer of a special pet food employs an interesting technique in a two-page spread that includes several illustrations. About 80 percent of the copy is devoted to useful general information that guides the reader in making an examination of his or her pet. Directions are given to examine a dog's mouth, teeth, paws, and other areas, with suitable comments, culminating, finally, in a column of type selling their product. Of course, a logical link between the diagnostic guidance and the selling copy is established quite clearly, so that the earlier copy is very much a lead for the "commercial." Dog lovers can hardly help reading this copy with great interest.

Using Imperatives

The copy referred to uses imperatives freely—e.g., "Raise your dog's upper lip to view the teeth." Of course, not all copy lends itself to this, but it is a forceful style when it can be introduced, and many advertisers take advantage of it. Unfortunately, it is not used as often as it could be, however; it could be fitted in much more often than it is.

Strangely enough, even the most independent individuals and executives who manage large organizations tend to lethargy in many ways, while they also tend to respond to imperatives such as those listed below (abstracted from a variety of print advertisements):

Get a head start on holiday beauty.
Call for a test drive today.
Call or send for your copy of our directory.
Reach these homeowners and your sales will grow.
Team up with a winner. Call today.

Invoking Emotions

Drama does not, of itself, sell anything but it does help the copy in at least two ways: it adds greatly to the overall impact of the copy and it adds an emotional appeal.

There is no question that emotions motivate human actions far more than do logical or rational considerations. The satiric humor that says, "Don't confuse me with facts; my mind is made up," is rooted in truth. We tend strongly to base our decisions on emotional drives and then rationalize those decisions to persuade ourselves that we acted intelligently and with good judgment. In watching a movie or reading a novel our interest is in almost direct proportion to the distress of the hero or heroine and the levels of villainy displayed by the antagonist or the perversity of ill- fortune arrayed against the protagonist. We must *identify with* that hero or heroine—understand and *feel* his or her fears, hates, aspirations, distress, loves, and other emotions. And it is only to the extent that most of us do or do not identify strongly that the story succeeds or fails. Even though we know—rationally—that we are watching or reading fiction and the characters are no more real than are the terrible disasters portrayed, we feel the distress. We succumb to what some writers have called a "suspension of disbelief" as a description of our ability to become virtually hypnotized into believing a fantasy—into an escape from reality for a little while, as we live vicariously with the protagonist and other characters.

The Choice of Themes

Emotional appeals are at the heart of most successful sales strategies, despite efforts to present them as appeals to reason. Overweight people are far less motivated by warnings about the health hazards of being overweight than they are by the desires to avoid embarrassment, to appear attractive, to like themselves, and similar emotional gratifications. Insurance advertising appeals to the prospect's need for a sense of security and the fear of disasters that might spell financial ruin. Computers are sold as the latest, the fastest, or the most advanced because experience has shown that *free, new, latest,* and many related terms have great emotional appeal for many. A commercial for a dishwasher detergent depicts the happy housewife being applauded by relatives and friends who are incredulous at the beauty of her dinnerware. As the late Charles Revson, founder of Revlon cosmetics, wisely put it, "In the factory we make cosmetics; in the stores we sell hope." Strategies evolve from themes that are based on either of two all-powerful emotional drives, fear or desire for gain, sometimes both. The MCI long-distance telephone service, for example, bases its appeal in a salesletter primarily on a gain motivation, although it includes a somewhat veiled fear motivator. The gain offered is 60 minutes free time and "guaranteed savings." The fear motivation, listed last, almost as an afterthought, promises that the customer will pay for only the calls he or she makes, "with no added costs whatsoever." That implies that competing long-distance services may charge for other things. They are wise to base the appeal on gain motivation here, however, because there is no really sound basis for a strong fear motivation.

In deciding on a theme and strategy, you must study the item to decide what strategy the item lends itself to most effectively—i.e., what the characteristics of the item are and how most prospects usually view the item and the prospect of purchasing such an item. Burglar alarms, locks, safes, fences, and insurance are "naturals" for fear strategies in advertising; the very nature of the items—how and for what purposes they are used—dictates the best strategic theme. Securities, lottery tickets, and franchises are clearly best suited to gain motivations. But there are many products and services that can be presented to prospects under either theme. Detergent, for example, is usually offered as a better product, one that produces (it is promised) brighter, cleaner clothes, clearly a gain motivation. But one advertiser sells a detergent quite successfully with a fear motivation, using the now-familiar "ring around the collar" commercial. The fear is that of embarrassment, and the motivation is, of course, to use the advertised product and so avoid experiencing the embarrassment. Correspondence courses can be sold with the promise of providing the means to a better life, but many training courses are sold as the means to become independent and furnish protection against the loss of a job. So there are three possibilities because while some items virtually force the fear-gain motivational choice on one, many items can be presented with either theme. But it does require a set of skills to find the most effective theme upon which to base a strategy, especially when most of your competitors trend to one theme, and you wish to go the other way.

Writing effective sales materials, then, is creative writing that requires more than effective writing skills or "wordsmithing" alone: it requires an entire set of skills, including a knowledge of motivation, analytical skills, creative imagination, and a marketing instinct. Fortunately, these can be acquired or developed, with enough effort. And as a starter on the road to such a development, you may wish to interrupt your reading at this point and work on the exercises suggested in the remainder of this chapter.

■ Exercises

Follow the instructions that introduce each of the following exercises. This is not a quiz, so there are no "school solutions" or "right" answers. (In fact, inasmuch as the entire field of marketing and writing marketing materials is far from an exact science, correctness is largely a matter of opinion.) The purpose is to direct your thinking about a number of important matters covered in this chapter. Unless you are quite certain about the correctness of your responses to each exercise, you will do well to review the chapter and note how well your answers match the messages in the original text.

NOTE: To make the exercise more interesting and encourage creative thinking, opportunities for constructed responses are provided. Feel free to write in answers where you think it appropriate.

Major Factors

All of the following are important factors (although not all the factors covered in the chapter) in writing effective sales materials, but some are more important than others. Decide which among these are the five most important factors and indicate your choices by checking them off.

- ☐ **1.** Correct spelling and punctuation
- ☐ **2.** Correct use of grammar
- ☐ **3.** Outlining
- ☐ **4.** Research
- ☐ **5.** Readability
- ☐ **6.** Strategy
- ☐ **7.** Theme
- ☐ **8.** Rhetoric
- ☐ **9.** Choice of words
- ☐ **10.** Headlines
- ☐ _____
- ☐ _____

Writing Style

Which of the following are the three most important style characteristics to strive for? Check off your choices.

☐ 1. Fluent and flowing
☐ 2. Highly literate
☐ 3. Dignified
☐ 4. Clear
☐ 5. Precise
☐ 6. Direct

Headlines

Decide and check off the two most important things a headline ought to do or be:

☐ 1. Be directed to a specific prospect
☐ 2. Get attention
☐ 3. Deliver the right message
☐ 4. Be properly positioned
☐ 5. Lead in to the body copy
☐ _____
☐ _____

Identifying Prospects

Check off those prospects you think would be the most appropriate ones for the offerings listed below.

1. Inexpensive desktop computers:
   ☐ Housewives
   ☐ Students
   ☐ Executives
   ☐ Farmers
   ☐ Teen-agers
   ☐ _____
   ☐ _____

2. Portable tape recorders:
   - ☐ Housewives
   - ☐ Students
   - ☐ Executives
   - ☐ Farmers
   - ☐ Teen-agers
   - ☐ _____
   - ☐ _____

3. Insurance:
   - ☐ Housewives
   - ☐ Students
   - ☐ Executives
   - ☐ Farmers
   - ☐ Teen-agers
   - ☐ _____
   - ☐ _____

Organization

There are many ways to organize written material, and the "best" way is not an absolute, but is dependent on the nature of the written product and on surrounding circumstances. However, match the items of the two columns below by writing the number of each left-hand item in the box beside the most appropriate right-hand items.

1. Sales letter
2. Brochure
3. Print advertisement
4. Press release
5. Speech

- ☐ Effect to cause
- ☐ Cause to effect
- ☐ Descending order of importance
- ☐ _____
- ☐ _____

Transitions

Write, rewrite, and/or edit (as you think necessary) whatever will create a suitable, smooth transition between the two paragraphs below:

The program includes two major activities, encouraging Federal agencies to develop useful consumer information. The Consumer Information Center (CIC) publishes quarterly the *Consumer Information Catalog*, distributed free to the public.

Federal Information Center (FIC) service is offered in five States. There are Centers in 34 other major areas, with 43 other cities connected to Centers by tie lines.

Translations

The following paragraph is in typical bureaucratese. Try your hand at translating it into clear, everyday English by eliminating surplus verbiage, simplifying sentence structure, and replacing the jaw breakers with shorter and more commonly used words.

Analysis of overhead is a two-step undertaking, involving the evaluation of projected or provisional indirect expenditures to establish a baseline of apparent reasonableness of allocability methodology utilized and the reasonableness of the stated necessity for proposed expenditures. The nominal goal of any such allocability methodology is to establish a ratio of such overhead or indirect costs to the productive effort in an attempt to make a determination of the most logical and equitable determination possible under the given circumstances.

Themes and Strategies

For each of the following items identify one of the two major themes, fear and gain, you think most appropriate, and write in a few words identifying at least one way you could implement that—e.g., fear/embarrassment or gain/money.

1. Jeans   ☐ Fear _____
                   ☐ Gain _____

2. Clothes   ☐ Fear _____
                   ☐ Gain _____

3. Automobile   ☐ Fear _____
                   ☐ Gain _____

4. Vitamins   ☐ Fear _____
                   ☐ Gain _____

5. Exercise machine ☐ Fear _____
                   ☐ Gain _____

CHAPTER THREE

The Typical Sales and Promotion Pieces

Sales and other promotional presentations are necessarily all visual and/or aural, the only two readily available avenues to human consciousness. Still, the presentations exist in an abundant variety of forms and functions, with some of them not even readily recognizable as sales or promotional tools.

■ A Potpourri of Sales Materials

There are a great many kinds of sales and promotion pieces used in marketing programs. "Piece" is something of a jargon term, used generally by writers to refer to almost any kind of writing that is shorter than a book—from a small print advertisement to a fat brochure. Here, the term is used in an even more general sense: as used here, a *piece* is any discrete communication item that is or can be used for marketing/promotional purposes. This necessarily includes an entire variety of print and aural media, since these are the two basic routes available to us in which to express our persuasive appeals.

Many of the materials referred to here are specifically and exclusively sales and promotional materials. But there are many others, materials with dual uses—that is, they are materials that were prepared for another primary use but found to be also useful for and therefore pressed into service to furnish direct support of marketing and promotional campaigns.

Sales Pieces

The fairly long list of materials most commonly used and recognizable as sales materials includes the following items:

advertising copy
broadsides
brochures
catalogs and catalog sheets
circulars
flyers
order forms
proposals
radio commercials
salesletters
TV commercials

Since many marketing campaigns are conducted by mail—in "mail-order" or "direct-mail" programs—many of these items are used together, along with sundry other items, to make up direct-mail packages. In addition to the salesletter, brochure, order form, and return envelope that are usually considered the obligatory minimum for a direct-mail package, many of the packages include sales messages on the outside of the envelope, several brochures, rather than one, and numerous other items, such as the following:

plastic cards simulating credit cards
calendars
decals and stickers
pens or pencils
folded leaflets saying "Don't open this unless you have decided not to order."
lists of testimonials
copies of press releases
reprints of relevant magazine and newspaper articles
newsletters
booklets
other novelties and giveaways

In connection with that last named item—"other novelties and give-aways"—I have had more than a few surprises at what I have received in direct-mail packages. So varied and expansive is the direct-mail business that I have gotten many unusual items. Some of the items appeared to be rather costly to include in a mass mailing. One was a plastic, but fully oper-ational digital timer/stop-watch, for example. Several times I have gotten audio tape cassettes in the mail, and on at least one occasion a videotape cassette.

■ Sales versus Promotion

Although not everyone distinguishes between and among the terms *marketing*, *sales*, and *promotion*, for our purposes it is useful to separate that last term from the first two and define it separately. For our purposes, then, sales and marketing pieces are those materials making a direct appeal for a specific order, such as a salesletter or sales brochure. Promotional pieces are materials designed to gain favorable publicity for a product or company. Typical promotional materials include at least the following items:

magazine and newspaper articles (and reprints thereof)
newsletters
press releases
photographs
press kits
product descriptions
specifications
annual reports

These materials are useful in all kinds of promotional and marketing campaigns, including inclusion in direct-mail packages. However, before considering the direct-mail package and direct-mail campaigns, it is useful to consider and discuss each major piece normally created and used for all types of marketing initiatives. So we will consider each one individually, in the order given.

■ Advertising Copy

Many people consider all material soliciting business—salesletters and radio or TV commercials, for example—to be advertising, and that conclusion is largely justified. However, for our purposes—to avoid unnecessary complexities in references—we will reserve the use of the term *advertising, advertising copy*, or *advertising piece* to refer strictly to print copy appearing in periodicals. Advertising materials appearing in other formats and environments will be identified by other, equally distinctive terms.

As is the case with many other sales and marketing pieces, advertising copy may have one of four direct and immediate purposes:

1. It may seek and request an immediate order for the item described as a direct response.
2. It may urge the reader to hurry to a retail outlet or showroom to buy the item described.

3. It may urge the reader to respond by requesting more information.

4. It may not call for any direct response, but may be what is often called "institutional advertising," merely promoting the product and/or company in general.

Advertising Seeking Direct Orders

All advertisers would like to simplify matters by asking the reader to send in an order immediately, in direct response to the advertisement. But there are three major factors affecting that: the size of the purchase and of the advertisement are two of those factors, and we will discuss a third one presently. But it is necessary to discriminate between small orders and larger orders, orders for items that are often referred to as "big tag" items.

Ordinarily, you cannot "pull" many orders for more than two or three dollars with a small advertisement—let us say an advertisement of one or two column-inches. Experience shows that it generally takes a full-page advertisement to pull orders of even $10 to $15 as casual purchases in direct response to advertising. It is normally quite difficult to generate direct-response orders much larger than that; a dozen pages will not produce direct orders for an automobile or refrigerator. These are "big tag" items, and it takes a great deal more than even the largest and most persuasive print advertisement to sell such items with a single appeal. There are exceptions, of course, because there are different conditions. "Big tag" is a generic and qualitative term, and it is not easy to quantify it. In some circumstances, a $50 item might be considered to have a big tag, whereas in other cases nothing less costly than a refrigerator would be considered a big-tag item.

Nevertheless, Sears, Montgomery Ward, Spiegel, Fingerhut, Bloomingdales, Neiman Marcus, and other well-known retailers who sell general merchandise and do repeat business with their customers are frequent exceptions. They can run advertisements and pull mail and telephone orders for sizable orders—at least, for moderately large items. But even they do not often sell really big tag items via a single advertisement. The average prospect simply does not part with hundreds of dollars spontaneously and without considerable thought.

Another exception is the case of the name brand item. Prospects may very well respond with spontaneous mail or telephone orders if you are selling an item with a large national reputation, one that is well known as a costly, quality item—a highly respected watch or a costly perfume, for example—as long as they (the prospects) are aware of the reputation and value of the advertised item.

There is still another exception: you see full-page advertisements for fairly costly items, wherein neither the item nor the advertiser is known to the prospect, not even by reputation. These are advertisements that are run again and again. Obviously, they must produce enough business to be worth running over and over. In such cases, the mere fact that they run over and over, plus the obvious fact that they are usually expensive advertisements, in full color and with other impressive embellishments, reassures the prospects that the advertiser is reliable and the offer legitimate. Familiarity and apparent stability have that effect on prospects. Many advertisements that do not return their insertion costs the first time or two that they are run eventually pay off very well when they have been run long enough.

Note the difference in these cases. In the first case, with only $10 or $15 at stake, the customer is not asked to undertake a large risk. In the other cases, with much more at stake, there are factors that engender trust in the advertiser so that the prospect is willing to undertake a much larger risk. It may be the great faith that an established customer has in the seller, it may be the reputation of what is being offered for sale, it may be the persuasive power of the copy (let us hope that it is that!), or it may be any of several other factors that generate confidence in the seller. That can be the factor that makes a difference. Still, never lose sight of the fact that under the best of circumstances it is not easy to sell big tag items directly from a print advertisement.

Advertising Seeking Other Responses

There are several conditions under which an advertiser does not seek orders directly or, at least, profit-producing orders are not the prime motivation of the advertising. That is, there are advertisers who do not necessarily expect to even recover all costs from orders resulting from the advertising. Frequently loss leaders or items offered at great discounts are offered. These offers are designed to achieve either or both of two ends: create a new sales lead, and/or create a new customer. In fact, the seller of general merchandise is well aware that most prospects will be rather cautious in ordering from them by mail or telephone for the first time, so initial orders are likely to be small ones. For that reason alone the item may be sold at well above its direct cost and yet be a loss leader because the profit is not great enough to return the cost of the advertising. The true profits, in that case, are in the new customer's future purchases. At least that is the rationale and the hope of the advertiser.

The Quill Corporation, a large mail-order supplier of furnishings and other items for businesses, invites new customers to provide their bank identification for immediate credit on their first order, an apparently quite effective means for creating new customers. A large mail-order merchant selling general consumer merchandise runs many small advertisements offering name-and-address labels at low cost. This is his or her means for generating prospective customers. The names of those ordering the mailing labels are added to the regular customer list and solicited for additional business after that. This is a type of inquiry advertising, but has at least one major advantage over inquiry advertising based on giving something away free: the prospect that submits an actual order, however small, is almost always a far better prospect than the one who requests something that is free. In fact, the former is actually a *customer* and, moreover, a *mail-order* customer, while the latter is not. The distinction is an important one. Customer lists are—rightly—considered the most valuable mailing lists one has, and lists of customers who buy by mail are especially valuable to those who market by mail.

These are not the only situations in which advertising seeks other responses than immediate orders, however; there are other marketing strategies, such as generating leads for items that cannot be sold by mail. Two typical examples are automobiles and houses. Both are situations in which the sale depends on bringing the prospect to the showroom or house (although there have been automobile salespeople who have driven the cars to the prospect).

This is a special problem, since it requires the prospect to do something, to undertake a specific course of action. It is rather well accepted by advertising specialists that the easier it is for the prospect to act, the less resistance to acting he or she will exhibit—i.e., the more likely it is that he or she will place the order. It is for this reason of making it easy for the customer to act that many advertisements include such conveniences as a postage-paid card for the prospect to fill out and drop in the mail. It is also for this reason that many advertisements do not require checks or cash in payment, but are quite willing to charge the customer's credit card or even, in some cases, to bill later. And it is for this reason that many advertisers offer a toll-free telephone number to call.

In the face of this philosophy, advertisers recognize the need to do something special to motivate the prospect to overcome his or her inertia and actually leave his or her home for the journey to the automobile showroom or the real estate development. Advertisers show a great deal of ingenuity in creating inducements to action in such cases. When the new model automobiles are out, some dealers create a virtual circus atmosphere in their showrooms, with balloons, beverages, even hot dogs dispensed freely to prospects and their families. But they also make psychological appeals to those who happen to take a great interest in automobiles and their features, by descriptions of all the features that are so new that they are revolutionary. They also offer test drives, urging prospects to visit and experience a new thrill. Some even urge prospects to visit all other dealers first so that he, the dealer, can prove that he has the best offer of anyone to make.

Builders of tract houses—whole developments—conjure up many inducements of their own, some similar, such as the circus atmosphere. They offer free gifts—small appliances, trips, and other lures—hold contests, and also hold out the inducement of inspecting the very latest in houses to those who make almost a hobby of visiting sample homes in new developments.

Invitations To Request More Information

There are many situations that fall between the two extremes described. For one reason or another, the advertiser wants to induce the prospect to ask for more information. This can be for any of several reasons:

☑ The advertiser wants to pre-screen prospects.
☑ The advertiser does not want to invest in large space advertising.
☑ The advertiser's primary objective is to build a mailing list for general purposes.
☑ The advertiser wishes to build a mailing list as the basis of a specific multi-stage campaign.

In the first case the advertiser wants to qualify the prospects to screen out those who are not serious prospects but who may be only idly curious. This is sensible when a great deal of time-consuming and costly effort—possibly including many telephone and/or in-person calls—is required to follow up leads and close sales. A great deal of time and money can be wasted on this if the leads are not good. It is far better, usually, to pursue a dozen leads that have been pre-screened and are known to be good than to pursue two or three dozen leads of uncertain quality.

In some cases each sale requires a highly specialized, multi-stage direct-mail campaign. It may be one that requires especially costly literature. (I have known of direct-mail campaigns wherein each package cost several dollars, for example.) This is another case where pre-screening to qualify prospects carefully is a must.

Pure inquiry advertising, such as that under discussion here, can usually be done effectively with relatively modest advertising space and budgets. It may be simply a waste of time and money to contract for a great deal of space in such cases.

Some advertisers wish only to build a general mailing list for direct-mail purposes. The screening in such cases is rather light and general.

This last is another, quite special case of the need for elaborate pre-screening of prospects. In some cases there are only a relatively few prospects among the general population. Securities dealers, for example, must seek out and carefully qualify rather specialized prospects. This would be especially true, for example, for securities dealers seeking to find investors to subscribe to a new stock issue; such investors are not the everyday individual "playing the market" casually.

In a later chapter we will examine specific examples of print advertising and discuss the kinds of publications commonly used to carry different kinds of copy.

■ Brochures and Broadsides

For practical purposes there is no difference between a brochure and a broadside. The latter is an advertising presentation on a large sheet—usually at least 11 × 17 inches but more often much larger than that—that is folded to fit into an envelope. The very term *brochure*, on the other hand, is so general and describes so many different forms and formats that it would not be wrong to simply include the broadside as one type of brochure.

A Few Brochure Forms and Formats

First of all, brochures are of a quite enormous range of sizes, both in their planar dimensions and in their number of pages. There are many brochures that measure as little as 3 × 4 inches on the plane, but there are others that are as large as 11 × 17 inches. Some are pamphlets, made up of a single sheet that is folded to form a number of panels, while others are made up of many pages, sometimes including stiff covers and some sort of binding. Brochures, often known by more specific names, include at least the following common types:

  Annual reports
  Booklets
  Capability brochures
  Catalogs
  Circulars and flyers
  Item descriptions and specification sheets
  Product and service brochures
  Salesletters
  Stuffers
  TV and radio commercials

Annual reports are generally published by public corporations and are written ostensibly for stockholders, although there are many other uses for them. They provide both qualitative and quantitative data about the company, identifying officers and principal or key executives; listing and describing projects, products, services, and other major activities; providing financial reports; and otherwise relating what the law requires and what the management believes stockholders should know. Small corporations tend to issue small, simple, inexpensive annual reports, but large corporations often go to major expense to have thick and rather elaborate annual reports published, with costly color photographs and expensive papers. This is not only to impress stockholders and investors, however; many corporations print a large supply of their annual reports and use them throughout the year to support their fund raising, stock underwriting, advertising, PR activities, and other functions in a large variety of ways, with the annual report acting as a leading advertising and promotional piece.

Capability brochures are generally made up in standard 8-1/2 × 11-inch size and are usually of a limited number of pages—probably averaging 6 to 20 pages for all but very large organizations. They are prepared for the general purpose of demonstrating an organization's qualifications for carrying out a project or providing specific services and functions. They normally describe the organization in terms of its experience and resources, the latter including physical facilities, staff, and financial capabilities. They are often requested by prospective clients or customers to aid in developing a list of organizations to be invited to submit quotes, bids, or proposals. As in the case of annual reports, capability brochures vary in size and nature from small to large and from simple and inexpensive to elaborate and costly.

Catalogs can and do also vary widely in size and nature. Quill Corporation, for example, mails out a thick, bound catalog twice a year, but mails a mini-catalog announcing sale items every month and frequently mails other mini-catalogs and catalog sheets to announce mid-month special discounts and other sale items. Catalogs are most widely used for direct-mail marketing because they are well suited to that application, and they are most appropriate to marketing that involves a reasonably numerous line of products. However, some manufacturing organizations do not offer a large enough number of products to merit a full-scale, bound catalog, but they do, nevertheless, often publish catalog sheets. These are descriptive pages or folders, often bearing detailed technical specifications describing the products covered. Catalogs may be used also to sell services, although less frequently.

Circulars and flyers are usually single sheets, generally but not always 8-1/2 × 11 inches in format, advertising a single item or service. They are used in a variety of ways, often as enclosures in direct-mail packages, but also distributed as throwaways. Quite often they are used to distribute special discount coupons to shoppers—they can often be seen in the mailbox, addressed to "resident"—especially in some sales season, such as Christmas and other national holidays, for they are most often used for a single sale or special occasion.

Item descriptions and specification sheets are much more objective presentations than advertising copy. They are necessary for certain markets, such as in selling to other businesses, whose needs must be satisfied precisely and who therefore require detailed, quantitative and qualitative descriptions. In many ways they are like catalog sheets issued by manufacturing organizations, especially those manufacturing technological products.

Product and services brochures are written for the information of the buyer—the customer or client—to describe the product or service and, of course, to extol its virtues. They are normally purely advertising and promotion pieces, and are written along the lines of some appropriate marketing and presentation strategy.

Salesletters are probably the most commonly used and most abundant sales pieces. The salesletter is the heart of the direct-mail package, for one, but it is also used as the centerpiece of other sales and promotional presentations, and is often mailed alone as well. Later we will look at a few exemplary salesletters, but it is worthwhile considering some basic do's and don'ts of salesletters here:

Salesletters are sales presentations. They are not personal nor individual business correspondence, and so are not bound by the conventional rules for such correspondence. Recipients of salesletters are more likely to be offended than pleased by such salutations as "To whom it may concern," or the obviously insincere "Dear friend."

It is perfectly acceptable today, in salesletters, to simply omit salutations, if you are addressing a general audience. (Still, if you are addressing housewives or marketing managers specifically and have used a mailing list of such a specialized audience, you may address them as "Dear Housewife" or "Dear Manager of Marketing.")

It is also acceptable today to use a headline to begin a salesletter. In fact, it is quite a good idea to do so, and it is rapidly becoming a common practice among direct-mail copywriters. Consider Figure 3-1 as an example. Or consider the salesletter of a paperback book club that begins as shown in Figure 3-2, using both a headline and a salutation. In this case, the letter is actually in the form of a brochure, printed on both sides of a large sheet that is folded, so as to present a four-page letter. The illustration shows only the beginning of the first page.

This illustrates the great flexibility possible when you do not permit yourself to be bound by archaic practices that have become rigid rules for some people. There is no reason to permit intellectual rigor mortis to take over. The marketing victories go to those courageous enough to think independently.

"3 Books 3 Bucks" is something of a theme in this mailing, in fact, since it is repeated as the name of an offer, and is also the headline carried on a 15 × 23-inch broadside, an order form, and a little brochure. Finally, it is printed prominently on the outside of the oversized envelope that carries

---

HRH COMMUNICATIONS, INC.
P.O. Box 1731
Wheaton, MD 20902
(301) 649-2499

WHY LEARN EVERYTHING THE HARD WAY?

Thank you for your response. Whether you are a beginner in business or a business veteran alert for new opportunities there are many useful ideas and tips for you in the array of information I offer, and I am delighted to begin by sending you the enclosed two free reports as small samples of the entire line of guides to success.

Please read these thoughtfully, and read them over and over, too. You will find that there is more to be gained with each reading. Read, too, my own credentials so that you will know who and what I am, as you should before you place enough trust in me to buy what I offer for sale.

I don't offer get-rich-quick promises. It is only in a most rare case that someone is fortunate enough to earn a lot of money swiftly. The truth about success in business is that it takes time, patience. You need three things: something worthy to sell (product or service), a sane and sensible marketing approach, and perseverance. If you have and employ all three, you will succeed.

FIGURE 3-1   One example of salesletter style

the package, so that it ties all its elements together. That, incidentally, is an excellent idea, lending unity to the entire package. In this case it is also a good headline since it does express the offer and the proposition: three books for three dollars is obviously a bargain. (It is the typical book club offer, of course.)

---

3 BOOKS 3 BUCKS
ZERO COMMITMENT

Dear Reader,
Do you love good books? Do you want to keep up with the latest trends and discover new voices? And do you enjoy savoring the great ideas of the past?

FIGURE 3-2   Another, slightly different, approach

Stuffers get their name not from what they are intrinsically, but from how they are used. They may be circulars, flyers, small brochures, or even salesletters that are enclosed—"stuffed in"—with orders and/or invoices. The organization that sells a variety of products will usually stuff a number of such pieces of literature in with orders and invoices. However, there are other ways to use stuffers profitably.

One such way is with other people's invoices. Credit card issuers, for example, often include stuffers for other people's merchandise on any of several possible arrangements that makes the proposition profitable for both parties. That is, flyers and brochures can be stuffed in with invoices from credit card issuers and several others, or enclosed with periodicals, an increasingly popular idea, apparently, judging from the increasing frequency with which it appears to be used.

Still another, related idea is cooperative mailing. Although pieces enclosed in co-op mailings are not normally referred to as stuffers, the idea is the same: many others who mail to large lists regularly will "piggyback" your stuffer under some form of sharing arrangement. And there are also some direct-mail support or service organizations whose entire business is that of cooperative mailings: they do not mail at all for themselves, but only for those who participate cooperatively. The participants benefit by paying only a fraction of what a full mailing of their own would cost, and if they cannot mail as complete a package—they normally include a single circular or brochure in the mailing—they gain the compensating benefit of reaching a far larger number of prospective customers than they could have otherwise reached.

Probably the most popular form of cooperative mailing has been that of the card deck—a pack of perhaps 50 to 100 3 × 5-inch cards enclosed in a clear plastic envelope. (Have you not yourself received at least one of these?) As a refinement, many now send out a mini-catalog, in 3 × 5-inch format, in these types of mailings.

Of course, we cannot overlook radio and TV commercials, for these— especially TV commercials—are a major element in advertising/sales/marketing materials and activity. But here we enter into a highly specialized area of writing, one that requires both technical knowledge (of production) and a sense of what "plays well" visually.

Of the two, writing radio commercials is undoubtedly less demanding, for a much greater reliance is placed on the listener's imagination, as stimulated by the performers' presentations and the sound effects. In some ways, that is an advantage over TV, for the listener's imagination is sometimes far greater than the realism of the set in a TV production. In any case, both, and especially TV, are quite effective when used well.

A reason for this is that of all the symbolism that the human mind translates into motivational inspiration, the interpretation/translation of written language is probably among the weakest. Words alone take on added emphasis when delivered by a charismatic character, even if the charisma is real, rather than the result of hype. Consider whether Lee Iaccoca's now well known, "If you can find a better car, buy it!" would have had the same impact delivered by an actor. Probably not, of course; the mere knowledge that Iaccoca was head of Chrysler and by now had become a well-known and highly respected public figure gave the message an impact it could not otherwise have had. You must understand such considerations as these in developing your "Sunday punch" commercials. The impact on the public is much more an emotional effect than a rational one, and therefore not at all easy to calculate or even to predict in the most general terms; there are too many imponderables involved. But understand, too, that even when you are thoroughly experienced, advised by experts, and have tested exhaustively, you can still be surprised by the actual event and often are. So the final injunction is to observe results and be guided by them, regardless of every other factor—period. That is at once the frustration and the mystique of marketing, and what makes it more an art form than a science or methodology.

■ Promotion

Here, again, we must first agree on what our terms mean. Some use the term "promotion" or "sales promotion" to refer to and encompass every kind of material and activity that has sales as its end goal. For purposes of explanation, however, it is much more convenient to segregate the terms. For that reason we have covered as sales and advertising those materials and activities that bear the direct exhortation to buy and utilize space (if a print item) or time (if a broadcast item) that the advertiser has paid directly for. These are easily identified as part of or representing direct sales efforts. On the other hand, when we discuss promotion in these pages we shall be referring to indirect sales efforts, most of which are usually identified as PR—public relations or publicity-seeking activity. This is activity that draws attention to the organization and/or products or services as news or features, space and/or time that are not directly paid for. That is, it is activity that results in write-ups in newspapers and other periodicals, mention on TV and radio broadcasts, and other approving public notice of the advertiser's existence, activities, services, and products.

As in most cases when subjects are fragmented into subordinate classifications, you find some cases that straddle the lines drawn, so that those cases must be arbitrarily assigned to one side or the other. This is no exception, and I confess that some of the assignments I make here are arbitrary, made for my own reasons. That, however, does not change the chief idea, which is to distinguish the characteristics of each to facilitate examination and understanding.

Public Relations (PR)

The term *public relations*, more popularly referred to as PR, is a euphemism for activities and materials that have as their chief goal the gaining of publicity—favorable publicity, that is—for you (your organization) and what you do or sell. Originally the chief medium toward which that goal was directed were the nation's newspapers, of which there were many thousands. (The columns of print in magazines were a secondary and subordinate target.) The inroads made by radio and television broadcasting have whittled down the lists of newspapers, and many of our metropolitan areas—even the largest ones—today boast only one or at most two newspapers, where once there were five or six. Philadelphia, for example, had six daily newspapers when I was going to school there. Today it has one morning newspaper and the tabloid; even the venerable and at one time seemingly invulnerable Philadelphia evening *Bulletin* was finally forced out of existence a few years ago, leaving the field to a sole surviving morning newspaper, the *Inquirer*. (In most cases where only a single paper has survived it tends to be a morning, rather than an evening, paper.)

The Changing Media

The growth of news and specialty magazines further thinned the ranks of daily newspapers, and they are also targets for your PR efforts today. The newsstands of several decades ago were heavy with the pulp magazines of that era. (They were magazines that were printed on cheap pulp paper and devoted to genre fiction.) The newsstands bore relatively few smooth-paper, general-interest periodicals in those times. Today there are few pulps left, but there are a great number of smooth-paper, special-interest magazines, and while the failure rate is high, there seems to be an almost endless supply of new ones springing up.

There has also been an enormous surge of interest in newsletters, most of which are devoted to fields and subjects too highly specialized to receive more than scant mention in newspapers and other general-interest periodicals. These are an almost always overlooked target for PR, possibly because few newsletters have large circulation. However, in the aggregate, the total circulation of newsletters is quite high, and this can be turned to advantage. Try to bear this in mind, for we will return to the subject.

Today, therefore, PR must be directed to radio and TV, as well as to newspapers, newsletters, and magazines. The scene, and to some extent the targets, have changed, but the philosophy and main thrust have not. It—publicity—must still be *made* to happen by taking advantage of chance, where that is possible, but, primarily, by creating newsworthy events and making them readily available to the media.

A Few More Specialized Methods

There are some other methods. There are in Hollywood, for example, PR people who specialize in getting their clients' products and services displayed and mentioned in movies and teleplays. It is not by accident that in films you can so easily read the trade names of many products or that some specific organization is mentioned. PR specialists work full time at arranging such fortunate happenings. Many manufacturers make supplies of their products available to movie makers, even lending automobiles and other non-expendable items for the promotional value. Manufacturers supply items to TV game shows and contests for the same reason, although these now become borderline cases, since they are, in fact, paying for the advertising/promotional exposure with the products themselves, many of which are quite costly. In a slightly more indirect way, many business owners supply uniforms for local sports teams, with their (the manufacturers') names plainly inscribed thereon.

If you cannot find local events, shows, contests, and other opportunities to turn to your advantage for gaining PR, you can always create the opportunities. You can, for example, sponsor a contest without waiting for someone else by either proposing it to some organization or launching it yourself. The multimillion-dollar national contests of the magazine-sellers (e.g., Publishers Clearing House) are one well-known example, but there are many others. In these activities you begin to approximate the "newsworthy" approach to PR more closely, doing things that are likely to get you mentioned in the local press and elsewhere. Of course, this may also be a direct advertising/sales effort, as the Publishers Clearing House contest is, but that is one of those borderline cases I referred to earlier.

The Tools of Promotion

The chief tool of PR is the release, also referred to as a press release, publicity release, product release, and news release. No matter what other PR activity you devise and launch, you can almost always find room for—even a necessity for—the release. And many successful campaigns have been waged with the release alone.

The news/press/publicity release

The release is a simple enough idea. It is a handout, ostensibly news and feature material provided to editors at no cost. It is copy, double spaced for editorial work, which the harried editor can press into service for his or her publication/broadcast. Editors ought to be grateful for this manna from heaven. And they are, if the material is useful. Unfortunately, this is not always the case. (By far the vast majority of releases wind up in discard after only a brief glance at the lead, just enough in far too many cases to demonstrate the probable futility of spending more time in reading it.) In short, writers of releases are too, too human; they make mistakes. Figure 3-3 is an example of a properly written release. Unfortunately, many other releases exhibit the following major mistakes:

- ☑ The material supplied as a release is not "newsworthy." Not only is it not fresh and sparkling, but it is an unabashed "commercial," a blatant and unabashed advertisement masquerading as a news release. It is absolutely shameless self-promotion.

- ☑ The writer of the release shows no understanding of the editor's problems and needs. The release is single-spaced—a glaring revelation of an editorial or journalistic tyro at work—and is in no relevant or recognizable format, further evidence of amateurish incompetence—perhaps even nincompoopetence.

- ☑ The writer has not only failed to provide photos, where photos are clearly needed, but has not even furnished a "contact" name and number so that the editor can follow up to request photos or whatever else might be needed to put the release to use.

- ☑ The release has not had at least a cursory editing to ensure that spellings and usages are reasonably close to those generally considered to be acceptable practice.

- ☑ The release is woefully overblown and laboriously written. It is several pages long when the subject does not appear to merit more than a page or two. Even worse, it is not possible to get a clue as to the subject matter from the lead, i.e., without struggling on for at least a full page.

Many releases contain minor faults, such as the failure to signal the end of the copy with a –30–, ###, or END and the failure to furnish a contact name. These are not usually fatal if the release is newsworthy and reasonably well written. But we need to define those terms, *newsworthy* and *well written*, and we will shortly. But let us consider a special kind of release first, one that is much closer to a pure (and free) advertisement than are the releases we have been discussing.

Ventana Press

FOR IMMEDIATE RELEASE

FOR FURTHER INFORMATION:
Lynn Echnoz, 919/490-0062

GRAPHIC DESIGN BOOK FOR DTP RELEASED THIS MONTH

Chapel Hill, NC; February 1988--Looking Good in Print: A Guide to Basic Design for Desktop Publishing, a graphic design primer for desktop publishers, has been published by Ventana Press of Chapel Hill, North Carolina. The book will be of value to any desktop publishing professional who wants to design better-looking reports, advertisements, newsletters or other desktop published printed material.

"Documents don't design themselves, even with the best layout software," says Looking Good in Print author Roger Parker. "Graphic design is the missing link between desktop publishing and good-looking printed materials."

Neither hardware- nor software-specific, Looking Good in Print introduces the reader to the "tools of the trade"--white space, bullets, typefaces, rules, and more. A "design makeover" features before-and-after examples of improved design through the application of basic techniques. The book contains hundreds of invaluable tips and tricks for producing creative design. A special discussion of "10 Common Design Pitfalls" (and how to avoid them) can save hours of problem-solving.

Looking Good in Print has been chosen as a main selection of the Graphic Artists Book Club and as an alternate selection of the Writer's Digest Book Club. Because the initial printing

--more--

P.O. Box 2468   Chapel Hill, NC 27514   919/490-0062

FIGURE 3-3   Properly structured release

The product release

The product release is a special type, one that merits its own discussion. In most cases it finds a home in somewhat specialized publications, those that run special sections in which new products are presented and described, often with photos where the photo will add something. Product releases announcing household products, cosmetics, tools, and other items are usually well received by the appropriate periodicals. An item that is of special interest, one that is really news (e.g., the early pocket calculators and other products made possible by the revolutionary new silicon chips) will often find its way into the news columns of the newspapers, as well.

What Does *Newsworthy* Really Mean?

Obviously, it is a rare occurrence when truly "big news" appears in or results from a release. Releases are usually announcements of new products, statements by officials, word of business meetings, and other such things. Word of all of these things is news, of course, but not in the sense of a revolution, the merger of two giant corporations, or the creation of a new government agency. Those latter events are likely to be front page items, whereas the former ones are more likely to be brief items in a special section of the periodical or broadcast programming.

Newsworthy, in the context of this discussion, means merely worthy of being used—printed or broadcast—by the recipients. In fact, releases do not have to be news at all, except in the most technical sense of the word or because it is of significance locally; they may be, like feature stories in the newspapers, simply accounts that are interesting or amusing for some reason. The true criterion is that they are worthy of being presented to the public. They represent free editorial matter provided to publishers and broadcasters, and therefore need only to be as useful to the publishers and broadcasters as is the editorial material they normally pay for.

The question of what is newsworthy is not entirely separate from the question of writing quality. Even newsworthy releases can fail when they are not written well.

What Does *Well Written* Really Mean?

The pressures and constraints of writing advertising, sales, and promotional pieces, like those of the journalistic trade, make it unlikely that great literature can ever emerge from writing such materials. So "good writing" in this field does not refer to the generation of great eloquence or great thoughts. But it does refer to a proper command of the written language, an organized and coherent train of thought that makes a main point and subordinate points clearly, and a style characterized by easy readability. Each of these bears a bit of discussion.

A proper command of the language

If what you write is to be considered seriously, especially by professional editors, your writing must be entirely literate. Spellings must be accurate, punctuation used judiciously, and sentences clearly in possession of a subject and predicate. You must not say *principal* when you mean *principle* nor *its* when you mean *it's*. And that's only the beginning, for while you do need to understand and be able to apply the rules of *usage*—grammar, punctuation, spelling, rhetoric, etc.—there is a great deal more to writing well than the mastery of usage. It is quite possible to follow all the rules of usage flawlessly and still write quite badly. More than a few well-educated individuals manage that feat every day. The matters of style, coherence, organization, flow, and logic are even more critical than are the rules of usage.

Organization and flow

One of the basic rules taught in public schools as part of education in *composition* is that every paragraph must have a topic sentence. The topic sentence introduces the paragraph and announces the topic of the paragraph. It is the first element of the friendly, three-element advice so often offered to individuals as the basic rule of public speaking: "Tell 'em what you're going to tell 'em, tell 'em, and then tell 'em what you told 'em. "

But that philosophy is not confined to paragraph construction alone; it is a general truth for all writing. The first chapter of a book is its introduction. The first paragraph of an article or short story has the same function. It orients and acquaints the reader, explaining or at least intimating broadly what to expect.

Another term used widely to refer to this introductory material is *lead*. Every well-written piece has a lead of some kind. Note the topic sentence or lead of this paragraph. It introduced and defined the term, making it clear that this was to be the subject of the paragraph. Most normal human minds think in a logical and orderly flow, and we can understand new information easily only when it is presented to us in that way. That is, we can grasp a string of facts and perceive the body of the information when we understand not only the individual facts but how they relate to each other. The relation may be cause and effect or the reverse—effect and cause; it may be chronology, forward or reverse; it may be order of importance, order of magnitude, or some other order. For the presentation to be effective—easily and thoroughly understood—the receiver must understand the significance of the sequence or order in which the facts are presented and have some clue as to where the presentation is headed—the overall goal or objective. (That is generally stated in the lead.)

Readability

The matter of *readability* has become a subject of some interest today, especially since the easy availability of computers has made it rather easy to measure readability. Two of the most popular measures are the Flesch Index (*How to Test Readability*, Rudolf Flesch, Harper & Row, New York, 1951) and the Fog Index (*How to Take the Fog Out of Writing*, Robert Gunning, Dartnell, Chicago, 1964).

Both use formulas based principally on measuring sentence length and word length (syllable count) to judge the complexity of the writing. This is admittedly only a rough measure of readability because there are many other factors:

- ☑ Readability varies from one individual to the next, depending in such things as the reader's prior knowledge of the subject, the degree of his or her interest in the subject, and his or her reading ability.
- ☑ Readability is also a matter of aids to reading and understanding, such as illustrations, tables, anecdotes, and writing style.
- ☑ Finally, there are many other inherent problems in measuring readability because results are obscured by the program's efforts to read matrices or tables, headlines and captions, figures, and other non-textual presentations. So readability can vary according to the nature of the material.

Despite these problems and shortcomings and with these limitations in mind, the measures are still quite helpful. At the least they give you a good clue as to how dense or difficult your text is, and in the case of releases and other sales/promotional material the materials tend to be primarily, often entirely, text.

There are a number of computer programs available to read text in a computer file. They fall generally into two classes, those that are relatively sophisticated and furnish a great deal of information about the text sampled (usually including some diagnostic data to help the writer correct problems), and those that are relatively simple and fast, reporting only scores. Figure 3-4 illustrates the kind of readability report offered by a simple program. Note the estimated grade levels of several popular publications. (*Reader's*

NOTES	LEVEL
HIGH READING LEVELS	18 17 16 15 14
ESTIMATED LEVELS OF POPULAR PERIODICALS	
	13
	12
Wall Street Journal	11
	10
Reader's Digest	9
	8
People	7
	6
National Enquirer	5

FIGURE 3-4   Readability scales. The text sample had a reading level of 10.7

Digest, usually represented as grade level 8, rather than 9, is often cited as representing an excellent readability standard.) Note the score reported for a sample text measured with this convenient and speedy little program. It scored the text at 10.7, just a bit below the readability of the *Wall Street Journal*.

Figure 3-5 illustrates a much more sophisticated readability program, one that not only offers a good bit of information but also identifies problem words and offers synonym lists to help the writer find simpler words to substitute for the problem words and so reduce the readability scores to better levels.

For the sample shown, the grade level is low, which makes the readability high. On the Flesch index the score is in direct proportion to the readability level, with 100 the maximum score. (So you look for low numbers if you are using the grade-level index and high numbers if you are using the Flesch index.) The results are summarized in both figures and in the graphic chart, "Index Summary," which runs from indicators of low readability at the left to those of high readability at the right.

The estimated grade-level 6 of the sample text may strike you as rather low for an adult audience, but the fact is that 8th- to 9th-grade level is about

```
=============== MAXI-READ  Summary ===============
  Readability  VERY LOW     LOW     AVERAGE     HIGH     VERY HIGH
  Summary::::  |_____+_____+_____+_____+_____█|
```

```
      Approximate GRADE LEVEL:    6  |   +---[   Index Summary   ]---+
             The FLESCH INDEX:   86  |L  0|_____+_____+_____+___█_|100 H
  Personal Tone-% Personal Words:  3  |O  0|_____+_█___+_____+_____|10  I
     Percent SESQUIPEDALIAN WORDS:  4  |W 15|_____+_____+_____█___|0   G
Average # of WORDS PER SENTENCE:  13  |  18|_____+_█___+_____+_____|7   H
Average # of SYLLABLES PER WORD: 1.3  |2.5|_____+_____+_____+___█_|1.0
```

```
  # of 'SENTENCES':   21    # of WORDS:   292   Total # of SYLLABLES:   365
```

```
  SESQUIPEDALIAN WORDS  |  The Following Words may be ADDING TO COMPLEXITY.
  ──────────────────────|Maximum Shown:  250 Words/13 Char. per Word|──────
```

Reference	MAXI-READs	Directory	Sesquipedalia 6MMMMMMMMMMMM
Exceptions	analyses-Assu	Exceptions?	continue...

|DONE!   [F1]=Interpretation HELP   [F5]=Synonym List   SPACE=Return To MENU

WORD	SYNONYM(S)	WORD	SYNONYM(S)
Abandon	Desert, Leave	Confederate	Ally
Abbreviate	Cut, Shorten	Conspicuous	Visible, Clear
Accelerate	Hurry, Speed up	Contaminate	Infect, Pollute
Acceptable	Pleasing, Welcome	Contemplate	Look at, Consider
Accident	Mishap	Convenient	Fit, Useful
Accomodate	Adapt, Fit, Suit	Conversation	Talk, Speech
Accomplish	Do, Finish	Demonstrate	Show, Prove
Acknowledge	Admit, Allow	Derivation	Source
Adjacent	Next to, Near	Deteriorate	Decay, Lessen
Advantageous	Good	Determine	Decide, Find out
Alternative	Choice, Option	Duplicate	Copy
Amalgamation	Union, Group	Economical	Frugal, Saving
Ambiguous	Vague, Unclear	Educate	Train, Teach
Anticipation	Hope	Effervescent	Bubbly
Appropriate	Fitting, Suited	Elementary	Easy, Simple
Approximate	About	Eliminate	Get rid of, Omit
Capricious	Odd, Fickle	Elucidate	Clarify, Explain
Combination	Mixture, Union	Embellish	Enhance, Adorn
Comfortable	Pleasant	Employment	Work, Job
Communicate	Write, Tell, Say	Encourage	Urge, Support
Compensation	Payment, Reward	Encumbrance	Load, Burden
Competent	Able, Fit	Endeavor	Try, Attempt
Comprehend	Know, Grasp	Enormous	Immense, Huge

|PRESS: ESC to QUIT   Any other key to continue . .page 1 of 3

FIGURE 3-5   MAXI-READ readability report and portion of synonym list. (Courtesy RWS & Associates)

right for the general public, even for professional people. The point of this is not that the average adult cannot handle language at higher grade levels, but that the higher grade level requires more effort by the reader. But the less readable or more difficult the text, the more likely the reader will skip past it if he or she has no compulsion to read it. Moreover, even when the reader is inspired to read the material, he or she will not normally work very hard at understanding it—will not pore over it or study it intensely— and so is likely to miss the message. You see evidence of this every day, as friends and acquaintances report what they think they have read in the newspapers and magazines, and you wonder where they could have gotten such false notions! Pressed as we are today, with so many things competing for our attention, we tend to read rather hastily.

The simple principles of simple writing

The principle here is to make it easier to understand what you have writ- ten rather than to misunderstand it. Avoid cleverness, subtlety, misplaced humor, ponderous language, complex sentences, overly complex charts and tables, scholarliness, and every other impediment to rapid and easy understanding. Deal with one idea at a time. Say what you have to say— make your point as directly as possible—and stop. Stay at about the 8th- grade level; that is the right one for most purposes. If you must depart from that, do so by being more readable, not less so.

Readability and related facets of the art of writing were covered here in connection with the writing of promotional materials because those are ordinarily the longest pieces you are likely to write, but the principles apply to everything you write. In fact, they are even more important when you write brief pieces because it is more difficult to write an effective small advertisement than to write an effective salesletter or brochure. However, one of the largest pieces of writing you are likely to be called upon in writing promotional materials is the newsletter, a publication often used as an effective vehicle for promotion.

Newsletter Writing

In general, newsletters exist because they provide their readers a specialized information service. They fall generally into about six broad classes:

1. Digests of useful ideas, tips, and data from a variety of published sources. The reader is spared the impossible chore of trying to read all those original sources to glean this information.

2. Specialized information on subjects either not covered in most publications or covered too scantily to be of value to those with special interest in the subjects.

3. Advice and "inside" (or alleged "inside") information and tips, but primarily advice.

4. An information exchange from the leadership and among the members of a membership organization.

5. An information medium in large business organizations, circulated to employees.

6. An information medium for your customers, your prospective customers, and other publishers.

The subjects vary enormously, across the whole spectrum of human interests. There are many newsletters bearing information and advice on the stock market and other investments. Also popular are newsletters on marketing, management, antiques, coins, stamps, and the various industries. There are few subjects that are not covered. Howard Penn Hudson, publisher of the *Newsletter on Newsletters* and other publications about newsletters estimates that there are about 100,000 newsletters in existence.

The newsletter as a PR tool

Obviously, it is the last-named class of newsletters that we are interested in here, for that is the kind of newsletter used as a PR or promotional tool. Written and used properly, such a newsletter is a powerful tool and can be used in more than one way. On the one hand, it is an excellent PR medium in general, carrying news of your organization to individuals and to other organizations, as well as to other publishers. It thus serves as a kind of press release. (You make it clear to other publishers that they may quote from or use items from your newsletter freely, with "attribution"—i.e., acknowledging the source. But it may also be used as a kind of salesletter or even as a direct-mail package sent out freely to customers and prospects. It is your own publication, and you can do with it what you wish, although you should observe certain principles and practices that we shall discuss briefly here. But first let us touch on some highly practical matters you must consider.

Frequency of publication

Newsletters range, in frequency of publication, from daily to annually: there are newsletters published every day, once a week, once a month, once every two months (bimonthly), once every three months (quarterly), once every six months (semiannually), and once every 12 months (annually). And there are even some published "occasionally"—at the publisher's whim or convenience.

By far the most popular publishing period for newsletters is monthly, and probably the runners-up are bimonthly, quarterly, and weekly, in that order. The decision as to frequency, the publishing schedule, is arbitrarily the publisher's, of course, but there are a number of factors to consider in making the decision. Here are a few of the principal ones:

- ☑ It would be rare that a newsletter published for PR would be published more frequently than once a month. (Many are bimonthly or quarterly.) You should probably not consider a more frequent schedule than that.
- ☑ To succeed, the newsletter must not be total advertising matter, but must have enough useful information for the reader to persuade him or her to work through the newsletter. Therefore, you must consider how much information flow you have to pass on—i.e., can you sustain a monthly newsletter by producing enough useful new information every month, throughout the year?
- ☑ How much of your resources are you willing to devote to the task of preparing the newsletter and distributing it? Are you willing to sustain an effort (i.e., cost in dollars and your time) every month?
- ☑ How much of our budget can you commit to distribution (primarily mailing) of each issue? A monthly newsletter requires twice as much as a bimonthly, of course.

Size

Most newsletters are in an 8-1/2 × 11-inch format, usually printed on both sides of one or more 11 × 17-inch sheets and folded to make four pages. That is usually the minimum size, although many newsletters are six, eight, and even more pages. The consideration of size (in number of pages, that is) is, again, an arbitrary one you make, but you must be guided by practicality. For the most part, they are the same considerations as those guiding your decision as to frequency of publication—the amount of material you expect to have to present, the resources you can spare, the budget you are working with, and other such factors. However, while it is difficult to change the frequency of publication once you adopt a schedule, you are under no compulsion to publish the same number of pages in each issue. Many newsletters vary in the number of pages in any given issue, controlled solely by the circumstances surrounding each issue.

Distribution

Because newsletters normally provide specialized information for a specialized audience, information they could not get easily elsewhere, the total number of readers from the commercial newsletter tends to be relatively small and the subscription price relatively high. That is not the case here, however, since your newsletter is free (although it should bear a stated subscription price to stress that it has a value, although the reader has been favored with a free copy). The number of copies you distribute is up to you.

Overall, the effectiveness of even the best newsletter is in some ratio to the number of copies distributed, for probability statistics play an important role in all marketing and promotional efforts. It is in your direct interest, that is, to maximize the distribution by any and all means possible. Distribution of a newsletter, which is usually primarily via the mails, would normally follow the same routes as distribution of your salesletters, direct-mail packages, releases, and brochures. That is one of the advantages of a well-done newsletter: it can serve in all these capacities quite well. You may therefore distribute your newsletters via the mails, but you can also get effective distribution of many copies through several other avenues, all of which you should employ:

☑ Make copies freely available at conventions, trade shows, association meetings, and other such conclaves.
☑ If you have dealers or distributors see that they each have a supply to distribute by whatever means are available to them.
☑ If you have sales people on the road make sure each has a supply to distribute.
☑ Enclose copies with any literature you mail out for any reason.
☑ Enclose copies with your invoices and quotations.
☑ Build a "comp" list of other publishers of newsletters, magazines, trade papers, and any other publication that reaches people who are suitable prospects for what your organization sells. Be sure to make it clear to all other publishers that they are free to pick up any of the material in your newsletter, but request attribution.

Probably you can find some other ways to add to your distribution. It helps to be always on the alert for new and better ways. For example, if you are invited to speak publicly, you can probably arrange to distribute copies of your newsletter and brochures to the audience or, at least, to have them made available on a literature table. You may also find that certain local groups, such as trade associations and business clubs would like to get a number of copies of each issue for distribution to their own audiences and attendees of their meetings. Depending on the nature of your newsletter, you may find the local libraries would like to place a supply on their own free-literature tables.

Content

Of course, your newsletter is promotional literature. You created it to help market your company's products or services, and the content is therefore necessarily advertising, even if low key or soft sell. At the same time, since you characterize and publish it as a newsletter, it cannot be 100 percent unabashed advertising matter. That would immediately destroy its usefulness. You must publish some material that is worthy of appearance in a newsletter and is definitely slanted to the reader's probable direct interest, whether that serves your own interests directly or not. It cannot be a pure salesletter, brochure, or advertising circular. Still, you do pay the bills for the newsletter and furnish it free of charge, so you are entitled to use it in behalf of your own business. My recommendation is that you devote not less than one-third of the content to true newsletter (editorial) material. That leaves you with two-thirds you can devote to selling your organization and products or services. Even then, you are likely to benefit more by devoting at least part of the remaining two-thirds to "soft sell" material, rather than direct appeals to buy. That is, material that promotes what you sell in the general terms of describing benefits produced by your products or services— applications-oriented explanations. (Examples will be presented in a later chapter.)

Miscellaneous Promotional Materials

There are a number of other items you can develop to promote your products and services. Following are just a few examples.

One whole class of such materials is that of reports or "folios." These are materials written as folders or brochures, usually only of a few pages, presenting several kinds of information, such as the applications notes just suggested for the newsletter and/or other material that would normally be of interest to your customers and bear some relation to the business of your organization.

Articles written for publication in periodicals are useful for PR. Even if the periodicals are not those typically read by your customers, you can make excellent use of reprints of those articles sent out as part of your promotional literature.

Speeches written to be presented by members of your organization as part of an in-house lecture bureau or at association meetings and similar occasions are used widely for promotional purposes.

■ Resources Required

There are two ways to get these materials produced. One is to do all the creative work—writing and illustrating—in-house with resident staff. The other is to vend the work to consultants and/or other firms who specialize in such work. And many firms adopt hybrid systems, doing both by producing some of the materials in-house but "contracting-out" the more highly specialized items, such as newsletters and speeches.

Sources for Creative Talent

Even then, a wide variety and combination of methods is possible. There are many firms, small and large, who operate with staffs and physical resources to handle all or any part of such creative work on their own premises. But there are also many consultant specialists who will do part or all of the creative work on your own premises, using your own physical resources. Some of these consultants are generalist writers who will undertake virtually any writing task, while others specialize in newsletters, speeches, direct-mail literature, or other distinctive kind of creative writing. (A resource list of such outside services and specialists appears in an appendix.)

The resources required to do this creative work in-house are principally human resources, rather than equipment of any kind. There is ordinarily not enough illustration required to justify a full-time illustrator, unless you have one or more illustrators on-staff for some other reason. Therefore, most firms who do not otherwise employ illustrators vend such work or bring in a consultant or part-time illustrator, as needed.

Much the same can be said for writing. Whether you keep one or more writers on staff depends on how much writing work you have. It is not difficult to vend this work out too. However, there is a problem here, in that you must either find a writer or writers who are competent in designing and writing materials for sales and PR, or you must have someone on staff who is expert enough to provide specific direction and careful guidance to ensure the right results.

This is true even when you hire a major vendor to help, such as one of the leading advertising firms. Many of the disasters in advertising campaigns are not really the fault of the advertising agency's account executives and copywriters; they are the result of inept guidance and direction by the client. Clients sometimes insist on copy that pleases them for the wrong reasons—perhaps because it flatters them or because it is artistic—rather than because it is effective. And sometimes it is the client who thinks up the cute and clever headline that spells disaster for the advertising copy.

It is essential, then, that whether you do the work in-house with your own staff or use others, outside specialists, to do the work, that you understand what you need and want.

Physical Resources

There is one kind of physical resource that is a must today: the desktop computer with suitable word-processing, desktop-publishing, and other relevant software. But along with that you must of course have someone who knows how to use them effectively. When so equipped, even the small organization can do in-house much of the work that they would have been forced to contract out only a few years ago.

■ Exercises

As in the previous chapter, a few exercises are offered here to help you determine whether you have grasped all the main points made in this chapter and, if not, what you need to review. Also, as in the previous set of exercises, provision is made to write in your own answers in most cases. There are no "school solutions"—answers—here either. Unless you are quite sure of your answer, you will do well to go back and review the relevant text.

Major Types of Sales Materials

Check off those items you believe to be the major sales pieces.

☐   **1.**   Envelopes with outside copy
☐   **2.**   Catalog sheets
☐   **3.**   Sales letters
☐   **4.**   Proposals
☐   **5.**   Order forms
☐   **6.**   Brochures
☐   **7.**   Reports
☐   **8.**   Advertising copy

☐ 9. Circulars
☐ 10. Flyers
☐ _____
☐ _____

Major Promotional Pieces

Check off at least three items used commonly as major tools for PR or promotion.

☐ 1. Calendars
☐ 2. Decals
☐ 3. Newsletters
☐ 4. Reports
☐ 5. Press releases
☐ _____
☐ _____

Sales versus PR

Write *P* or *S* following each of the following items to signify whether you believe the item to be a sales piece or a PR tool.

1. Magazine article _____
2. TV commercial _____
3. Speech _____
4. Catalog _____
5. Brochure _____

Direct Mail Packages

Check off those items following that are generally considered to be the obligatory minimum required for a direct-mail package.

☐ 1. Sales letter
☐ 2. Advertising novelty
☐ 3. Order form
☐ 4. Brochure

☐ **5.** Return envelope
☐ **6.** Broadside
☐ **7.** Catalog sheet
☐ **8.** Product description
☐   _____
☐   _____

A Few Basic Truths and Untruths of Sales and Marketing

Write in *T* or *F* (for True or False) after each of the following items.

1. The most effective advertisements are given CLIO awards.   _____
2. The most important thing in selling is to get attention.   _____
3. Body copy in advertising is more important than the headline.   _____
4. The only test of advertising is whether it produces orders.   _____
5. Sales copy on the envelope is a must in direct mail.   _____
6. Spelling out benefits is a must in all selling.   _____
7. You should never use a headline in a sales letter.   _____
8. Effective advertising and selling offers proofs of the claims.   _____
9. Inquiry advertising is a waste of money.   _____
10. The headline should summarize the appeal.   _____

Readability

Check off those items you believe are important rules for making your copy highly readable.

☐ **1.** Use short, direct sentences.
☐ **2.** Illustrate main points, both verbally and graphically.
☐ **3.** Use impressive words and an elegant style.
☐ **4.** Present long and highly detailed explanations of every point.
☐ **5.** Use picturesque language and lots of anecdotes.
☐ **6.** Use terse, telegraphic style.
☐ **7.** Use active voice.
☐ **8.** Use passive voice.
☐   _____
☐   _____

Releases

There are several "rules" for writing a good release. Check off those you believe to be important ones among the following.

☐ **1.** Use a high-quality paper for your releases.
☐ **2.** Always include a headline.
☐ **3.** Double-space the copy.
☐ **4.** Use telegraphic style.
☐ **5.** Provide a "contact" name and number for follow-up.
☐ **6.** Indicate at the bottom of the page whether there is or is not more copy to follow.
☐ **7.** Date the release.
☐ **8.** Be sure your name is prominent.
☐ _____
☐ _____

Writing Quality

There are major and minor elements in writing well. Check off those you believe to be the major or most important ones.

☐ **1.** An effective lead
☐ **2.** Rhetorical flourish
☐ **3.** Transitions
☐ **4.** Spelling and punctuation
☐ **5.** Grammar
☐ **6.** Organization
☐ **7.** Illustrations
☐ **8.** Eloquence
☐ _____
☐ _____

Readability

Check off that grade level range ordinarily considered to be most suitable in writing intended for the public in general.

☐ **1.** 6-7
☐ **2.** 8-9

☐ **3.** 10-11

☐   _____

☐   _____

Newsletters

Check off those items following that you believe to be important things to consider in deciding to publish a newsletter.

☐ **1.** The title you will use
☐ **2.** The schedule or frequency of publication
☐ **3.** The size of the newsletter
☐ **4.** How much advertising you can crowd into it
☐ **5.** How you will distribute it
☐ **6.** What resources you must commit to it
☐   _____
☐   _____

CHAPTER FOUR

The Essentials of Persuasive Writing

Sales and promotional copy must, rather obviously, be persuasive if they are to be successful. The "proof and promise" discussed earlier summarizes the basic method for being persuasive, but there is a great deal more to be said on the subject of implementing that concept.

■ A Common Denominator

The most important word in an advertisement or other sales appeal is *you*, the direct address to the reader. We all need to be recognized. We all have egos that need gratification. We all need to feel appreciated, to love and be loved, to "belong," to be "in," to feel worthy. Perhaps it all adds up to a need to feel some sense of security, not only in the physical sense of feeling reasonably assured of being warm, fed, clothed, and housed, but also—perhaps even more intensely—in the sense of emotional security. If there is any single factor that we share universally it is that need for such assurances. And much as some of us might wish to deny it and try to do so, we are ruled far more by our emotional needs and drives than by reason. Effective sales presentations—*persuasive* presentations, that is—always have as their central element a basic appeal to the prospect's emotions.

■ The "Secret" of Salesmanship

A deep and complete understanding of that is a large part of the "secret" of supersalesmanship. It is what the late Elmer Wheeler had that led him to such achievements that he came to be recognized and acclaimed for years as "America's greatest salesman." It is what enabled him to develop such a deep understanding of customer motivation as he expressed in what was probably his most famous dictum to other salespeople, "Sell the sizzle, not the steak." It is why he could so brilliantly solve the problem of a frustrated retailer, stuck with a large inventory of slow-moving long underwear, by posting a sign on a large display of that underwear, saying, "They don't itch."

■ Greed, The Motivator

So powerful is the emotional appeal that in the hands of experts it can even cause countless individuals to completely abandon reason and do totally irrational things. It is the reason that confidence games work on so many people: the expert con artist usually has little difficulty in persuading the victim to believe what the victim eagerly *wants* to believe—he or she can realize material gain (usually money) without earning it, something for nothing. That is the basis for all con games, and the success of the swindler depends entirely on his or her success in convincing the victim that the promised something for nothing will materialize if he or she (the victim) supplies certain assets—money—to seed the miracle.

The routine is always the same in swindles based on greed, at least in principles and basis phases: interest the victim in the prospect of getting something for nothing (i.e., money), "prove" it true—convince the victim that he or she will, indeed, get something for nothing—and present a convincing case of the necessity for certain money from the victim.

Greed overpowers reason. The victim wants so much to believe the promise of rich reward that he or she practices self persuasion. The wish to believe is a powerful stimulator.

■ The Desire for Gain

Of course, the foregoing explanation was not intended as advocacy of such deception in developing outstanding sales materials but merely to accentuate the basic principle of persuasion. But there is a counterpart in normal sales effort, with the most common motivator being the human desire for gain, and the principles and elements—promise of gain and proof—the same. The word *sale*, for example, is a direct appeal to that desire, as are many other terms in common use—e.g., *discount, free, save,* and *special offer.* These terms never wear out, evidently, no matter how often used.

These are not the only terms that appeal to the desire for gain, however. Any promise of a reward or direct benefit is such a term. The current sales literature (their "January Tabloid") on my desk from the Quill Corporation offers several excellent examples, such as these:

TURN YOUR PRINTER INTO A HIGH-SPEED LABELING SYSTEM!
A/V EQUIPMENT MAKES YOUR MESSAGE MORE MEMORABLE!
ECONOMICAL WAYS TO INCREASE TRADE SHOW TRAFFIC!
STRETCH YOUR FILING CAPACITY. . . AND YOUR BUDGET!

Note that each of these headlines incorporates a promised direct benefit in its wording. But although promises of gains are by far the most common class of motivators found in advertising and sales copy, there is at least one other major class of motivator.

■ Fear, The Motivator

Fear is as powerful a motivator as—and quite possibly even more powerful than—the desire for gain. Perhaps it is, in a way, the same motivator because it usually incorporates the promise to provide a remedy for that which is to be feared. But the immediate focus of the basic message is, nevertheless, on that which is to be feared. And in those cases where such an appeal is a natural fit, as it is in many cases, it is a powerful mechanism indeed.

The sale of alarm systems—burglar and fire alarms, primarily—must almost inevitably be based on fear, for it is fear—caution—that impels most of us to buy alarms. There is a gain factor—peace of mind or, at least, a greater sense of security—but that results only from the fear that threatens one's peace of mind and causes a sense of insecurity. Insurance is very much in that same class. The gain side is that it is a kind of investment or saving, but one less beneficial than several other methods of investments and saving, and so insurance advertising and sales literature is almost invariably based on fear motivation: a provision for coping with disaster.

With a little creative imagination it is possible to find persuasive fear motivations for many other services and products. Perhaps the best known of these is the "ring around the collar" TV commercial. A quite ordinary household product, a laundry detergent, becomes the hero (or is it heroine, in this case?) of the plot, in which the villain is a dirty shirt collar that other detergents allegedly do not clean properly. The menace is fear of embarrassment. Fear is divided between husband and wife: for him, the embarrassment of having others notice his unclean shirt collar, and for her, that of doing a poor job in the laundry room.

A kind of lighthearted commercial—did the advertiser originally intend it as a humorous satire or was it presented with serious intent?—it was obviously taken seriously enough by viewers to make the product highly successful. The proof is that after a long run it ended its appearance, but after a hiatus it made its ubiquitous appearance on the TV screens once again. That is a rather reliable sign that a commercial works well.

It is not very difficult to find fear motivators for many other products and services. Banks can base arguments for saving or investing on the fear of depression and unemployment, for example, as can vocational schools and franchisers. Dance studios can alarm prospects with the fear of always being a wallflower. Clothing manufacturers can base advertising on the fear of being ridiculed as a wearer of old-fashioned or out-of-style clothing. It is always possible to find a down-side. Nor is there necessarily any need to be deterred by the fear of being more than a little far-fetched in such projections. No one goes up to even a friend, let alone a stranger, to inspect and criticize his shirt collar; yet, the commercial does work well.

◼ What Is the Real Persuasiveness Factor?

How much is the success of any given commercial due to the inherent persuasiveness of the copy and how much to sheer repetition (for repetition is most definitely a factor)? That is difficult to say. Certainly, no intelligent adult really believes that strangers will look at a man's shirt collar and scream in disgust and outrage at finding "rings." Still, women do buy more of the product when the commercial is airing than when it is not. *Something* about the commercial is producing that result.

The simple fact is that many allegations made in and by advertising/sales copy are absurd, far beyond the bounds of credibility by any normal standard. Strangely enough, most people understand and *accept* that as something to be expected in such presentations and tolerated in good humor. Surely, viewers don't truly believe that drinking a popular soft drink or chewing a given kind of gum will transport them to heavenly pleasures and sweet romance? And surely, advertisers do not expect to be taken literally when their messages make or imply such promises. And yet, a great many advertising and sales presentations are based on such promises, and they succeed. Why? The answer to that is enlightening, but we must first digress here to find it.

◼ What Are You Really Selling?

There is a discipline known as Value Engineering, which is also known by several other names—Value Analysis and Value Management, to name two of the more popular variants. It is a methodology, born of World War II, for improvement of value, applied originally in the engineering field, later extrapolated to and adopted in others. It is dedicated primarily to achieving results—e.g., engineered products—by less costly means, although the cost parameter it pursues is not necessarily in dollars; it can be addressed to reducing other costs—time, materials, or energy, for example.

The essential principle upon which the concept is based is simple. It is based upon a first effort to identify a product, service, organization, or other item in terms of what the item *does*, rather than what it is. It seeks to determine why the item exists—what its essential purpose is.

That is probably the most difficult task of the discipline. Those who teach Value Engineering always find this to be true. Possibly that is at least partly because the instructors tend to insist on using the technical term *function*, instead of focusing exclusively on such questions as *Why?*, *What does it do?*, and *What is its primary purpose?* Those are the questions that must be answered when seeking a definition of what the item does.

Soon enough, answering the question runs into another problem: most items do more than one thing. A wrist watch is ornamental, indicates the time, and, in some cases, also indicates the date. (Some watches do several other things, in fact.)

The question must therefore be further refined to determine what the *primary* or *main* purpose of the item is. Perhaps some people wear wrist watches for their decorative effect or to impress others, but the ostensible or clearly implied main function of a watch is to indicate the time of day. It seems clear that watches are designed by their makers for that function, and we therefore accept that as the primary thing the watch does.

We won't probe further into value analysis, interesting as it is, for the point has been made now: the first, most difficult, and possibly most important task is defining what the item does as its primary reason for existence. And it is precisely that idea we must adopt and adapt to our needs in finding motivators—principal benefits to promise—for our advertising and sales presentations. The question to answer is *What does [the item] do for [how does it benefit] the buyer?* And, as in the value analysis, we need to confine that to the primary or principal benefit. Other issues only confuse the main issue; they do not contribute to a useful answer.

There is at least one important difference between the kind of "what does it do?" in value analysis and the "what does it do?" in sales and advertising: in value analysis the search is for the practical function; in our application it is for the *most appealing or most motivating* function. In value analysis, "indicating time" will always be the primary function of a watch and serving as jewelry will be a secondary function. In our application, "indicating time" (accurately and reliably) will be what the watch does as a primary function only when it is an inexpensive or "practical" watch; when it is an expensive watch, keeping time accurately is less important than being a fine piece of jewelry, so that the latter becomes its primary function.

In short, the success of a sales presentation is linked inextricably with what is likely to be most appealing to the prospect. But that is most definitely a variable factor; the $10 digital watch is certainly directed to a different prospect than the $1,500 diamond-studded watch. Obviously, one is buying a timepiece, while the other is buying a bit of luxury. It is relatively easy to write a sales appeal to the buyer of a timepiece. The stress is on accuracy and dependability at a quite small price. The other sales appeal is much more difficult to write. It is readily apparent that the buyer of the latter watch is buying a piece of jewelry that also indicates the time of day, but the most persuasive, direct benefit is not easy to divine. Does that buyer wish most to impress others or to satisfy his or her own ego, for example? Even the answer to that question may make the difference between a highly successful presentation and a not-so-successful one. And there are other possible motivators. The problem is that it is difficult to find the most effective one. And the usual mistake is trying to play safe by including all the possible motivators. But the result of that attempted compromise is usually an unfocused and therefore fatally weakened appeal.

This is not to say that there are no answers. Far from it; there are very good answers. But they are not always the obvious ones. They are not—most definitely are not—compromises. In advertising, as in military operations, compromises are more likely to be the worst answers than the best. It is almost always far better to hit on the second-best answer than on a compromise.

Take note of how beer is sold in TV commercials, for they furnish some classic "do and don't" models. Do they sell beer? Superior quality? Of course not; they know they can't sell it, for customers know in their hearts that there is not a penny's worth of difference among the brands, regardless of the claims. No, they sell fun, companionship, good times with your friends, even a bit of romance, perhaps. Who can quarrel with that?

Is that different from what soft-drink bottlers sell the young crowd? No, it is the same thing. The only difference is age. Both sport on beaches, although beer drinkers sport and spark in taverns too.

So what are the advertisers selling? They are both selling the same thing—fun, good times, romance. They are selling one of the most basic of human emotional needs, the need to love and be loved, not only by the opposite sex but by everyone. It's universal, and you can't miss with that appeal when you can deliver it convincingly.

That isn't all of it. Smart advertisers know enough to focus sharply, to make only one promise at a time. (There is a strong temptation here to say, "Only one promise to a customer!") For other promises—other appeals and motivators—they go to other presentations. One, for example, has two outdoorsmen, in boots and jackets in the woods beside their tent, drinking the beer. That one is for the outdoors, macho crowd. Another is for the weight-conscious crowd, promising "light" beer. Each appeals to a market segment, as a separate "positioning" approach.

Positioning

At some point the concept of positioning must be addressed, and this is probably as good a place as any to start. In a nutshell—and it is admittedly not easy to create a nutshell definition about this idea—positioning is the act of creating an image of you, your organization, and/or your product/service in the mind of the public. With an almost unlimited reservoir of possible images, here are just a few examples of how an organization might wish to position itself:

An old-time, well-established, and thus honest and highly reliable service or supplier.

An eager youngster with modern ideas for today.

A corporation that cares about its customers.

The company of today.

The company of tomorrow.

The positioning may not be of the organization per se; it may be of the product or service the organization offers. It might assume an almost infinite variety of chief attributes to distinguish it, including these few examples:

An old, reliable product/service.

A modern, new-idea product/service.

A modern, new-discovery product/service.

A revolutionary idea.

An honorable tradition.

A product that promotes romance.

A product that promotes greater security.

By now you may have noted that positioning and the promise or the benefit have a great deal in common—appear to be almost the same thing. They are, of course. Revlon, for example, manufactures and sells cosmetics, but all of their products are calculated to help the women who buy and use them become more attractive, so the products enhance romance. That is the position sought for both the organization and its products.

On the other hand, Prudential Life Insurance long ago adopted the Rock of Gibraltar as its symbol, and displays that symbol regularly in its commercials and other advertisements. The position or image it wishes to convey is one of reliable solidarity, a reassurance to customers of total security in dealing with the company.

Allstate Insurance uses the extended, cupped hands symbol for much the same reason, as an assurance that the customer is in "good hands" when dealing with Allstate. Like Prudential, Allstate wishes to inspire prospects to have great confidence in the company.

"Positioning" is thus another term, perhaps even another approach to our concept of the appeal to the prospective customer. For unless the "position" is one that helps motivate the prospect to become a customer, it is a waste of time and money to pursue it.

In the end it comes down to the same thing: customers do not want to buy the item itself; they want to buy what it *does*—not a new automobile, but the peace of mind resulting from driving a new car or the prestige of exhibiting it—perhaps of an *expensive* new car (Cadillac? Mercedes? BMW? Ferrari? Continental?)

It was the pleasurable prospect of never having to sit behind the wheel of my old clunker—and never having to change a flat tire on it or struggle with starting it on a cold morning again—that compelled me to buy my first new automobile, even when I was not sure that I could afford to spend almost all my reserve cash on the down payment for a new car. (The law required one-third down at the time.) It was much more emotional drive than practical necessity that caused me to buy my first—and my second—computer system, too. I rationalized my need to retire my faithful, old Selectric typewriter because I wanted to join the crowd and feel that I was in step with the times; a full-page advertisement in the *Writer's Digest*—my "bible" of many years—was largely responsible for my decision.

The Medium as an Influence

The medium in which a sales appeal appears plays an important role in the sales process. In the case of my decision to buy a computer, the *Writer's Digest* was an important factor. There is only one other major or nationally circulated writer's trade journal, and it is somewhat specialized, so it is not amiss to consider *WD*, as the *Writer's Digest* is often referred to, to dominate in its field. Having read *WD* for nearly 50 years, I have come to have a high regard for everything that appears in its pages, and I was thus highly impressed with the advertising that appeared there for the Morrow computer, which I soon went out and bought, consigning my battered old typewriter to a well-deserved rest.

Whether the Morrow advertisement would have been equally persuasive had I read it elsewhere is problematical, but I was certainly more disposed to regard it favorably when it appeared in a favored journal. In fact, I might not have paused to read it at all had it appeared elsewhere than in a journal I have read faithfully for many years. Morrow was wise overall to run their advertising in *WD* because word processing—writing with a computer—has been from the beginning the most popular use of desktop computers even in business offices where writing is an incidental activity. It was thus quite sensible to appeal directly to writers in their most popular journal.

Again, What Are You Really Selling?

By now it should hardly be necessary to return to the question posed earlier, that of what you are really selling (although there is another point to be made shortly in answering this question again). Obviously, you are selling some end benefit, one with an emotional content that is the greatest influence: beer or soft drinks because they mean fun, romance, perhaps even being macho; a new automobile because it means peace of mind, a sense of security, a feeling of accomplishment, or showing your friends that you are successful; insurance because you need to feel secure or free of the guilt of failing to provide for your family; and other items for equally satisfying, emotional reasons, the practicality of which is usually only incidental. That is, you are not selling beer or soft drinks; you are selling fun and romance. You are not selling automobiles; you are selling peace of mind or sense of accomplishment. You are not selling insurance; you are selling a clear conscience or a sense of security.

Even that ignores a major point because you are, in fact, not truly selling even these emotional benefits, for you are really selling only the *promise* of these benefits. You can't package and deliver the benefits themselves; you can only assure prospects that they will derive and enjoy the promised benefits, so it is the promise itself that your customers buy! It helps to understand and remember this in writing copy. It provides you a deeper understanding of the problems you must solve with your words.

The Role of Reason

Are there then no rational considerations in the decision to buy something? If emotion is all there is in the appeal and the buying decision, why does the automobile salesperson work so hard at explaining the great value of the model you have already decided you like and indicated the probability of buying? Why the technical discourse on its features, and the arguments for the extras, which have already seized your fancy?

Those are secondary arguments, you will notice, laid on you only after you have shown a clear tendency to favor a given model. You have already made a tentative buying decision, usually revealed by an obviously heightened interest, but you are still, after all, an adult and a rational being. You now need a bit of reassurance, some rationale that your tentative decision is a wise and practical one. The technical treatise is provided to help you in this. For you do need to feel easy about your decision, especially when the decision is a major one, involving a major commitment.

Perhaps there are a few buyers who are in such total command of themselves that they suppress their emotional drives and make buying decisions based on pure reason. If so, they are very much in the minority among buyers. It is far more likely that those buyers who firmly assure themselves and others that they make their decisions on a purely rational basis are practicing a bit of self-deceit. In any case, you must deal in probabilities—the average or typical reactions of buyers—and you will not go far wrong in addressing emotion-based motives with the primary promise and supplying proof to satisfy the buyer's need for rationalization.

■ Wants and Needs

The word *want* originally meant lack of—"for want of a nail, the shoe was lost," for example. In its popular use today, however, the word is generally interpreted to mean desire. And so we tend to discriminate sharply between *wants*—desires—and *needs*—indispensable requirements. In marketing, however, even that distinction becomes blurred, and we assume that buyers have a need for everything that can be bought, even the item or service that is obviously a luxury.

Sales professionals often tend to identify an entire class of needs as *felt* needs. These are the needs that people agree in advance they have, before anyone suggests it to them. The need for food is a felt need, for example. But the need for some given food item, especially if it is a new item being introduced, is not a felt need. The "need" for it must be created by whatever means we normally use to persuade prospects to begin to feel a need.

Making a need felt or persuading prospects to want something is one way of describing what sales and advertising are all about. Filling an order for a customer who walks in and asks for Williams buffered aspirin is not selling. Persuading that customer to try Rhinestone's Special Compound instead of Williams buffered aspirin is selling. Persuading that customer, who came in only for the aspirin, to buy a vaporizer also is selling. Those are actions that create needs.

There are some experts who insist that needs cannot be created, that you cannot sell a prospect something the prospect does not really want, at least subconsciously. That's probably true enough, but the argument is really an exercise in semantics, for every day people are being sold goods and services they did not feel a need for until it was suggested to them. Call it the creation of needs, the raising of subconsciously felt needs to the conscious level, or simply educating the customer about some product or service; the effect is the same.

You might consider the proposition that progress creates new needs. There was no need for a radio before radio was invented, before anyone knew that such a device was possible. The need only arose with the advent of the device. Who went out and said, "I need a TV set" before TV sets existed? In that sense, if in no other sense, some make an argument for the creation of needs. But there is still another way to look at this and gain yet another useful insight into what we are really trying to do with our sales and advertising appeals.

Basic Needs and New Needs

It is now well recognized that we all have certain basic needs, physical and emotional. We all need food, shelter, clothing, warmth, love, security, recognition, companionship, belonging, and a few other things. The means by which we satisfy these and, for that matter, the degree to which we are able to satisfy these vary widely, even at some given period, such as today. The differences are more discernible over long time periods, however, as manifestations of progress and change. The need for heat in cold weather, for example, was once satisfied by open fires of natural flammables—brush and wood. A bit later, as humans began to live in human-made structures, rather than in caves, wood fires were kindled in fireplaces. A bit later, central heating, usually with hot-water systems, became available, and these were soon fueled with coal, later with oil. And today houses almost universally use gas heat with warm air, rather than hot water.

Progress: The Better Way

The point here is simply that despite the steady evolution from the open wood fire to the modern, clean, thermostatically controlled, automatic gas heating system, all that has changed is the means of satisfying the same basic need for heat. The need itself has not changed. A better means has been provided; however, and the public has embraced it immediately, making it an instant success.

In short, we can extrapolate a principle from this that there is no such thing as a new need. Needs are always basic and immutable. Progress consists of finding or inventing better ways to satisfy those basic needs. In general, the public recognizes those ways as better (when they are, indeed, better) and embraces them, producing a market success. On the other hand, when the buying public does not agree that they are better ways, they are market failures. It is truly that simple—and that complex.

What Does "Better" Mean?

This puts us back in the semantics arena, for *better* is certainly not a precise or easily defined term. But it is not useful to us in improving our copy writing unless we succeed in defining it somehow. Is gas heat truly "better" than oil or coal? How? Why?

Only once in a while are you fortunate enough to be able to offer something that is unique and better in some self-evident way. That was true of the xerographic office copier, for example. Earlier methods—carbon paper, thermographic, wet processes, and others—were awkward, messy, laborious, slow, and produced poor copies. The early Xerox® copiers produced copies of less than good quality, but were relatively fast, easy to use, and would copy on ordinary paper found in all offices instead of special paper. The earlier copiers disappeared from the market quite rapidly, and the new competitors did not do at all well until the original patents expired and competitors could build true clones of the leader, who had by now developed far better machines producing copies of quite excellent quality.

Now bear in mind that while all these copying machines were new inventions, they did not satisfy a new need: the need for copying documents was an old, long-standing one. Prior to that time, most offices used carbon paper, a messy and awkward expedient. Formal documents were often sent out to a local blueprint shop to be copied by a process known as making a photostat of the original, involving a camera and special equipment and producing an excellent, albeit costly, copy.

This new method was also relatively expensive, compared with some of the alternatives, because the early users could not buy the machines; they could only rent them by paying a per-copy charge. But the new machines were better—that is, they satisfied the basic need for copies in a better way. Users obviously agreed for the company experienced a rapid success. But how were they "better?" Let's delay answering that question for a moment to consider what "better" means.

Remember, first of all, what our objective is: we are trying to find the most effective ways to make our copy persuasive, to induce readers to become buyers. It is they, the readers, who must be convinced that whatever it is we offer is somehow better than what they are now using or what competitors are offering. We should base our approach, our strategy, on an analysis that takes into account the following items:

- ☑ Recognition of the basic need that must be satisfied
- ☑ How that basic need has been satisfied traditionally
- ☑ How our competitors are satisfying or offering to satisfy the need
- ☑ How we propose or promise to satisfy the need
- ☑ What is better about how we propose to satisfy the need

In short, we must conduct a sensible analysis to decide what we can promise that achieves the desired result in some better way than otherwise possible. We must decide how our product or service is better, e.g., is it:

Cheaper?
Safer?
More effective?
More convenient?
More easily available?
More prestigious?
More reliable?
More attractive?
More durable?

Analyze the situation, based on the facts you now have available, and ask yourself that question with regard to the new Xerox copier described here. How, would you suppose, was the copier better in the eyes of the buyers? Pause before going on to the next paragraph, survey the list of possible "betters" here, and choose one as your answer to why xerographic wiped out its competition almost overnight. But remember, as you do, that it is emotional motivations, not rationales, that are most effective.

The xerographic copier was not cheaper, not more readily available, certainly not more reliable than the earlier methods, nor was the copy it produced greatly superior in quality to some of the others. It was more effective, but that "better" does not have much emotional content; *effective* is a rational word. The one true "better" that fits the requirement is *convenient*. The xerographic copier was infinitely more convenient than any other. And convenience is a powerful motivator indeed. It accounts for the success of gas heat over all others, it accounts for the immediate success of the Seven-Eleven convenience stores, it accounts for many, many commercial successes. Never underestimate it. People generally prize convenience above many other advantages, and they will pay for it.

Despite this, don't be misled into believing that it is that easy to decide what "better" means. It is not easy because "better" is not an absolute; it is a variable. That is, there is more than one kind of "better," because there is more than one kind of customer.

Who Decides What "Better" Means?

There are two significant factors you must recognize in defining or identifying what is better. One is that it can not be defined by you; only the customer can decide what is better. Like proof in advertising, it exists only as, and if, the customer perceives and accepts it. Two, it is an emotional factor, for all the logical, rational proof in the world will not persuade anyone who does not want to be persuaded, anyone who has an emotional bias against believing what you claim to be an advantage or a benefit of some sort. Some customers, for example, will almost automatically be attracted to the item with the lowest price. But there are others who shun anything resembling a bargain, convinced that there are no bargains, that anything advertised as a bargain must be shoddy, or that buying anything that is low priced is beneath them and demeans them. Because many—perhaps most—customers have biases of one sort or another, it is relatively easy to persuade customers who want to believe, if you can manage to cater to their prejudices. So even arguments of quality and value sway some prospects because of their emotional content for those who need/want/get some ego gratification out of believing that they have gotten the highest quality or made the best deal in their purchases.

Don't confuse that with rational decision-making. There are those—you may have known some yourself—who brag about how cleverly they bargained and negotiated a good deal or found a wonderful source, unknown to mere mortals. Some will thus brag about how little they paid for something, as evidence of their shrewdness, while others will brag about how much they paid as evidence of its high quality and their good taste. For example, buyers of VHS videocassette recorders and buyers of Beta models have long argued over which is better, probably as evidence of their superior judgment in buying the one they argue for. For many who are eager to demonstrate their superior judgment or superior "connections" and "contacts" as buyers, convenience may be secondary when it clashes with those other emotional desires. In fact, some of the latter kinds of buyers actually look down on and sneer at convenience stores and bargain prices. But they are a different class of buyers, and you cannot usually attract more than one class of buyer with any single approach. There are many different classes of buyers, and it is essential that you understand this truth when you plan your copy.

You Can't Please Everybody

All of this illustrates the maxim that you can't please everybody. That is certainly true of any given piece of copy. This is one of the basic mistakes some people make in writing copy, either with some approach or argument the writer believes to have universal appeal or by incorporating several different appeals into a single presentation. It does not work. Too broad an approach simply has no focus, and few prospects will recognize their own interests in such an appeal. Two or more totally different (and possibly even conflicting) approaches in a single presentation dilute both/all and serve only to confuse all the prospects as to whether their interests will or will not be served by buying what the presentation offers. Certainly, you are not likely to persuade both the bargain hunter and the quality-conscious buyer with the same copy.

That is not to say that there is not an answer to the problem. There is. If you find that you have more than one major class of prospective buyers to whom you should address your appeals, the proper way to go about it is to develop separate presentations, with separate definitions of what is better and what the benefits to the buyer are. Not only must you develop a sales argument and a definition of better from the customer's viewpoint, but you must understand all the prospective customers and their individual viewpoints. In some cases this may be a matter of analyzing the potential market and deciding who your best prospects are, but the reverse may also be true: it may be a case of deciding which market(s) you wish to pursue. You can take a single product that almost everyone can use and package it— using the term "package" both literally and figuratively—for more than one market.

■ Packaging Considerations

One common example of alternate packaging can be found in almost any supermarket chain. Most such chains have a number of products "privately packaged" for them. That is, they have a manufacturer or processor prepare their normal product with the chain's label. Usually the product is identical, but the version packaged for the private label sells for considerably less than the nationally advertised brand. As another example, there is on my own kitchen table a small TV set bearing the label of a large and well-known mail-order firm that also runs a chain of retail stores. A relative of mine has an identical set with the label of the manufacturer. It is obvious that the manufacturer private-labeled a quantity of these sets for the retail chain, which does not manufacture anything.

It is not unheard of for a manufacturer to package and market his own product under more than one label. I clearly recall a major distiller selling his leading brand of rubbing alcohol in a rather fancy bottle, but also selling it in plain bottles, under another label, at slightly less than one-half the price of his "name brand" rubbing alcohol. That is not an unusual practice in the business world. The simple fact is that when you buy goods today you cannot always be sure where, how, and by whom they were actually manufactured. Frequently the labels and the prices are the only differences among several similar items.

There are also "generic" brands, especially in the patent medicines and pharmaceuticals businesses. If you read the labels of the some of the brand-name products and those of their generic counterparts, you will have trouble finding any difference in components or directions for use, or any other evidence of significant differences between them. The chief difference appears to be in packaging, using that term in a rather special sense, having no relationship to its container and wrappings.

What *Is* Packaging?

In some uses, *packaging* refers to the physical wrappings—box, paper, labels, and other such material—which surround the product. In other cases, it refers to the dispenser or permanent housing—the metal case in which a lipstick is mounted and from which it is dispensed or the cabinet/ housing of an appliance. And in still other cases it refers to the manner in which the product/service and the offer is presented.

In many cases—lipstick, perfume, cologne, and a number of other cosmetics are representative of such cases—the package is far more costly than are the contents, although the price is represented as the cost of the content.

To a degree, the same generalization is true for many cases where *packaging* refers strictly to the advertising and/or promotion by which the item is presented, especially when great effort is made to achieve a certain special aura or effect. A candidate for public office, for example, is "packaged" by his or her political consultants and strategists when seeking the nomination. The candidate who wins the nomination is even likely to be later repackaged by the sponsoring political party in pursuing votes from the public, since the objectives have changed. (The first objective was to win his or her party's nomination; the second is to win the popular vote, quite a different matter.) Both kinds of packaging, not entirely different in principle from the "positioning" concept discussed earlier in this chapter, are often decisive. When it succeeds in identifying the candidate with benefits the party wants—usually the ability to win the general election—the contender becomes a nominee. When it succeeds in identifying the candidate with benefits the voters definitely want—and "identifying" means, here, persuading the voters that electing the candidate will produce the benefits—the effort is a success. On the other hand, the opposition may manage to do a more effective job of packaging the candidate as representative of probable undesirable results if elected, so packaging can work both ways.

Beer advertising illustrates this kind of packaging well. Beer is packaged in most TV commercials as the favorite drink of fun-loving working people and sports enthusiasts, both men and women. For the most part it is directed to the blue-collar class, with only half-hearted efforts to make it appear a beverage favored by professionals and executives. That may or may not be an accurate representation, but it does cater to and conform with the popular conceptions, and so meets with little skepticism or resistance.

Automobile advertising, on the other hand, shows definite class consciousness in another way: commercials for the large, high-priced luxury automobiles manufactured in the United States tend toward a snob appeal, packaging the cars as the choice of successful, cultured men and women, while commercials for mid-range automobiles (mid-range in both size and price) tend to lay stress on the product as a family car. Obviously, the advertisers have an image of the class of customer most likely to be attracted to their product and thus wisely address those customers with their advertising and promotional appeals.

Controlling Factors in Packaging

As in all things, there are right and wrong ways to package. And as the first item that must be considered, you must make a realistic assessment of the true nature of the item: what kind of item is it *inherently?* The ancient saw about the foolishness of trying to make a silk purse out of a sow's ear and the equally shopworn admonition to refrain from gilding the lily are both quite appropriate here: the first is a practical impossibility, and the second is overkill. (Lilies are quite beautiful enough; they don't need gilding, and are only diminished by it.)

Rolls-Royce automobiles are not heavily advertised, nor even are other (less costly) luxury automobiles, such as Cadillacs and Continentals. But that does not apply to automobiles alone. I can recall buying a piano for my children, and being directed by others to a Gulbrandsen as among the "top of the line" (for I have all the musical expertise of a Martian and would not have had the faintest idea of where a Gulbrandsen stood in the hierarchy of quality pianos). I was received in the showroom in Philadelphia with the haughtiness that a Gulbrandsen presumably merits, almost with indifference, and I was thus properly awed and made to realize that being permitted to buy such an instrument was itself a privilege not accorded everyone.

Of course, that is a bit extreme, but I have not exaggerated here by much. There are purveyors of high-quality and costly items who work hard at appearing to be almost disinterested in selling them because they believe that is the right image to present to their prospective customers. That is, they cater to customers who want to believe that they are trading in truly "exclusive" emporia and would not trade anywhere that was not so packaged. The customers expect a special kind of aura when they visit such establishments: deep carpets, a sound-deadened room in which all conversation is necessarily hushed, impeccably dressed salespeople, an abundance of chairs and sofas for patrons to rest upon, and, usually, no price tags in view anywhere.

Translating that kind of package or image to paper is not easy. It is usually done by very "soft sell" paper with special messages, using such subdued headlines as "Special Showing" and such copy as "James Martell and Company will show their exclusive new fall line of ladies' jewelry on Tuesday and Wednesday, September second and third, between one and four p.m." The copy says, between the lines, that the merchandise is expensive and suitable for only the discriminating and wealthy. It's unabashed snob appeal, but it's effective to sell a certain kind of merchandise to a certain kind of customer.

The kind of customer you wish to pursue and the kind of items you wish to sell must match, obviously. You can't handle dime-store merchandise and pursue a Park Avenue clientele as a practical matter, nor can you sell many luxury foreign automobiles to factory workers. But even between the extremes, selling across a wide spectrum of prospective customers, there are many classes of customers, and you can package your line, at least as far as your sales literature is concerned, in more than one way to maximize your sales.

■ Exercises

Once again a few exercises are offered here to help you make sure that you have mastered the most important points covered in this chapter and to help you determine what you must review, if anything. Use your best judgment and, again, don't hesitate to write in your own answers where you think it appropriate to do so.

Motivators

Check off True or False for each of the following items:

		True	False
1.	The most persuasive quality in sales literature is the logic of the sales argument.	☐	☐
2.	Reason and emotion are equally powerful motivators.	☐	☐
3.	If the promise is powerful enough you don't need proof.	☐	☐
4.	Headlines must do more than get attention.	☐	☐
5.	When greed comes in, reason flies out.	☐	☐
6.	Many advertisers use fear quite effectively.	☐	☐
7.	Effective sales messages sell what products or services do, not what they are.	☐	☐
8.	Positioning can be used to support either the promise or the proof, perhaps both.	☐	☐
9.	The medium does not matter if the copy is strong enough.	☐	☐
10.	It is up to you to decide what is better about your product or service.	☐	☐

Critical Factors

Check off those items in the following list that you believe to be usually critical factors in persuading readers to buy what you offer.

☐ 1. Logical arguments
☐ 2. Promised benefits
☐ 3. Fear
☐ 4. Price
☐ 5. Packaging
☐ 6. Claims
☐ 7. Endorsements
☐ 8. Hyperbole
☐ _____
☐ _____

Persuaders and Attention-Getters

Certain individual words seem to never lose their effectiveness as attention-getters and persuaders. Check off those words in the following list that you think fit this description.

☐ 1. Free
☐ 2. Great
☐ 3. Sale
☐ 4. Exclusive
☐ 5. New
☐ 6. Mighty
☐ 7. You
☐ 8. Only
☐ _____
☐ _____

Selling the Sizzle

When the great salesman Elmer Wheeler advised others to "Sell the sizzle, not the steak," he meant which of the following:

☐ 1. Hype up your message.
☐ 2. Use attention-getting techniques.
☐ 3. Learn the secret of salesmanship.
☐ _____
☐ _____

Booby Traps to Avoid

Check off those following items that you believe to be serious, perhaps fatal, mistakes in advertising and sales presentations.

☐ 1. Using humor.
☐ 2. Slanting appeal to everybody.
☐ 3. Using "me" instead of "you."
☐ 4. Failing to use humor at all.
☐ 5. Being clever in writing copy.
☐ 6. Being clever instead of selling the product.
☐ 7. Basing the copy on claims of excellence.
☐ 8. Not using enough hyperbole.
☐ _____
☐ _____

Important Major Copy Characteristics

Prospects are persuaded most easily by your presentation when your copy (strike out the inappropriate or incorrect term):

1. (appeals to their self-interest) (makes impressive claims)
2. (is subtle) (is highly specific)
3. (flatters them with scholarly language) (uses the simplest language possible)
4. (is highly general) (offers details)
5. (is highly formal) (is highly informal)

Rank the Persuaders

Some of the following items are important motivators or persuaders in advertising and sales copy. Assign numbers (1 for highest or most important) to the three you think most important.

- ☐ 1. Claims
- ☐ 2. Promises
- ☐ 3. Prices
- ☐ 4. Recognition factor
- ☐ 5. Headline
- ☐ 6. Body copy
- ☐ 7. Testimonials
- ☐ 8. Attention-getters
- ☐ 9. Proofs
- ☐ 10. Convenience

Do and Don't List

Strike out the inappropriate or incorrect words in each of the following statements.

1. It (is) (is not) possible, in most cases, to appeal equally to all prospects with a given presentation.
2. Most people (are) (are not) persuaded by appeals to reason.
3. Basic wants and needs (change) (do not change) in time.

4. Many people are persuaded (more) (less) by price than by most other factors.

5. Many people are persuaded (more) (less) by convenience than by most other factors.

6. It (is) (is not) possible to "create" needs, in the broad sense.

7. Finding the "better" feature upon which to base your appeal means (anticipating) (shaping) the customer's perception correctly.

8. To sell to more than one class of customer you must (broaden your standard presentation) (develop additional presentations).

9. "Packaging" refers primarily to (the wrappings and containers) (the entire image you create) for the product.

10. "Positioning" is, essentially, (explaining your offer to the prospect) (creating an image of yourself or product).

CHAPTER FIVE

Examples and Exercises: Advertising Copy

Advertising is a world all its own, and yet it is a world that can be explained and understood, as its work and methodology can be, in common sense terms that anyone can grasp and apply to his or her own needs.

■ Some Catch Phrases of Advertising and Copywriting

The sales/advertising world (I choose to combine these, as far as a study of copywriting is concerned) has developed its own jargon. Almost every specialized field does. Let's start by looking at a few of these special terms, what they stand for, and what they really mean.

AIDA

"AIDA"—(get) Attention, (arouse) Interest, (generate) Desire, and (ask for) Action—was presented earlier as a concept that explains and rationalizes advertising for many, if not most, advertising copywriters. I offered you what I believe to be a simpler, more easily understandable, and more useful concept in its place, Proof and Promise, a bit more "catchy" as a phrase than Promise and Proof, the chronological order in which they must normally appear in copy.

My quarrel with AIDA is simple enough: it describes, by implication and extrapolation, at least, certain results to strive for—what ought to happen as a result of our advertising efforts. But it does not even suggest a means for achieving those results—*making* them happen. It does not answer the pertinent questions: *How* do I get attention? *How* do I arouse interest? *How* do I generate desire? It brings to mind the probably apocryphal story of the late Wall Street financier, Bernard Baruch, who is alleged to have explained that making money in the stock market was quite simple: one had only to buy low and sell high! *Très simple?*

And so it was with the hope of suggesting in quite simple and easily understandable terms the means for getting attention and arousing interest and desire to buy that I offered Proof and Promise as a replacement for AIDA. (I admit that I am always suspicious of these clever pronounceable acronyms, spelling out familiar names and ideas, as having been generated before their rationalizations were.) Admittedly, Proof and Promise does not cover AIDA's "ask for action" element, which is not an unimportant element, but is not really at the heart of the true sales and advertising essence: *persuasion*. Nor does it cover some other important elements we will want to cover, as we proceed, but neither does AIDA, for that matter. But let us go on.

"Positioning"

"Positioning," the advertising industry's jargon for image-making, is a concept championed in many speeches and writings by two advertising executives, Al Ries and Jack Trout. Their many writings include their popular book, *Positioning: the Battle for Your Mind* (McGraw-Hill, 1981), a book that has become something of a minor classic. (In fact, the authors take credit for popularizing the concept of positioning, if not actually inventing it.) They and others acclaim this as a new idea that has brought and/or will bring fundamental and significant changes to advertising, and they make a point of stressing that positioning is something one does to the prospect's mind, rather than to anything else. They say, for example, that the term "product positioning" is a misnomer because, while "positioning starts with a product," positioning means influencing how the prospect views the product, so it is doing something "to the mind" of the prospect, not to the product. Positioning does mean change, say the authors, but it is changes made in the name, the price, and the package, so as to change the "position" (image?) of the product in the prospect's mind. In fact, the authors go on to state that the changes are "cosmetic," made to secure a "worthwhile position in the prospect's mind."

Some of the logic escapes me, especially that reasoning behind the statement that it is incorrect to call the concept "product positioning." But stating that the change is merely cosmetic is even more jarring, since it suggests that the change is relatively unimportant or, conversely, that cosmetic change *itself is* important. I find both these ideas to be unrealistic, for "cosmetic," to most people, suggests superficiality. Moreover, if positioning is what the authors claim, it seems to me that it is incorrect to say that it starts with a product. Positioning ought to be an equally valid idea when applied to a service or to the advertiser's organization. (Later, the book does talk about positioning a leader, a company, a service, and even a country. But by then they are beginning to extrapolate the positioning concept to many other fields of endeavor in addition to advertising *per se*.) In fact, so-called "institutional advertising" does meet the overall description of positioning a company. That's the kind of advertising that does not try to sell any specific product or service—often does not have a product or service the individual consumer would be interested in or able to buy—but merely to raise readers' consciousness of the existence of the advertiser and to create or reinforce a favorable image. Hughes Aircraft Company is one who does this month after month in a leading news magazine *(U.S. News & World Report)*, but many other large corporations also do such advertising for no apparent reason other than general PR.

Motivational Research

Exploring what motivates prospects is a matter of great interest in the advertising industry for rather obvious reasons. Hence, the industry has tended to invest in research in this area, especially in exploring how prospects react and respond to advertising messages. One of the classic stories is that of the test of Kool cigarette advertising, in the days before cigarette advertising was banned from TV. The commercial contemplated and offered to the test audience as a prototype offered a graphic illustration of the familiar Kools package rushing forward to fill the screen and burst a chain that appeared before it. The intended message was "Break the hot-smoking habit," as a plug for the mentholated Kool cigarettes. Unfortunately, the message a test audience inferred from the commercial was "Stop chain smoking." Obviously, that was not what the advertiser had in mind!

The story illustrates an important principle: it is almost impossible to predict with any certainty what an audience will infer from or how they will react to a given advertising message. Test audiences confound us regularly by inferring meanings other than those we intended and reacting differently than we had hoped. The only reliable way to be sure that we are *communicating accurately* and invoking the responses we want is to test and act according to the results. That will be even more apparent, although neither more nor less true, when we discuss direct mail because direct mail lends itself far more readily to testing than does print advertising. (You will better understand why when we discuss direct-mail copywriting.)

In fact, "motivational research" consists more of devising means for testing advertising copy than it does of pure research into what does, in fact, motivate people. We already know pretty well what motivates people; what we don't know is how to judge the meanings most people will infer from our copy and how they will react to it. Therefore, we need to devise effective tests to actually determine and measure the typical or common reactions to and interpretations of what we write and project with our copy. This is what *motivational research* is really all about, and it is a worthwhile and well-justified activity, even if a misnamed one. Testing is, in fact, an absolute necessity in creating effective copy, and I would be derelict, indeed, if I neglected to discuss it. We will therefore shortly return to a more extensive discussion of this most important subject.

Demographics

Demography is the science of people—statistics concerning people, to be more exact. A demographic study reveals statistical data on ages, occupations, economic status, educational achievements, residential characteristics, and sundry other data defining and/or profiling the individuals. It has many uses, of course. If, for example, your product or service is of use only to dentists or only to those with graduate degrees, you want to seek out that population of prospects for directing your message or appeal.

In print advertising you go after the general public—advertise in publications the general public reads—if what you are selling is of general interest so that almost everyone is a potential buyer. But if you are offering something that is probably of interest to only a given class, you seek out media that are directed to that class of readers. For example, among the several trade journals I read regularly is *Government Computer News* because it covers two of my interests, the government and computers. The advertising in this periodical is primarily of computer hardware and software. Much of it is, not surprisingly, slanted to the interests of federal agencies and of those who sell or wish to sell computer-related products and services to those agencies.

On the other hand, *MIS Week* is also a computer periodical, but is specialized in a different way, focusing primarily on those readers with interests in information management, wherever they are and by whomever they are employed. (MIS is a relatively old acronym for *management information systems*.) Advertising in this periodical tends to be of software and systems in that field, although there is also general computer advertising.

Still another computer periodical is *Network World*, a tabloid that specializes in computer communications, and it carries advertising that is predominantly relevant to that special field of communications between and among computers, especially in formal networks.

Every Monday the business section of the *Washington Post* is a thick tabloid with heavy advertising of computers and related products and services, but they are all directed—obviously—to the small, local business and the individual consumer.

Each of these periodicals features computers and related items, and yet each is highly specialized in one way or another. And in most cases the advertising departments of such periodicals as these can furnish detailed demographic information about their readers. That is usually especially true of the "controlled circulation" periodicals, those trade journals sent without charge to those who "qualify" by virtue of being good potential customers for the advertisers. (Now you know why you must fill out that little questionnaire to qualify for a free subscription: that is how the periodical gathers that demographic data for its advertising department!)

■ Testing

I am constantly dismayed when reviewing well-written how-to books on advertising, authored by knowledgeable specialists, to discover that they neglect the subject of testing, frequently not even mentioning it. Yet the classic Kool cigarette case is only one of many tales that could be told to illustrate the importance of testing. The most knowledgeable advertising expert can easily guess wrong on how prospects will react to copy.

This does not mean that advertising experts do not test, especially those in the direct-mail field. However, testing print advertising is somewhat laborious and difficult, compared with testing direct mail, as you will see later, when we discuss testing direct-mail sales literature. There are two basic techniques you can use, clumsy though they are. One of these is the "split run," wherein the publisher runs two versions of your copy, each in one half of the edition. Of course, you will have coded your copy in some manner so that you can evaluate the results in terms of the differences in response.

The difficulty in this is the deadline problem. Most periodicals require you to submit your copy weeks, even months, before the issue appears, so that testing print advertising in most periodicals other than daily newspapers takes a great deal of time.

One alternative is to run more than one version of your copy in a given edition. In this case, you can run as many versions as you wish, coding each to measure and evaluate results. Again, this takes time and is rather costly. Still, both methods work, and despite their cost they are quite likely to be a great deal less costly than advertising mistakes can be.

Some people try to test copy by trying it out on a selected audience that is, it is hoped, truly representative of the intended audience for the advertising. The special audience is asked to read the advertising and fill out a response card—complete a little questionnaire that is designed to reflect and measure their response.

Unfortunately, such audiences are rarely truly representative, and the "Hawthorne effect" is a major factor, as a rule. That, named after a test conducted in a Hawthorne, California, industrial plant, revealed that the mere knowledge of being part of a test group or experiment distorts the reaction of the group members so that their response cannot be considered typical. (It is analogous to the "uncertainty principle" of Werner Karl Heisenberg, which maintained that the mere introduction of a test instrument distorts results so that no test can be 100-percent accurate in whatever it tests.)

There are, in any case, two important considerations in all copy testing:

1. The various versions of the copy and the conditions must be exactly the same, except for a single factor, the variable being tested. (You must test only one thing at a time.)

2. Each version must be coded in some manner that enables you to make positive identification of each test version and relate it to the relevant set of results, for accurate measures and comparative evaluations.

There are common sense reasons here. You must test only one thing at a time, for example—the price, the promise, the proof, the terms, or other aspect. That is, of course, the only way you can be sure what factor accounts for a difference in results. That is also why it is important to run the tests in the same edition. The season, some special feature in a given edition, or some other imponderable and unanticipated factor may influence the results. It is that which adds to the difficulty in testing print advertising. The only truly sound and reasonably reliable way to test several variables in your copy is to run several advertisements simultaneously. And even then you must try to get them presented in the same areas of the publication, for place and position of an advertisement in a periodical can itself be a major factor. (For example, it is commonly accepted that there is a distinct advantage in having your newspaper advertisement appear "above the fold" in the newspaper—in the upper half of the page—because it is more prominent there, so, presumably, more prospects will read the copy.)

You run into the effect of seasons on results, too. The advertising that produced poor results in October may produce excellent results in February. That may be because the advertised item has some seasonal appeal or significance, or it may be—again–due to some imponderable factor. Business people often assume that the weeks immediately following Christmas will be "slow," except for those exchanging gifts, but in some years they are completely wrong, and January proves to be a prosperous month. For the same copy, running it in January 1988 may produce great results, while running it in January 1989 produces poor results. Why? We can rationalize—and we probably will—but the truth is that we simply do not know. So you cannot even use last year's data, if you want to be reasonably sure; you must run your tests again.

Even so, given all the foregoing and assuming that you have tested your copy thoroughly, should you now "roll out"—launch a full-scale advertising campaign, making the main investment and major budget commitment thereby? Maybe. It depends on at least two factors: whether you have a large enough bankroll to do that, and whether you want to do that even if you do have the budget for it.

Joe Karbo, testing his "Lazy Man's Way to Riches" idea, resorted to an excellent device that may or may not be viable for your own circumstances. He advertised his book of that title *before he wrote it*, so that he could judge whether the response was great enough to justify writing it and "rolling out" a full-scale campaign, which he evidently could well afford, judging by the claims he made in his advertising. That was a viable option for him, as it is for others in many cases, because he knew that he could write and publish the book on short notice and so satisfy the orders that came in from his test runs, if necessary. (It proved to be necessary, happily for him.) Had the orders been inadequate, on the other hand, he would simply have returned the money to the customers with an apology and gone on to another idea. (Karbo was of that school of mail-order entrepreneurs, like the well known Joe Cossman, who prefer to deal with one item at a time in their promotions.)

I myself used a variant of that idea in writing and publishing my own first mail-order book, *Anyone Can do Business with the Government*. I explained in my initial advertising that I was still writing the book, but that anyone who would send in a prepaid order immediately would be guaranteed a copy of the first run off the press, plus a bonus (which was a subscription to a companion newsletter I launched, although I did not know at the time just what the bonus would be). It was a quite successful approach, with enough advance orders, with prepayments, to help greatly in defraying printing and other publishing expenses, an excellent self-financing or "OPM" (other people's money) approach to financing a venture.

On the other hand, Ted Nicholas, launching his successful self-published book, *How to Form Your Own Corporation Without a Lawyer for Under $50.00*, was more cautious and measured in his approach. He kept careful records of his advertising, as he relates in a subsequent self-published book, *How to Self-Publish Your Own Book & Make it a Best Seller!* and proceeded quite deliberately, step by step, under the guidance of those results. In that subsequent book he reveals another way to test and evaluate advertising, albeit on a more gradual and more long-range basis. He advocates a well-established method that many careful entrepreneurs use, and it also serves as a test and evaluation measure, but on a longer-range basis. Figure 5-1 illustrates, in a hypothetical example, how such a system works. You can see quite easily in this example which advertisements paid out and which did not. But you do not know, from these scanty returns, why one medium or one insertion did well, while another did not.

Key	Periodical	Issue	Cost	No. Orders	Sales
Dept A	Moneysworth	1/82	750	160	2,392
Dept B	Income Upportunities	2/82	1,257	87	1,300
Dept C	Popular Mechanics	2/82	3,286	379	5,666
Dept D	Money Making Monthly	3/82	1,055	266	3,977
Dept E	Star MO Journal	3/82	356	81	1,211
Dept F	Farm Journal	4/82	435	97	1,450

FIGURE 5-1   Typical record-keeping of advertising results

So you do not really know what to do with and about the data you collected. In this small sample *Moneysworth* and *Popular Mechanics* appear to have paid off, while *Income Opportunities* did not, but only by running several advertisements in each and making long-term comparisons can you be sure that you are getting data for *replicable* results, the true objective of all testing. Consider Figure 5-2, for example, in which the data collection continues and begins to reflect other data from which you can begin to draw a few conclusions.

From Figure 5-2 you can begin to see the various influences and their effects: which media produce what kind of results, whether there is a seasonal influence (although that is not easy to detect over a brief period of a few months), and other factors. Some advertisers do this monitoring in only the early phases of a campaign and then assume that they have the data they need to run the rest of the campaign. I believe in doing it throughout the campaign because there are imponderables, factors you cannot anticipate and which may very well change abruptly during the campaign. The insertion that has pulled well in several issues of a given periodical may suddenly drop off sharply in response, for example. Or a change of season may have an effect you did not anticipate. Continuous monitoring alerts you immediately to changes and enables you to react appropriately. Monitoring of your advertising and the results it produces is like accounting in that respect: it is *management* information, data upon which to base decisions.

Keys

Coding advertisements so that you can determine which advertisement produced which results is not difficult. In the trade, such coding is generally referred to as "keying" your advertising. If you review any advertising that invites direct orders from readers and viewers, you can see for yourself that each is keyed in some manner, instructing the reader to address "Dept GHJYK" or mark the envelope "eggbeater," for example.

Key	Periodical	Issue	Cost	No. Orders	Sales
Dept A	Moneysworth	1/82	750	160	2,392
Dept B	Income Opportunities	2/82	1,257	87	1,300
Dept C	Popular Mechanics	2/82	3,286	379	5,666
Dept D	Money Making Monthly	3/82	1,055	266	3,977
Dept E	Star MO Journal	3/82	356	81	1,211
Dept F	Farm Journal	4/82	435	97	1,450
Dept G	Moneysworth	5/82	750	123	1,845
Dept H	Income Opportunities	5/82	1,257	85	1,275
Dept I	Popular Mechanics	5/82	3,286	399	5,985
Dept J	Money Making Monthly	5/82	1,055	185	2,775
Dept K	Star MO Journal	5/82	356	87	1,305
Dept L	Farm Journal	5/82	435	107	1,605
Dept M	Moneysworth	6/82	750	120	1,800
Dept N	Income Opportunities	6/82	1,257	87	1,300
Dept O	Popular Mechanics	6/82	3,286	386	5,790
Dept P	Money Making Monthly	6/82	1,055	165	2,475
Dept Q	Star MO Journal	6/82	356	89	1,335
Dept R	Farm Journal	6/82	435	102	1,530
Dept S	Moneysworth	7/82	750	111	1,665
Dept T	Income Opportunities	7/82	1,257	92	1,380
Dept U	Popular Mechanics	7/82	3,286	453	6,795
Dept V	Money Making Monthly	7/82	1,055	266	3,977
Dept W	Star MO Journal	7/82	356	99	1,485
Dept X	Farm Journal	7/82	435	122	1,830

FIGURE 5-2   More complete records accumulated

The obvious keying is via listing "department" numbers or letters, but there are many more subtle ways of keying advertisements, such as these few examples:

☑ Variations in spelling—"H. Green & Co." versus "H. Greene & Co." or "H. Green & Co." versus "Howard Green & Co." etc.

☑ Adding a suffix to an address, such as "P.O. Box 1377" versus "P.O. Box 1377-A." (This can, however, confuse some Postal Service personnel.)

☑ Adding a room number to or modifying a room number: "1121 Grant Blvd." versus "1121 Grant Blvd., Suite 312" or "1121 Grant Blvd., Suite 312A."

☑ Product-name differences, such as "Magic Vitamins" versus "Miracle Vitamins" or simple price differences.

Other Test Methods

Some people test their copy in other ways. One is to leave the copy for a day or two and work on other things, returning to review your copy when it is not so fresh in your mind. The theory here is that you will be more objective now in reviewing and revising it.

Some writers find that reading their copy out loud enables them to judge it more effectively, or to read it out loud to others and ask for their reactions.

There are still other "tests" employed. But all these "other" tests suffer the same problem: they aren't really tests at all; they are merely ways of trying to *judge* the effectiveness of your copy. Do they help? They probably do to some extent, when used in conjunction with the kind of tests described earlier, but their limitations must be recognized: they do not produce measured results, the only true tests.

Included in the many books written by advertising people about advertising—many of them *how-to-do-it* books—is a wealth of speculation and rationalization. Many of the authors work hard at trying to analyze why certain headlines worked, while others did not. Especially, they work at examining the cases where a change in the headline of an advertisement made a major change in results. The case of the headline, DO YOU MAKE THESE MISTAKES IN ENGLISH, for example, has been reviewed and studied frequently because it is an outstanding example of a long-lived advertising headline. Still, the long-term value of such analyses appears to be minimal, for we are still unable to construct a reliable methodology from it. We continue to benefit from and depend on actual tests to justify the roll-out of a campaign. The lessons we infer from our analyses probably make it somewhat easier to write good headlines—at least, we derive a few dos and don'ts from them—but, unfortunately, they do not lessen our dependence on tests for making final judgments.

That is not to say that we have nothing to learn from these cases. We certainly do learn a few things. But what we learn are primarily principles. The practical application of the principles is still experimental—trial and error—in each case. For example, we now accept that the word *you* is an important one to readers and should be a focal point in a headline when possible. We know that *free, sale,* and *now* are words that tend to command attention and inspire action, and they appear to never wear out and lose their effectiveness. And yet, much depends on how the words are used in a headline and on other circumstances that are not directly linked to the wording. An issue that is prominent in the news at the time may have a great effect on how a reader reacts or what a word comes to connote. It is virtually impossible now, for example, to use words such as *gay* in their classic sense. Too, readers often exhibit a totally unexpected reaction to a sales message, and that reaction may be the opposite of what you wish. A few years ago the key words in a TV commercial that had heavy exposure was an exclamation from a housewife to another actress, "Please, Mother, I'd rather do it myself!" Readers found it humorous, and soon half the comics on the tube, as well as many individuals in private conversation, were spouting jokes based on the "I'd rather do it myself" line. In effect, then, they were laughing at the commercial itself, and that pretty well destroyed the usefulness of the commercial. No viewer would now take it seriously, of course.

■ Mail-Order versus Direct Mail

Many people use the terms *mail-order* and *direct mail* interchangeably. Not so Norman King, writing in his book, *Big Sales from Small Spaces* (Facts on File, 1986). King makes a distinction between the two, and he justifies that distinction quite well. He points out that mail-order advertising is advertising in a periodical (often in a section labeled *mail-order*), addressed to the public at large, soliciting orders by mail. Direct-mail advertising is advertising literature sent out to individuals on a mailing list, soliciting orders by mail. The difference, therefore, lies solely in how you advertise, at least in your initial approach.

A Few Variants and the Pros and Cons of Each

This author does not mention radio and TV solicitation because his book is about small-space advertisements—confined to mail-order advertising in print media, that is. But radio and TV commercials are also mail-order advertisements because they, too, advertise via the mass media, rather than by some direct approach, and so they are philosophically identical with what was designated here as mail-order, in contrast to direct mail: radio and TV commercials are addressed to the viewing public at large and they, too, solicit orders by mail. But here the resemblance between the two forms of mail-order advertising ends, for one depends primarily on printed words, while the other depends primarily on sound—spoken words, sound effects, and music—and motion—moving graphic illustrations. At the same time, both do require copywriting skills, albeit the writing disciplines required are markedly different from each other, for the two media are themselves so different from each other. Both are visual—their sole commonality, in fact—but on TV the visual effect—the whole presentation—is transitory, lasting for a few seconds or a minute or two, at most. But the print presentation is more or less permanent, at least until the reader is finished with this edition and discards it. He or she can read and reread the presentation many times, even clip it out and save it. (I have personally known people to do this and send orders in as much as two years after the advertisement appeared!) TV commercials must be repeated (and usually are), often with frank admonitions to viewers to get pencil and paper and prepare to write down an address and ordering information. Too, an advantage of print advertising is that it can include a coupon type of order form or even a separate, insert type of order form, with postage prepaid, to make it almost childishly easy to order. This is itself not an inconsiderable factor favoring print advertising.

On the other hand, TV and radio advertising have certain special appeals. It is easier and more convenient for the prospect to watch, listen to, and understand a broadcast message than it is to read one, and the public has gotten into the habit of enjoying this easier way of absorbing ideas. Sound, color, graphics, and motion have much greater impact than do mere words in ink on paper (although print may include color and graphics). Even animation and/or puppets can become quite popular, as evidenced by the enormous public enjoyment of and enthusiasm for the current "California raisins" commercials and the continuing popularity of all Walt Disney cartoon characters. Too, the appearance of a trusted public figure—a popular movie, TV, or sports star, for example—as an advocate testifying for a product is also of some difficult-to-calculate (but large) influence. Who would question either the judgment or the sincerity of Bob Hope, the late John Wayne, or another well-known hero of our time?

What Is "Good" Copy, in Either Case?

Remember always that we cannot—should not—equate the quality of sales and promotion pieces with literary skill, for literary skill has nothing to do with quality when it comes to advertising and other sales copy. Grammarians were quick to point out that the well-publicized Winston cigarette slogan, "Winston tastes good like a cigarette should" was ungrammatical; the rules dictate that the sentence should read "Winston tastes good *as* a cigarette should." Winston management and advertising officials were amused because the advertising slogan was working for them in its popular, if ungrammatical, form.

In short, the only measure of quality in sales copy is its success or lack of it. If it works—if it *sells* the product effectively—it is good copy. There is no other criterion of quality. Success, therefore, does not depend solely on writing skill. There are other factors that are influential in whether the copy "works" (sells) or not. The choice of medium, for example, may be a decisive factor. But it is not even that simple. In opting for a radio or TV commercial, the time or day of broadcast can be a decisive factor.

It is often critically important to remember these various characteristics and the advantages and disadvantages of each when writing for each of these media, and to use the strengths of each to best advantage. Exhibit 5-1 is offered to help you bear these factors in mind or to refresh your memory and the factors you should consider when writing for these media. It presents an organized set of basic characteristics and pros and cons or advantages and disadvantages for each. Of course, there are no absolutes: writing for each of these media requires that you weigh these factors against the characteristics of what you are trying to sell, the nature of the prospects you wish to reach, and related factors. The exhibit therefore offers only general guidelines for you to consider, guidelines that you must examine more thoroughly for actual application.

■ Exploring the Guidelines

One thing to keep in mind is this: don't forget who your audience is. The bulk of the radio audience today, consisting of those listening in their automobiles, are not in a good position to jot down an address or telephone number. If your sales depend on people remembering a number, think long and hard about making a major effort via radio commercials. One thing you can do is to try to find mnemonic devices to help radio listeners remember, or furnish other help. For example, if you are advertising a product sold locally, list some of the major outlets or mention that it is sold in most department stores or whatever is the case. This helps the listener who does not remember the name to find the product. If you are listed in the local Yellow Pages directory, mention that as an aid. Try to find devices—tags that are easy to remember. For example, an advertiser whose telephone number is 841-2676 might advise listeners to dial 841-CORN. (Advertisers often make a deliberate effort to get telephone numbers that lend themselves to such mnemonic devices.) Repeat the product name, the address, the telephone number, and/or whatever is critical several times—as often as possible. Try also to use some dramatic or otherwise outstanding sound—voice, music, or special sound effect—in connection with information you especially want the listener to note and remember. The association with another sense in this manner also serves as a device to help the listener's recall. At the same time keep the commercial as short as possible—preferably not more than one minute—consistent with these considerations and the message you must deliver. It's quite easy for a listener to switch to another station, especially with the pushbutton and "signal-seeking" convenience features of automobile radios today. Moreover, if your advertising need lends itself well to short commercials, a series of frequently repeated short commercials is generally more memorable than a few lengthy ones. (Repetition usually helps in all forms of advertising.) Listeners are less likely to tune out short messages—are more tolerant of them even if they are less than sparkling and entertaining—and more likely to remember them when they are repeated frequently.

Medium: Radio

Basic Characteristics: Sound—voice, music, and sound effects only.

Pros: Great impact possible with judicious use of sound, a charismatic narrator, and enhancement of listener's imagination. Relatively inexpensive, especially as compared with TV, because costly sets not required and often narrator can do several voices.

Cons: Listener must be asked and reminded to remember product name, if going to retail outlet to buy, plus mailing address and price, if ordering by mail. Not as easy to remember mailing address with aural stimulation only as with visual (TV) stimulation. Basically transitory in effect; if listener does not act at once he or she will probably not act at all. To overcome this, commercial must be run frequently over extended period.

*　　*　　*

Medium: TV

Basic Characteristics: Sound—voice, music, and sound effects–sight, and color.

Pros: Great impact possible with judicious use of sound, a charismatic narrator, and good visual effects. Easier for viewer to remember mailing address than in case of radio because visual impact is greater, especially when reinforced with narration of text on screen, and address may be left on screen for a time to permit viewer time to get materials to write it.

Cons: Relatively expensive, as compared with radio and print, especially when costly sets, animation, and/or special effects are required. Listener must be asked and reminded to remember product name, if going to retail outlet to buy, plus mailing address and price, if ordering by mail. (Less of a disadvantage than in case of radio, but greater than in case of print.) Basically transitory in effect; if viewer does not act at once he or she will probably not act at all. To overcome this, commercial must be run frequently over extended period.

*　　*　　*

Medium: Print periodicals

Basic Characteristics: Visual only, but color and special devices possible.

Pros: Relatively inexpensive, especially in comparison with TV. No need to be highly repetitive since print copy always available for rereading. Many readers postpone action but save copy and order at later date, often much later. Can also include postage-paid order form, a valuable asset.

Cons: Listener must be asked and reminded to remember product name, if going to retail outlet to buy, plus mailing address and price, if ordering by mail. Not as easy to remember mailing address with aural stimulation only as with visual (TV) stimulation.

EXHIBIT 5-1   Some basic guidelines on media

With TV you can do all these same things, but here you can use special visual effects, in addition to showing the product often enough to maximize the probability that the viewer will recognize it. There are many animation techniques, for example, that have more impact than mere human narrators and are thus more memorable.

Getting Attention

Audiences for advertising messages are usually not captive audiences. They tune in the station for music, news, movies, or other program material, not for the commercials, of course. It is necessary to induce audiences to listen, view, or read advertising, and there are a number of ways to do so.

The best way, by far, is to make the lead or headline itself of such direct interest to most prospects that their attention and interest is captured at once. For years every man who was ever cowed by a burly bully actually enjoyed reading the Charles Atlas body-building advertisements, in which he claimed that he was once a "97-pound weakling" until he built his body up and became a "strong man." Men enjoyed the advertisement because it depicted, in cartoon-strip form, the victim getting his revenge, after being humiliated by the bully and then going to Charles Atlas to have his muscles built up. It was a dramatic story and it satisfied the fantasies of many men yearning to be of heroic physical dimensions, as well as in their daydreams.

Of course, it is not always possible to achieve this ideal in copywriting. But that does not alter the need to somehow induce the prospect to listen to, watch, or read the sales message. Many advertisers use humor or, at least, mildly amusing commercials to get attention and arouse at least initial interest. Hopefully, if the commercial is a bit amusing, rather than deadly boring, the viewer will watch it instead of going to the refrigerator or chatting with others during the commercial break.

Other Attention-Getting Devices

Humor is only one way of attracting attention and inspiring some initial interest. However, do not be quick to turn to indirect devices, for they, like cutting prices, are signs of failure in a way: their use should not reflect a lack of resourcefulness and creativity in writing copy. Try, always, to build the attention-getter and interest arouser into the copy itself to the maximum extent possible. Following are two other ways it can be done rather easily.

Drama

Dramatic effects can be introduced in the opening of any kind of advertising or commercial, even by the judicious choice of headline type. A single word, large and stark in black ink on a field of white, is dramatic in itself, whether the word is or is not in itself a dramatic one, such as WAR! However, do try to use dramatic words, as well as dramatic presentations. (Drama is conflict, so words that describe or refer directly to conflict are inherently dramatic.) For example, here is an idea how that concept could be used in the headline of a pesticide advertisement:

DEATH & DESTRUCTION!
to household pests with
Bug-Death spray.

In radio and TV commercials sound and pictures can be used, of course, to heighten the effect. Many commercials use film clips and tape segments from movies, newscasts, and even old newsreels, as an inexpensive way of creating a dramatic opening.

Nostalgia

Nostalgic openers are often effective. Fondly remembered music, sound, words, scenes, and other memory-stirrers are excellent for getting attention and arousing interest. For those who remember the old radio drama series titled *Inner Sanctum*, recreation of the famous creaking-door theme is instantly recognizable. Some other sounds used, in both a serious vein and in a humorous reference include the theme music and signature hammer-and-seal clang from the early TV show *Dragnet* and popular rock-and-roll music of the fifties and sixties. But many commercials use music from the days of World War II, often with scenes from those days—e.g., jitterbug dancing in service clubs, as well as scenes of the forces in the field.

In using nostalgia themes you must be sure that you are using the right ones, the themes that have the nostalgia characteristic for those you want to appeal to. The rock-and-roll music of the fifties and sixties have meaning and appeal to those who were teen-agers in those years; they have no memory of *Inner Sanctum* or World War II days. Even though they know about those days and have seen the scenes and heard the music, it is not nostalgic for them. At the same time, those old enough to remember those days are rarely nostalgic for the fifties and sixties. Nostalgia is for fondly remembered times, most often for early years.

A Pitfall to Avoid

The mistake many make in using various devices, such as those we have been discussing here, is overdoing it, making the advertising or commercial perhaps even more entertaining than the editorial matter or the program that is being interrupted for the commercial. Why is that a mistake? It is a mistake because if the commercial is too entertaining the viewer remembers the commercial but not the product. Many of us today remember that now-famous line, "Please, Mother, I'd rather do it myself!" but have no idea at all what product the actresses were advertising. And I personally watched the "ring around the collar" commercial many, many times and recalled it readily enough, but without being able to identify the product. The gimmick, which, by the way, depicted a dramatic situation, as did the Charles Atlas advertisement, had seized my attention, but it became a distractor, rather than an aid. As a result, the product had really never registered in my consciousness until I deliberately set about determining what it was! In fact, it was only when I attempted to use that commercial as an example in an earlier book that I even realized that I did not know the name of the product.

But that is not the only mistake. Overdoing the use of a substitute device is also a mistake because as the copywriter, if you strive especially to be amusing or entertaining, you often lose sight of the true purpose of the copy and produce great entertainment but not very great "sell copy." That is, such devices have a built-in booby-trap that you can avoid only by being conscious that it is potentially always there. Therefore, use such devices when necessary, but judiciously, never allowing yourself to lose sight of or stray far from your central message, which is to sell your product or service.

■ Ideas and Creativity

We have been discussing the presentation of ideas, but we have not discussed how to *get* the ideas to present. That is a subject of some importance and is, moreover, one that produces many surprises. Here are a few basic, generally accepted facts about creativity that will probably include a few surprises:

- ☑ There are no truly new ideas. All new ideas are actually old ideas that have been adapted and/or modified in some manner to improve them or to make them more suitable for a modern world.
- ☑ Everyone–but *everyone*–has the potential for being creative and coming up with new ideas.
- ☑ We are much more creative as children than we are as adults. Our society, with its standards and educational system, tends to stifle our natural creativity or instincts for it.
- ☑ In general, the higher our level of formal education the less our instinct for creative thought.
- ☑ It is the courage to reject conventional wisdom, to think independently, and the faith to believe in an idea that are even more critical and necessary to ultimate success than is the vision to perceive a new truth.

Why Are We Not All Creative?

All of this can be demonstrated to be perfectly logical, but that discussion is well beyond the scope of our work here. Suffice it to point out that our educational system tends to teach what is purported to be absolute truth, rather than teaching a questioning and questing attitude, so that the average student and/or graduate has little encouragement, much less motivation, for seeking new truths. Quite the contrary; such a quest is definitely discouraged. History is replete with accounts of how naysayers attempted to shout down such hardy freethinkers and pioneers as Lister, Pasteur, Semmelweiss, Fulton, Edison, Bell, Ford, Kettering, and many other achievers who had the courage to ignore the doubters and shouters and go on to reach their goals.

On a much smaller stage we must all fight the same battle when we want to try out a new idea. Gary Dahl faced ridicule when he got the idea of asking the public to pay him $4 for a smooth beach pebble in a little wooden crate with a tiny brochure that explained how to care for the "Pet Rock" contained in the tiny wooden "cage." But enough people were willing to buy a Pet Rock to earn Gary Dahl a reported $1 million or more within 90 days. Were Dahl's customers buying a rock in a box? No, they were buying a good chuckle that they could share with the friends to whom they sent the new "in" item, as a new and different gift idea.

To get ideas for marketing you must understand what and why people buy. Charles Revson, founder of Revlon cosmetic products, put it succinctly and accurately when he observed, "In the factory we make cosmetics; in the stores we sell hope." And another shrewd marketer remarked that people do not buy quarter-inch drills; they buy quarter-inch holes. That distinction between what you sell—your viewpoint—and what the customer buys—the customer's viewpoint—sums up the essence of sales and marketing. I once functioned under the delusion that my clients were buying my expert help and counsel in writing proposals and my expert guidance overall in selling to the government. My practice picked up rather sharply when I finally realized that what my clients wanted to buy was my help in winning contracts, whatever the means for doing so, and I then began to sell them what they wanted to buy. It made a surprising change in the response of prospects to my sales literature for both my consulting services and the newsletter I was publishing.

Is There a Method for Being Creative?

We are, in fact, all creative when we permit ourselves to be, when we abandon our fears of being "different," our fears of swimming upstream, our reluctance to abandon the supposed security of conventional wisdom—that which everyone else (apparently) embraces as Ultimate Truth. The chief barrier to individual creativity is that chained thinking in which we have been indoctrinated throughout our lives. In our society it takes a bit of courage to cast off those shackles, to start thinking independently. Either through laziness or through fear of disparagement—that nagging sense of insecurity that most of us are never totally free of—we tend to take the easy way out and cling to those tired old cliches and platitudes that represent conventional wisdom—"slow and sure," "tried and true," and all the other worn-out expressions of reverence for the "good old days" and all the old, simple answers. But that is yesterday's wisdom, and it is not immutable. There is always a better way waiting to be discovered. (We call that discovery *progress*.)

In this case, it is not really too difficult to get new ideas, for we are not trying to invent revolutionary new products or to change the course of history, as some of our great ancestors did. We are merely seeking better ideas for our advertising and sales strategies to improve our literature, to help our prospects perceive the advantages we have to offer them. What we really want to do here is simply to perceive needs from the viewpoint of the prospect a bit more effectively than we have been doing in the past. And that means analyzing what the typical prospect wants as an end result. For the fortunate few who are blessed with the instinctive genius for inventing and using the inspired sales message, there is no problem. For the rest of us, fortunately, there is a discipline, a methodology, that we can put to work to help us here; we do not have to rely on the uncertainty of pure intuition or inspiration. It is not that difficult to be as creative as we need to be when we put that methodology to work. Nor is it difficult to master that methodology. It has a few simple rules, easy to learn and easy to apply to all situations:

1. Define, in the simplest possible terms, what the product or service *is*.
2. Define, in simple terms (one noun and one verb only) each thing the product or service *does* or can do. (Make a list.)
3. Analyze the list to select that thing/those things that offers the greatest benefit/s to the buyer.
4. Find the proofs of benefit/s.
5. Construct the promise and proof for the headline and copy.

■ First Step: Definition

Probably the most difficult part of the process are the first steps, deciding what a product or service is and does, especially in the uncompromising terms of a single noun and verb. But it is critically important that you do so, as you will see, if you are to avoid the trap of lapsing into hype and other claims you cannot substantiate or "sell" to the prospect.

Let's take a simple case of trying to sell what is almost an antiquated device to some people, a "quality" (expensive) fountain pen. Forced to the uncompromising objectivity of the noun-verb requirement, the value engineer will state that a fountain pen is a writing implement and what it does is "make marks." (It does not "write"; humans write, but pens make marks.) That definition is valuable for value engineering; it is valueless for us. Why? Because it is not a definition that invokes or points to a sales argument. We must find a definition that is a legitimate statement—we need to be able to back it up—but offers the prospect a benefit that will motivate him or her to buy. That, after all, is our objective. And today there are dozens of inexpensive pens—throwaway pens—that are as effective for writing as are the costliest fountain pens. We have a problem selling quality fountain pens today. We must look at what *else* a quality fountain pen is and does if we are to find a persuasive sales argument for our advertising copy.

That a fountain pen, even a quality fountain pen, is a writing implement is of little significance because there are so many effective and inexpensive writing implements now available. However, let us first list what it is:

1. Ink pen.
2. Writing implement.
3. Fountain pen.
4. Status symbol.

Yes, a quality fountain pen was always a status symbol. Before the era of ball-point pens and felt tip pens, *any* fountain pen was a status symbol, and there were dozens of inexpensive fountain pens on the market. (The old thick-barreled Sheaffer, with its distinctive white dot, was probably the "top of the line," and the student who carried and used one of those was regarded with some envy and perhaps even awe by fellow students.)

Probably many of the cheapest felt- and ball-tipped pens today are the equal of the best Sheaffer in writing quality. But the Sheaffer is still a status symbol, a prestige item. And that is probably the only way it can be sold today—by appealing to that instinct to own a symbol of success and of good taste. Were I planning a campaign to sell an item of this type I would not consider any other approach, for I think no other approach would work well. Bear in mind that the true motivation is always emotional and not rational. Therefore, the "prestige" and "status" appeal, and, in this case, I would direct that appeal to those most sensitive to the need for symbols of status, the young professionals struggling to become established and respected in their professions—lawyers, accountants, physicians, architects, engineers, and others of that class. A good color photograph of the pen with appropriate copy—perhaps something along the lines of the below, a frank admission, might be quite effective:

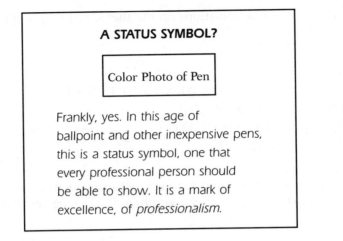

This is a reasonably conservative approach. There are others, approaches that are more heavy handed, less tactful. Here, for example, are a couple of such ideas:

The photo is of a young professional—or even of a not-so-young professional or executive, the reader to whom the advertisement is directed—seated at a conference table with somewhat older individuals, each of whom is writing with what is obviously a quality fountain pen, while the younger executive is using what is obviously a throwaway ball-point or felt-tip pen, and looking a bit uncomfortable. In fact, several of the other executives are staring a bit incredulously at the cheap pen. An exaggeration? Most certainly. But so are many, if not most, successful advertisements. Exaggeration is not a handicap. Quite the contrary; it is usually a necessity. The headline? Maybe it could be something along the lines of IT'S PART OF YOUR APPEARANCE, LIKE THE SUIT YOU WEAR AND THE SHINE ON YOUR SHOES. (Don't be afraid of long headlines, if they do the job. Injunctions against long headlines are in the same class as those against solid text: they are based on mythology about advertising.)

You can easily go the opposite way. All the others in the photo are using cheap felt-tip and ball-point pens, and the reader is proudly using a quality pen, while the others are staring admiringly at him and his pen. The headline:

I WAS SO PROUD TO FLOURISH MY BLANK-BLANK FOUNTAIN PEN.

Once you seize the main idea you can come up with many headline and copy ideas. (The copy should follow the lead established by the headline, of course.) Here are a few variations on the theme (with appropriate illustrations, generally):

THE BLANK-BLANK PEN GOES WITH THE WHOLE IMAGE
DON'T LEND IT OUT. YOU WON'T GET IT BACK.
MAKES YOU 10 FEET TALLER
YOU GET THE *FEEL* OF QUALITY
YOU *KNOW* IT'S QUALITY

These ideas can all be used for print advertisements, but some can be made particularly effective as TV commercials, using motion and scenes with actors.

■ Analyzing the List

We have defined what the product is and what it does now. That is, we have defined several things that it *is*, but each thing that it *is* invokes a different thing that it *does*. If it is a pen, it makes marks, for example, but if it is a status symbol, it inspires self-confidence, lends prestige, advances one's career, and/or otherwise does something for the individual far more valuable than making marks. And that, defining what the item does for the buyer, is the critical point in creating the copy, for that is creating the promise, the reason for buying the item. These headlines (and, presumably, the body copy that would follow and reinforce each headline) are really saying such things as these:

Here's how to gain respect.
Your associates will admire you.
Your career will be advanced.
You will gain self-confidence.

Don't underestimate the importance of promising such things as these, especially that latter one of helping the prospect have greater faith in himself or herself. I can recall meeting a young man some years ago who had saved his money and bought himself a $250 suit when a good suit cost about $75. He wore that suit only on the most important occasions, such as when he was to be interviewed for a new job. He explained to me that when he wore that suit it transformed him in a quite marvelous way. He *knew* that he was wearing a suit of such quality that only the most successful men normally wore such a suit. It made him feel 10 feet tall, he told me; he was sure that he could do nothing wrong and he was the equal of any man, including the one interviewing him.

■ Finding Proofs of Benefits

"Proving" that buying what you sell will produce the benefit you promise is a necessary step—it must always be there in some form—but it has its own set of variables. The amount and quality of proof is never an absolute, but depends on several circumstances, the first of which involves establishing a better definition of what we mean by that word "proof."

The proof required is not an absolute, such as is required by scientists in formulating a scientific law and declaring something to be a scientifically established and verifiable fact. Nor is it proof such as that required in a court of law, which establishes a well-defined and carefully constructed set of rules to minimize error. It is, instead, *whatever the prospect will accept as proof*, and that, in turn, depends on four variables:

1. The weight of the evidence offered as proof—the inherent credibility of the presentation, as compatible with the other two factors named here.
2. The characteristics of the prospects (demographics, to a large extent).
3. The nature of the promised benefit.
4. The trade-off—what the prospect is asked to risk.

It is no news to anyone that we humans have a strong tendency to believe that which we want to believe. Logically, therefore, the more we want to believe something, the less evidence or proof we require to be convinced. And that is true to a certain extent, but it has its limits. It is limited by the sophistication of the prospect and by the inherent believability of the promise. For example, a midwestern mail-order publisher has recently sold a book that promises readers that they can make $25,000 a year as readers for book clubs and publishers, and as a result many book clubs, agents, and publishers who were listed in the book have been receiving applications for such employment. They report that most of the letters received are from writers who appear to be barely literate, which is itself a revealing fact. Few more highly educated people believe the promise because it is contrary to their everyday experience and judgment.

On the other hand, the late Joe Karbo reportedly enticed more than 600,000 readers to send him $10 each for a 70-page paperback promising to reveal an easy way to riches. (He advertised it as *The Lazy Man's Way to Riches* in his headline.) The little paperback book proved to be Karbo's own version of "positive thinking" and little else. But he drew orders from some well-educated readers because he was a master copywriter, and his copy was highly persuasive.

In general, then, the more attractive the promise of rewards, the less proof required, unless the promise is so extreme as to be hard to believe, in which case the opposite condition prevails: the more proof required. The same conditions prevail with respect to the sophistication of the prospects: the less sophisticated, the less proof needed. Moreover, the greater the risk required of the prospect—e.g., the higher the investment required—the greater the amount of proof and persuasion required.

But the nature of the proof and of the presentation is important, too. Some types of proof are more persuasive than others, although even that is a variable, according to who is the prospect, as you will see. Here are some basic kinds of proof you can offer:

Your guarantee

Your statements with suitable hyperbole

Logical argument

The general credibility of your presentation overall

Testimonials and endorsements from typical users

Testimonials and endorsements from public figures

Testimonials and/or endorsements from technical experts

Statements from respected institutions and/or known experts

Statements from government agencies

You can judge for yourself the relative merits of each of these classes of proof. There is no absolute significance to the order in which they are listed here, but the first two items are the least effective persuaders, ordinarily. True, there are those who will believe what you promise simply because the name of your organization is well known or even merely because they saw it "in black and white." (There are still some ingenuous people who think that anything appearing in formal print must somehow be entirely true and accurate.) Most people, however, require somewhat more impressive authority than mere assertion before they will accept your promise, especially when you are asking them to undertake whatever appears to them to be a risk. That might include asking them to spend a substantial amount of money, dye their hair, try a new patent medicine, or be the first to wear a new and different style, as just a few examples of kinds of perceived risks.

The other obstacle to acceptance of your promise is the promise that appears too good to be true. For example, most of us are reluctant to believe in miracles, and the prospect of suddenly becoming rich does appear to be a miracle of no mean proportions, although we would like very much to believe it could happen. That is why the magazine distributors running a contest offering multi-million-dollar prizes must spend hundreds of thousands of dollars merely to urge all of us to open the contest envelopes and enter our ballots. The difficulty in believing that they have even a slender chance of winning anything leads many to reject the entry blank even though participation is free. Many even doubt that the contest is genuine. They may be heard to say, "Ah, they don't really give millions of dollars away." They don't even want to get their hopes raised by entering the contest and be eventually disappointed at not winning, so they work at persuading themselves that it is all a sham and a waste of time to even enter. The advertising is therefore designed primarily to persuade prospects to believe in the validity of the contest by presenting past winners of the major prizes. That persuades many of us to read the literature, thereby increasing the probability that we will enter and that some of us will order a few subscriptions.

That device of presenting past winners to testify to the legitimacy of the contest is a direct form of testimonial. In this case the advertising is done on TV, and the past winners are introduced and then present their testimonials personally. In print advertising the testimonials are presented in printed statements, of course, preferably using their names and cities, where possible.

The most effective testimonial or endorsement, ordinarily, is that of a well-known figure—an entertainer, sports star, public official, even an author, although relatively few authors, even highly successful ones, become well known to the general public.

The next best testimonial or endorsement is that of an authority figure of some sort—a scientist, physician, engineer, mechanic, or whatever is appropriate for the advertising. In TV commercials you usually do not have to identify the individual specifically; the costume does that—e.g., a white laboratory coat, a suit of hospital greens, a blue mechanic's coveralls, etc. And where it is possible to do the photography against the appropriate and recognizable background—in a laboratory, hospital, or shop, for example— the believability rises further.

In print you would handle it somewhat differently, even if you are not permitted to use the individual's name. (You must get written permission— a release–to use people's real names.) Following are examples:

> *I prescribe Smooth-On ointment regularly for my patients with stubborn skin problems. — Dr. E. M., Pawtucket, RI*
>
> *We sell a lot of Xtra-Lube at my service station, and I use it in my own car.* — HRJ, service station owner, New York City

There is, of course, the testimonial statement from the ordinary customer, which is similar to those shown here but does not identify the occupation of the individual whose initials are used. (Of course, if the customer is willing to give permission, it is better to use his or her full name.)

There are some other kinds of evidence that are less direct but may be more or less inferred by you as testimonials or, at least, used by you as additional credentials. For example, where an item you are selling or the practitioner of a service you offer must be inspected, approved, and/or licensed by a government agency, a statement specifying that fact is accepted by many people as a kind of testimonial or at least good evidence that you and what you advertise are legitimate. Plumbers, for example, are invariably licensed by their local governments, and many are licensed in more than one jurisdiction when their normal service area includes more than one. In this area (suburban Washington, DC), for example, many plumbers are at some pains to advise prospects that they are licensed in Maryland, the District of Columbia, and Virginia. Drug advertising may mention that the item advertised has been approved by the Food and Drug Administration. Advertising for certain kinds of equipment may specify that it meets the most exacting government standards and specifications.

Another badge of merit that is useful is an identification of affiliations. Most professional people belong to a professional society or association, as do many businesses and their owners. Statements of such memberships included in advertising are themselves credentials that are akin to testimonials, helping the prospect gain confidence in you.

■ Exercises

As in previous chapters, the exercises that follow are provided to help you make sure that you have mastered the most important points in this chapter. Again, choose the answers you believe most appropriate, but don't hesitate to write in your own answers where you wish to. But also do not fail to reread the chapter or portions of it if you find yourself uncertain about answering the following items and, above all, think hard about any item that causes you to pause. Remember, this is not a test for which the answers are clearly evident in the text. In some cases you will find answers plainly stated there, but in many cases you will have to read between the lines to find the answers. The objective of the exercise is not to test your recall or to persuade you to memorize items in the text; it is to encourage you to think about the meaning of what you have read here and interpret that in responding to these exercise items, as you will interpret it in applying this information later.

Positioning

Positioning is an important idea, but it is one that is, unfortunately, not always well understood. Check off True or False for each of the following statements about positioning.

		True	False
1.	Positioning applies only to products.	☐	☐
2.	Positioning applies only to services.	☐	☐
3.	Both products and services can be positioned.	☐	☐
4.	Positioning is what you do to the item.	☐	☐
5.	Positioning is what you do to the image of the item.	☐	☐
6.	Institutional advertising is positioning.	☐	☐
7.	Once a position is established, it cannot be changed.	☐	☐
8.	Positioning is what you claim the item is or does.	☐	☐
9.	Positioning is what the item actually is or does.	☐	☐
10.	Positioning is what customers think the item is or does.	☐	☐

Demographics

Strike out the inappropriate phrase in each of the following statements about demographics or write in one of your own.

1. Demographic factors are important (only when selling specialized items) (in all cases) (_____).
2. The chief use of demographics is in choosing (the best prospects) (avoiding advertising mistakes) (_____).
3. The importance of demographics (is greatly overrated) (is most useful in political campaigns) (_____).
4. You can usually get demographic information from (the Census Bureau) (magazine advertising) (_____).
5. The use of demographics data is most likely to (save you money) (cost you money) (_____).

Testing

The subject of testing offers and copy is not usually covered seriously in most books on how to write good advertising copy. Following are some multiple-choice items dealing with the subject of testing. For each one, make the choice you think most sensible.

1. Testing your offers and advertising copy is
   - ☐ more reliable than experience and judgment
   - ☐ not as reliable as experience and judgment

2. Testing advertising copy and offers in print media is
   ☐ difficult
   ☐ easy
3. Testing print advertising copy is
   ☐ expensive
   ☐ inexpensive
4. Testing print advertising
   ☐ takes a lot of time
   ☐ can be done quickly
5. The best test is
   ☐ with a test audience
   ☐ in a split run
6. To test effectively you should
   ☐ save time by testing several things
   ☐ vary only one item in each test
7. If done properly, testing is
   ☐ absolutely reliable
   ☐ still subject to unpredictable variables
8. Once you roll out the campaign
   ☐ you do not need to monitor or measure results any more
   ☐ you should continue to monitor and measure results
9. If you run the same campaign each year
   ☐ you do not need to test after the first successful campaign
   ☐ you need to test every time you run the campaign
10. Broadcast–radio and TV–advertising
    ☐ does not need the same kind of testing
    ☐ should be tested the same way

Pros and Cons of the Different Media

Broadcast advertising—radio and TV commercials—is necessarily different from print advertising because the media are different. One—print—is visual only; another—radio—is aural only; and the third—TV—is both visual and aural. However, those are only basic differences, and there are different characteristics and qualities deriving from these and other basic qualities. For each item in the next exercise, check off all the phrases that apply to the item. Use the extra space provided to write in an additional characteristic that applies (i.e., advantage or disadvantage).

1. Print advertising has the advantages that it
    - ☐ has inherently greater impact than the other media
    - ☐ is easier than the other media to key
    - ☐ is easy to test
    - ☐ can be reread and kept for future reference
    - ☐ _____

2. Radio advertising has the advantages that it
    - ☐ has inherently greater impact than the other media
    - ☐ is easier than the other media to key
    - ☐ is easy to test
    - ☐ has great potential for dramatic impact
    - ☐ _____

3. TV advertising has the advantages that it
    - ☐ has inherently greater impact than the other media
    - ☐ is easier than the other media to key
    - ☐ is easy to test
    - ☐ has potential for multi-sensory appeal
    - ☐ _____

Just as each medium has advantages, each has disadvantages. Check off the appropriate boxes and write in additional notes for the following items.

4. Print advertising has the disadvantages that it
    - ☐ has inherently less impact than the other media
    - ☐ is awkward to key effectively
    - ☐ is difficult to test properly
    - ☐ _____

5. Radio advertising has the disadvantages that it
    - ☐ has inherently less impact than the other media
    - ☐ is awkward to key effectively
    - ☐ is difficult to test properly
    - ☐ _____

6. TV advertising has the disadvantages that it
    - ☐ has inherently less impact than the other media
    - ☐ is awkward to key effectively
    - ☐ is difficult to test properly
    - ☐ _____

On Creativity

Advertising copy is not great literature, but it can be highly creative in the hands of an imaginative writer. Decide which of the following statements about creativity and creative copywriting are true and which are false.

		True	False
1.	To be truly creative an individual must be born with the talent.	☐	☐
2.	Creativity tends to increase as we mature.	☐	☐
3.	The more educated we are, the more creative we become.	☐	☐
4.	The enemy of creative thinking is conventional wisdom.	☐	☐
5.	We can become more creative by working at it.	☐	☐
6.	The greatest problem solutions are the simple ones.	☐	☐
7.	Creativity is thinking differently.	☐	☐
8.	New ideas are always revolutionary ones.	☐	☐
9.	A poor headline can be salvaged by good body copy.	☐	☐
10.	A good headline can be destroyed by poor body copy.	☐	☐

A Few Essentials of Good Copy

A good advertising presentation loses no time in defining or describing what you are selling. That means determining what an item is in terms of what it does from the buyer's viewpoint. For each numbered item below, select from the choices given, the definition(s), description(s), or descriptive slogan(s) you would use in selling it. (You may check off more than one choice or write in one of your own construction.)

1. Electric frying pan
   - ☐ The modern, easy way to cook
   - ☐ The easy clean-up frying pan
   - ☐ The secret of being a gourmet chef
   - ☐ The way to a husband's heart
   - ☐ _____

2. A business magazine
   - ☐ The latest inside business information
   - ☐ The key to business success

☐ What top-level executives read
☐ News before it becomes news
☐ _____

3. A portable or laptop computer
☐ Take your office on the road with you
☐ Be _really_ in touch all the time
☐ Travel with an easy mind
☐ Laugh at busy telephone lines
☐ _____

4. A new perfume
☐ A new and different scent
☐ Let 'em eat their hearts out!
☐ The perfect gift
☐ Be the first to wear it
☐ _____

5. An office chair
☐ It's a _President's_ chair
☐ For the chair-bound executive
☐ Almost as good as a backrub
☐ An orthopedic breakthrough
☐ _____

Credibility and Proof

Even the most skillful copywriting requires that quality of credibility to be effective. Respond appropriately to the following items, as instructed, and write in items of your own if you believe it necessary.

1. Check off those items most likely to help in establishing credibility in your copy.
☐ Smooth and professional writing
☐ Generous use of adjectives and adverbs
☐ Testimonials and endorsements
☐ Simple language
☐ _____

2. Rank-order the kinds of testimonials, writing the numbers in the boxes, with number 1 the highest priority.
☐ From satisfied buyers
☐ From technical specialists

☐ From famous individuals
☐ From government agencies
☐ _____

3. Check off two items below that help generate confidence on the part of the reader and thus enhance credibility in your copy.
☐ An impressive company name
☐ A listing of superlatives
☐ A clearly stated guarantee
☐ Detailed explanations
☐ _____

4. Which of the following items impede credibility and thus increase the requirement to prove that you can deliver on your promises? (Check off your choices.)
☐ Ponderous and difficult writing
☐ Generous use of hyperbole
☐ Extravagant promises
☐ A lack of illustrations
☐ _____

5. Which of the following ideas are myths? (Check off your choices.)
☐ Short headlines work best
☐ Advertisements need lots of white space
☐ The more you tell, the more you sell
☐ People won't read long advertisements
☐ _____

CHAPTER SIX

Examples and Exercises: Direct-Mail Copy

Direct mail is not only a major industry, it is a highly specialized world of dedicated practitioners who make almost a mystique of their professions as specialists in this romantic world of direct mail.

How Different Is Direct Mail from Mail-Order?

In the previous chapter I reported how author Norman King distinguishes *mail-order* from *direct mail*. A great many people, even among those who are themselves involved directly in advertising, mail-order, and direct mail, do not make this distinction; for them, it is all "mail-order." For our purposes, however, the distinction is important because despite many basic similarities, each of the two is based on a different method for recruiting new customers. In that chapter we focused primarily on media advertising, print and broadcast, for attracting buyers. In this chapter we shall concentrate on sending out packages of sales literature to individual prospects, using mailing lists.

In their most basic concept, advertising and sales activities have a great deal in common. All are based on a "numbers game," on the probability that if an appeal or presentation is made to a sufficiently large number of prospects, even a relatively small percentage of positive responses will produce enough sales to support the effort profitably. The real difference between the two is more a matter of degree than of kind, based on the constraints of each method. Media advertising is costly, in terms of space (for print media) and time (for broadcast media), and so the major reliance is on numbers—on reaching many, many prospects, so that even a fraction of one percent is a significant number. Direct mail, on the other hand, has different constraints. An important one is a minimum cost per piece mailed, whether that piece weighs one ounce or only a fraction of an ounce (for first-class mail), so it is wasteful to package less than the full allowable weight of sales literature. (An ordinary number 10 business envelope can carry five sheets of typewriter paper, with as much as 5,000 words worth of sales literature, within the one-ounce limitation.) So direct mail generally depends on getting a somewhat larger percentage of return—favorable responses—as a result of doing a much more intensive selling job in each presentation.

There are other points of similarity although the practical methods of implementation differ. Take the matter of demographics when ordering advertising in print media, for example. You address this at different levels. First, the type of publication: almost anyone or everyone is likely to read the daily newspaper of any metropolitan area, but people with specialized interests read the *Wall Street Journal*, for example. And you can narrow that further, at a second level of discrimination, by dictating where in the newspaper—e.g., business pages or sports section—your copy is to appear. And you choose other types of periodicals in the same way, going to succeeding levels by studying the publishers' demographic information about their readers.

Selecting direct-mail prospects according to characteristics is not greatly different, except for the probability that you can get greater precision in marketing by direct mail. That is because mailing to a list of names automatically provides better control, since most mailing lists are more uniform in a demographic sense than are the readership lists of periodicals. (And the identification of the "listenership" and "viewership" of broadcast media is never better than an estimate.) For example, virtually all those whose names appear on the membership list of an association of engineers are likely to be engineers. And it is usually possible to get mailing lists much more highly specialized in selection criteria than this. Mailing lists can be sorted by zip codes, for example, if you want to mail only to certain specified areas. They can be sorted by profession or occupation, by income, by buying history, and by sundry other tags, according to how the names were originally coded.

▪ Where Mailing Lists Come From

There are dozens of mailing list dealers, large and small. Most of the lists they offer for rent belong to others—publishers and mail-order houses, for example—so the dealers are really brokers, working on a commission basis. (They are dealers or brokers, to you, when you are the customer for the list, but they are "list managers" when they solicit you as a list owner to permit them to broker it.) For example, in the current issue of *DM News*, a direct-marketing trade journal, the Direct Media List Management Group, Inc., offers to rent a list of people who have bought ball-point pens from Union Pen & Pencil Co., another of mail-order buyers of Thayer greeting cards, and another of those who have bought office supplies from Reliable. For some purposes you do not need to go beyond this first level in choosing lists of acceptable prospects. That might be especially true in some cases, such as that of the Thayer list, where you have two indicators of buyer characteristics: one is that the names are those of greeting card buyers, and the other is that they are mail order buyers, a not unimportant fact to note.

Measures of Mailing List Quality

Not all mailing lists offered are the property of others. In some cases the renter owns some or all of the lists. That does not mean that the list is necessarily less valuable than one that is the property of another organization, but it does mean that you do not know a great deal about the list, whereas you know something immediately about a list of subscribers to a popular magazine or one of the customers of some prominent firm. Ergo, the customer list of Bloomingdale's by Mail or the subscriber list of *Tennis* magazine is likely to be more valuable and command a higher rental fee than an "anonymous" list alleged to be that of bank vice presidents or of credit card owners. But there are other indices of value (and price):

- ☑ A list of customers—buyers—is more valuable than a list of applicants or inquirers.
- ☑ A list of people with a stated high-income level is more valuable than one with no income level stated.
- ☑ A list of people who have bought recently—within the past 6 months—is more valuable than one without information on buying history.
- ☑ A list of those who have spent $50 or more is more valuable than one of those who have spent only $10.

By far the most valuable list is, usually, your own customer list, especially a list of current or recent customers. And the second most valuable list often proves to be your own list of inquirers. In fact, in many cases the best list is the one you have accumulated yourself as a result of your own inquiry advertising.

Combining the Methods

It is here that we begin to see the hybridization of the two methods, mail-order and direct mail. That is, some entrepreneurs use media advertising to collect mailing lists to use for direct-mail campaigns. This is sometimes the most effective—even the most practical—approach to a by-mail venture for one or more reasons:

1. There are some cases (such as in one of my own campaigns) where you cannot find really suitable mailing lists offered and you are compelled to seek some other means for finding a useful mailing list.
2. There are cases where the combination of methods is by far the most economical way to go—the least costly way of acquiring suitable mailing lists.
3. You may have decided that you want to or must own the mailing lists. (Brokers normally rent their lists and will not sell them, although the list of names of any who become your customers becomes your property.)
4. You may find it possible to make substantial numbers of sales while acquiring names for your mailing lists.

■ Alternative Methods

There are several alternative methods for collecting your own mailing lists. The one used most frequently is that of inquiry advertising. This is simply advertising—often very modest advertising, even classified notices—that invites the reader to send in his or her name to be put on a mailing list! The invitation is not that bluntly stated, of course; it usually says something that, it is hoped, will arouse the reader's interest, and then invites the reader to send for more information. It may even offer some special inducement, such as promising a free report or a newsletter.

Many who advertise to invite inquiries defray the postal expense by requiring inquirers to provide an "SASE"—a self-addressed stamped envelope. In fact, I have used this method myself, and in one case it proved to be most wise because I drew about 3,000 inquiries! In postage alone that is nearly $700.

There are others who have even better approaches to the problem of cost in gathering names for mailing lists. Some entrepreneurs, such as mail-order merchant Walter Drake, have an even more effective approach. They collect the names of prospects at little or no cost—perhaps even at a slight profit— by offering a loss leader, such as a supply of good-quality return-address labels at a modest price. Thus they not only defray the costs of gathering the names, but they are gathering the names of *customers*, not merely inquirers. Consider what this means:

1. Every name on the list is that of a mail-order buyer.
2. Every name on the list is that of a customer.
3. Every name on the list is that of a *satisfied* customer.

(Obviously, the Walter Drake organization appreciates the difference between making sales and making customers!)

There are still other ways of creating your own mailing lists. There is the method we shall call *compilation*. That's a simple term and a simple idea. It means simply compiling names by other than the two methods just described. Names are drawn from a variety of sources, essentially dependent on your individual resourcefulness. One prime source for such names, for example, are the membership lists of pertinent organizations. Another source is the telephone directory, especially the Yellow Pages.

In my own case, when I was seeking to build a mailing list for my first newsletter subscription campaign, I turned to periodicals that were heavy with advertising and began to mark up the names of those advertisers whom I thought to be good prospects for my own solicitation. If that appears to be a rather tedious and difficult chore, it was. But it was also fruitful; I began to win subscriptions almost immediately, as I began to mail to those on my growing list. And as I gained experience and learned what kinds of prospects responded most enthusiastically, my compilation grew more and more efficient.

The advantage of that method is that it is based on compiling a list of prospects of known characteristics. If you have an offer that, you believe, would be most appreciated by optometrists, you can select a list of optometrists from advertisements in periodicals, in the yellow pages, and in other directories. (Most communities today offer directories of local businesses and professional services. There are at least three that I know of in my own community, in addition to at least a half-dozen weekly "shopper" tabloids.) In fact, you can probably find directories devoted entirely to that profession, and it is likely that there is a professional association of optometrists. You may be able to buy a copy of the membership list; some associations do make those lists available for a price.

The hypothetical optometrist as the chief prospect represents a rather narrow target field. Usually, your prospect field is more generalized than that—e.g., independently practicing professionals—so the field is much greater, but the actual selection and compilation process may be more difficult in that it requires a great deal of knowledge on your own part to make the discriminations. That may be why many people in the direct-mail field believe that compiled lists are of much lesser value than those representing someone's customers. However, the criterion of quality usually stipulated is that of the name being that of an individual demonstrated to be a buyer, rather than a "looker" or shopper who rarely buys. And it is true enough that there are individuals who inquire frequently and buy infrequently. That is why the names of those who are demonstrated by their past performance to be mail order buyers (or "direct-mail" buyers, if you prefer) are usually more valuable than are those of inquirers. And the names of inquirers are supposedly of greater value than are those compiled from directories because inquirers are at least individuals who have demonstrated an interest in something offered by mail.

Another Measure of Quality

Many list brokers use another measure of quality. They represent the quality of their lists by the rate of deliverability or, conversely, by the rate of "nixies," undeliverable names and addresses. Those are people who have moved, died, or whose addresses are simply incorrect. Brokers who value their lists in this manner often make claims of less than 5 percent nixies and/or guarantee to provide five additional names for each nixie. Obviously, however, this is a subordinate value. The first value is the appropriateness of the list to your needs.

The Ranking of Importance

Many direct-mail experts consider the suitability of the mailing list for your needs to be the number-one consideration, all other factors thus being of secondary importance. They tend to believe, that is, that when a direct-mail campaign is not a success the mailing list should be the prime suspect as the cause for failure. And the logical corollary of this is, of course, that with a good enough mailing list, success is all but ensured.

I tend to quarrel with this concept on two grounds.

First of all, I think it is futile to decide which of several critical factors is more "important" than the others. The failure of any one spells the overall failure of the campaign, so who can say which was the most important contributor to the failure—or to the success, if success it turns out to be? It is, in fact, rather dangerous to think this way because this kind of thinking may blind you to other problems.

Second, in terms of pure logic, the first thing to consider is the promise itself: is it truly appealing? Exciting? Motivating? The best mailing list is of no use if the promise does not arouse the prospect's interest. Ergo, my own tendency is to be concerned first with what I promise—my offer. And yet you cannot test your offer properly without a valid mailing list.

It is thus something of a chicken-and-egg proposition. A good offer cannot be tested without presenting it to a qualified set of prospects—a good mailing list—and a good mailing list cannot be tested without making a good offer to those on the list; both ingredients are necessary in a kind of symbiosis to make the whole proposition a worthy one. However, in most cases it is much easier to determine whether the mailing list is a good one and/or to find a good list than to determine whether the offer is such. Let us then consider what constitutes a good offer.

■ What Is An *Offer?*

Before we can have an intelligent discussion of what constitutes a good offer we need to establish what an offer is. But searching through a half-dozen excellent how-to books on direct-mail marketing, I searched in vain for even a definition of an offer as used in marketing, much less a discussion of it. Only in the last book (*Direct Marketing Success*, Freeman F. Gosden, Jr., John Wiley & Sons., Inc.) did I find a discussion, limited although it was, of the offer. And that definition was presented in connection with the "40-40-20 rule," which holds that marketing success depends 40 percent on the right prospects (i.e., the right mailing list, in this case), 40 percent on who/what you are and what you offer, and 20 percent on the presentation. And in that second 40-percent category, says the author, the offer is the most important element.

Not surprisingly, the offer was defined rather conventionally—as the terms proffered for the projected sale, that is, the price, delivery, discount, special sale, or whatever you wish to proffer. Undoubtedly you will find this used as the common definition of the term, for it is classic and logical: a sales presentation is, indeed, an offer to sell something on some stipulated set of terms. Nevertheless, I find it useful to use the word *offer* to refer to something else, for reasons that I hope to make clear in a moment.

I quite agree with the author of *Direct Marketing Success* that the offer, as it is defined in his book, is highly important. In fact, I happen to think that the offer, *as I will define the term here*, is the most important element of the entire presentation. For I use that term to refer to the promise: what I promise or offer to *do* for the customer—help him or her lose weight, make money, find happiness, become more secure, win respect, or otherwise gain some tangible benefit. It is because I think that the promise of a benefit is by far the most important part of the presentation that I wish to reserve that word *offer* to refer to it.

The special terms I offer the customer—two for the price of one, a bonus free gift, a special discounted price, a double-your-money-back guarantee, or other such manna—I then refer to as *the proposition*.

What is the purpose of establishing a special meaning for the word *offer*, and why replace it with the word *proposition?* Simply this: I firmly believe— and I think that belief is based on ample evidence—that the proposition or set of terms is far less motivating to the average prospect than is the attraction of the offer and the hope of attaining it. That is, if the prospect believes in the offer and finds it sufficiently attractive, the terms (as long as they are within reason, of course) are not important. A prospect will pay $25 as swiftly as he or she would pay $10 to get something he or she truly desires. On the other hand, if the offer is not sufficiently enticing, sale prices, discounts, bonuses, free gifts, and other special benefits will not induce an order.

I believe that you can find enough evidence for that concept to adopt it as a premise. Let's look at some evidence for this premise that the offer (as defined here) is by far the main determinant in the marketing appeal, far more than the proposition (also as defined here).

First of all, consider the case of the neighborhood convenience store, of which the ubiquitous 7-11 stores are most representative. Without a doubt most of the patrons know that they can probably buy a bottle of milk or carton of cigarettes for less money at most supermarkets, but they choose the convenience store even when the supermarket is nearby. Why? The answer is simple enough: *convenience*. Convenience is the benefit; it is what the convenience store offers, of course. You can park your car almost at the door, and everything is within easy reach almost from the moment you enter. Whether you want a cup of coffee or a six-pack of beer, it is conveniently at hand a few feet inside the door.

IBM electric typewriters dominated their market for many years, until the very letters *IBM* were almost synonymous with *typewriter* and were so used by many people. Whether their typewriters were technically superior to those of their competitors is moot; there is no clear evidence either way. But there is little question that they cost more. Yet, they outsold all their competitors combined. That was because they sold confidence. Their "secret" was unparalleled service—prompt response by courteous and well-trained repair technicians. But the customer was buying confidence that the typewriter would never be "down" for long, confidence in IBM and IBM service, that warm feeling of security that the great and comforting father figure, IBM, was at hand and would always be there when needed.

It isn't only IBM that has fostered that image. Allstate Insurance, with the cupped hands, has striven to create that same image. And Prudential Insurance, with its Rock of Gibraltar logo, has tried hard to instill in prospects that image of ageless stability. But there are other tactics in popular use.

Visit any supermarket or department store chain and you will find at least a few of their own products—products with their own brand names—offered. These are referred to often as "store brands."

Many "store brands" are identical with the "name brands" that they resemble. The store brand is often manufactured and packaged as a "private label" for the store that sells it, bearing the store's trade name. The "store brand" is invariably cheaper; it has been packaged to be offered more cheaply. Here, the customer who chooses to buy the more expensive brand is "buying the name"—buying confidence that the more expensive brand is better because the name is familiar, it is widely advertised, and it is the name of a large corporation. That is, the customer is buying an easy mind, based on the prejudice that a "big name" means superior quality.

It is not unusual for a product to sell poorly because it is priced too far below that of its competitors, leading many prospects to have serious doubts about its quality. When we have nothing else by which to judge quality, we usually use its price as the criterion. In fact, in testing, direct-mail specialists test price, as well as other factors, to find out which price is most acceptable to prospects, and it is not always the lowest.

To fully understand what that word *offer* really means we must explore the subject a bit further. By now it should be clear that customers buy benefits of one sort or another. In the case of the convenience store the customer buys the true benefit of convenience. In the case of IBM typewriters, the benefit is unfailingly fast and reliable service, which in many customers' minds equals greater quality. And in some other cases cited, the customer buys an easy mind, confidence that he or she is buying the best or, at least, the better quality.

Note that in at least some of these cases, what the customer is buying is not identical with the best characteristic of the service or product. Whereas, for example, a store brand is identical with a name brand, the best characteristic of the store brand is its lower price. However, the customer does not gain that benefit but opts for what gives him or her the satisfaction or mental comfort of what appears to be the better quality. And there are two significant things to note here:

1. The customer does get a real benefit—ease of mind, in this case.
2. The benefit results from the customer's *perception*.

The benefit the customer buys is always that which the customer perceives, whether that agrees with what the seller perceives as the benefit or not. You cannot decide for the customer what the decisive benefit will be; you can only ask the customer what he or she wants. That, in fact, is the true purpose of testing, to find out what the customer wants to buy, and the most important thing to test is the offer. (In fact, everything else that may be tested, even price, may be deemed to be part of the offer, since it contributes to the prospect's perception.)

Probably the successful marketer is something of a practical psychologist, for marketing does require an understanding of what "makes people tick"— why we act and feel the way we do. The professional psychologist will explain that aside from our natural physical needs, such as food, warmth, and shelter, we all feel the need to be loved and to have someone to love, to be recognized, to feel that we "belong," to feel important, and to feel secure, among other things. But we all also want convenience, we want to "keep up with the Joneses," and otherwise to feel at least equal to others, if not superior to some. (In fact, many, maybe most, of us need to find someone or something to which we can feel that we are superior, which accounts for much of the trouble in society.) But, in my opinion at least, we all suffer from some degree of insecurity, and many of our wants stem from that.

The analysis can be pursued even further, for even the concept of customer perception does not fully explain the motivation. The fact is that in many, if not most, cases, the customer is really buying the *promise* of the perceived benefit. When the customer orders, he or she has not yet received the benefit, but only the promise of the benefit, whether implied or stated directly. The name-brand buyer, for example, perceives—*assumes* or *infers*—superior quality, whether the manufacturer has specifically claimed superiority or not. And the customer infers that he or she will have an easier mind, where that is the perceived benefit, whether a specific promise or not. Ergo, we must discriminate between the promised or perceived benefits and the terms offered the prospective customer and the cost—terms—offered.

■ The *Proposition*

The offer does not exist in a vacuum. It is made in the environment of what I choose to call *the proposition*. That is the set of terms—the cost, payment arrangements, discounts, bonuses, and/or whatever else.

■ What Is a *Proposition*?

The attraction of an offer must be traded off against the price demanded. Within limits, the prospect will pay whatever is demanded if he or she can manage to meet the price and is sufficiently motivated. But the tradeoff is obvious: how much the prospect wants the benefit versus how much is demanded as the price. But don't make the mistake of believing that meeting the price necessarily requires a painful sacrifice; quite often the well-to-do prospect (for whom the price represents no practical problem at all) is the most reluctant to part with the price, for it is an emotional problem in many cases, not a true financial problem. Even wealthy people are often grudging in relinquishing their fond grip on a dollar, sometimes more so than are those of us who are in more modest circumstances. Nor should you be led astray by demographics. People who are definitely middle class, as indicated by their occupations and perhaps residences in neighborhoods of modest (and perhaps older) homes, often have more cash to spend—more "disposable income"—than people with large homes and apparent affluence. (Sometimes those styles of living actually make well-to-do people cash poor, with little disposable income.) It is therefore risky to base conclusions on external appearances or indirect clues, such as demographic indicators.

In a practical sense and within reasonable limits, then, price is often not the major determining factor. The qualified prospect, one who can manage the price, will agree to pay the price if he or she wants the item badly enough. (You must bear in mind that we are discussing these matters always with reference to *qualified* prospects, at least with respect to their ability to buy the item.)

Asking for Action

The proposition, therefore, is simply the set of terms—what the prospect must do to get the product or service—price, mode of payment, and alternatives—and what you propose to deliver for the money. That, in a great many cases, includes more than one inducement to buy, a subject we must discuss. But first a few words about the subject of "action" or asking for the order, as it relates to the proposition, for that bears on the subject too.

In face-to-face selling, the wise salesperson learns how to ask for the order. It is a fact that even the most masterful and persuasive sales presentation does not impel many prospects to say, "I'll take it!" Many people—perhaps even most people—are not naturally decisive; they want to take time to think, and they tend to postpone decision-making. And once the prospect begins to procrastinate—to put off making the decision—the probability is that he or she will never make the decision (the purchase, that is), so the order is lost forever in most of such cases.

This reluctance to decide immediately is probably the greatest single obstacle most salespeople must overcome. Therefore, the most successful salespeople are those who learn how to persuade the prospect to action, to actually making decisions and placing their orders without delay.

The classic wisdom in how to ask for the order is that it is a mistake to ask in a way that offers the prospect *yes* and *no* alternatives, such as, "May I write up the order now?" Rather, the question should be asked in a way that offers *yes* and *yes* alternatives, such as these:

"Would you like this in blue or red?"
"Do you want to take it with you, or shall I have it delivered?"
"Will this be cash or charge?"

Written sales presentations do not offer this advantage of continuous interchange of responses with a prospect. It is possible, however, to include features in the proposition that have the characteristic of offering the prospect alternatives, and it is quite a common practice to do so. One reason for doing this is to try to guide the prospect's thinking into a choice between *yes-yes* alternatives, rather than *yes-no* alternatives. Another is to press the prospect to make a decision, to act instead of procrastinating. That is the reason for the typical exhortations in direct-mail literature to "ACT NOW!" and "CALL TODAY!" Along with those imperatives are bonuses offered for prompt action—special discounts, free gifts, and other inducements to decisiveness and immediate action.

The Actual Terms

In normal business commerce the expression "terms" or "terms offered," as it is often expressed, refers strictly to payment. Between organizations doing business together as seller and buyer it refers to the length of time granted for payment and discounts offered, if any. In direct mail, most "small-tag" items are sold on a cash basis, the payment required with the order. For larger items, there are usually terms of some sort—a "time payment" plan. Without some financing plan, the sales figures would drop sharply.

The larger mail-order firms, such as Sears, Fingerhut, Spiegel, and Quill, have their own credit schemes. Quill, because it sells to other business organizations, ships the order and then bills to customers with approved credit. Catalog houses and others who sell principally to individual consumers offer time payment plans and usually accept major credit cards. Even the small direct-mail and mail-order dealers find it expedient to offer credit-card convenience—usually Visa and MasterCard—to their customers. It is generally believed that this increases sales by about 25 percent.

Many of the leading periodical publishers stress payment via several small payments. However, in direct mail, especially when selling directly to the individual consumer rather than to another business organization, the expression may have additional meanings. These may include not only credit terms, but also bonuses, free gifts, and other inducements, as cited in the following examples.

Periodicals often offer free sample issues in their quests for new subscribers. The proposition offered me by *TRIPS, the Travel Update*™ is typical. I can get two issues free, according to the order form, which says "Mail today for two trial issues, no cost, no obligation." Actually, if I sign and return the order card I have ordered a subscription, which I may cancel, without obligation, after the second issue I receive. It's quite typical of all such offers of free issues of periodicals; the *Wall Street Journal* recently made me a similar offer and I get such offers from other publishers more or less regularly. It is the wise expedient, from the sales/advertising viewpoint. If you send out sample issues with an invitation to subscribe, many will simply postpone doing so, even if they like the publication. A research service not too long ago reported that the practice of sending sample issues with an invitation to subscribe generally does not produce very good results. The promotion method described here is usually far more effective, and it is not difficult to understand why this is true: many people are not especially likely to go to the trouble of canceling a subscription already made, just as many are not especially likely go to the trouble of subscribing. Hence, this is making lemonade out of lemons, turning a disadvantage into an advantage. That is, since so many people are either lethargic or indecisive, it can be turned to advantage by making it necessary to take a positive action to cancel.

Book clubs take similar advantage of these common traits of lethargy, indecisiveness, and procrastination by sending members the "main selection" each month unless the member specifically requests that the main selection not be sent. And there is at least one computer-program club running a "program of the month" emulation of the book clubs.

Time magazine usually offers gifts, as well as credit terms. Currently, they are offering a desk telephone, and in an earlier campaign the gift was a digital desk clock. Fingerhut, a large direct-mail seller of general household goods, has for years offered free gifts with all purchases, including "surprise" gifts. And in my own direct-mail ventures, selling specialty publications I myself wrote and published, I gave many of my publications free as gifts or bonuses to make my offers more attractive.

Discounts and other "special sale" blandishments are another kind of effective inducement. There are several alternative ways in which you can offer discounts, each with its own advantages and disadvantages. There are, in fact, two basic approaches to offering customers special prices and discounts. One employs simple sale prices, unhampered by qualifications or special requirements of any kind, usually citing the list prices to emphasize the saving. The other uses a qualified discount or special price, the special price dependent on the customer meeting some special condition or taking some special action.

Each of these has its own set of variants. However, the word *sale*, along with the many adjectives commonly used with it, never fails to attract and excite a great many prospects; it appears impossible to wear out either the sale idea or the word itself. In fact, one seller of carpets in this area advertises a "special sale" constantly, throughout the year. However, there are dozens of commonly used "justifications" or reasons for sales, making the idea of a sale more credible. Here are just a few such "reasons" or kinds of sales in which special prices are offered without qualifications of any kind:

- ☑ Fourth of July sale
- ☑ Washington's birthday sale
- ☑ Weekend sale
- ☑ Going out of business sale
- ☑ Inventory clearance sale
- ☑ Labor Day sale

☑ Fire sale
☑ Our buyer's mistakes sale

Each of these ways offers certain advantages and disadvantages, of course, and some are suitable for only certain situations and uses. You could hardly expect anyone to take advantage of a quantity discount on an automobile purchase, for example, or even on such items as household appliances. This method of discounting is most suitable for goods that are consumed regularly, such as foods and medicines. For durable goods, the rebate plan is more suitable, although it is also used in selling consumables and soft goods.

Sales based on qualifiers of various kinds are also numerous. Here are a few of those:

☑ Quantity discounts (e.g., "cheaper by the dozen")
☑ Two for the price of one
☑ Second one at half-price
☑ Early bird dinner prices (in many restaurants)
☑ Cocktail hour prices (in restaurants and bars)
☑ One-hour sale
☑ Ten-minute sale (usually spontaneous and announced over a speaker system in the emporium)
☑ Unadvertised specials
☑ Senior citizen discount
☑ Rebates

The rebate has become a popular inducement and has spread from the marketing of automobiles, where it had its origin, to other goods, usually hard goods. It has at least two large advantages to the seller. As an offer, it enables you to publicize a low price. (The printed price usually has an asterisk beside it, invoking a footnote in small print that explains that this is the price after the rebate is deducted.) Yet, the average price received for the item will be substantially higher than that advertised because a great many buyers will not go to the trouble of sending in the form necessary to get the rebate.

■ The Direct-Mail Package

A fairly complete list of the commonly used sales and promotional materials, printed and otherwise, was presented in an early chapter. The direct-mail package generally includes a number of these pieces. Earlier in this chapter the case of the *Trips* magazine offer was cited to illustrate a typical sales proposition offered by periodicals. In fact, the entire package, mailed under a bulk mail permit in a number 10 envelope (regular business size envelope, that is) included the following items:

1. A four-page salesletter (two sheets, printed on both sides).
2. An enclosure—a single sheet, printed on one side only, as an example of the tours (listed thereon) that subscribers can learn of and enjoy.
3. An order form, which is a single card about 4 × 8 inches.
4. A "business reply" (postage paid) response or return envelope.

This all amounts to one ounce, and so qualifies for the lowest first-class postage rate. The package is a somewhat typical and reasonably complete, but relatively modest ensemble of direct-mail materials, as compared with the direct-mail packages sent out by many other organizations.

Another package, from the Mail-Order Market Place, also arrived in a number 10 white envelope, under first-class postage. It did not contain a letter, but did have three letter-size circulars and two smaller circulars. These materials offered mailing lists, a book on the circular-mailing business, and advertising space in a periodical.

In a highly successful direct-mail campaign of my own some time ago, mailed in a number 10 plain white envelope, I included a four-page salesletter (two sheets), a two-page circular (one sheet), and a combination circular and order form of four more pages (two sheets). That was a total of five sheets, which will fit into a business envelope and weigh one ounce, so it will travel at the lowest first-class postage rate. I was selling a newsletter subscription and three manuals in that package, and I made a "package deal"—a price for all that was considerably less than the total individual prices of the four items. ($100 for the full package, as against $142 for the several items sold individually.) It was a package wherein the approximately 1.5 percent response rate I experienced resulted in a satisfactorily profitable venture.

About Return Envelopes

The obligatory minimum complement of materials normally recommended for a direct-mail package is a salesletter of two or more pages, a brochure, and an order form. A great many direct-mail experts recommend strongly the inclusion of a return envelope, preferably a postage-paid one, and many even state that it is obligatory and its inclusion or exclusion makes a substantial difference in the response one may expect.

I am ambivalent about return envelopes. It is probably true that when you mail to individuals at their home addresses some will not have an envelope or postage stamp handy and so will not respond or will, at best, put off responding. And many of those who procrastinate will never get around to responding. So undoubtedly the return envelope makes some difference in those circumstances. On the other hand, when mailing to businesspeople at their office or business addresses, the situation is entirely different. It has been my experience that in that case the respondent rarely uses the return envelope but discards it and uses one of his or her own business envelopes. It is therefore a waste to include a return envelope in this latter kind of mailing unless something special in an envelope is required, as in some cases.

About Salesletters

In the typical direct-mail package the salesletter is the centerpiece, setting the tone and delivering the principal message. In fact, the sales-letter normally delivers the entire message, and the other materials reinforce it in several ways. The salesletter in the *Trips* package, for example, begins with a first page on what appears to be the publisher's regular letterhead, with a blurb under the letterhead, before the salutation. The blurb delivers the essence of both the offer and the proposition in three short lines:

Try two issues of TRIPS absolutely FREE. . .
. . . and learn how our readers enjoy
quality travel at up to 40% off!

The offer is, of course, a promise to enjoy quality travel at 40 percent below regular prices, and the proposition is to get two issues of the periodical free. The body of the letter does an excellent job of following up the blurb and the promise made in it. It starts immediately, after the salutation "Dear Traveler," with the promise that the reader will become a travel "insider," getting many kinds of special benefits as a result of the special "connections" they acquire through subscription to the publication. It then goes on for four pages, explaining numerous benefits in detail, urging the reader to subscribe and take advantage of the proposition, stressing the risk-free nature of the proposition. (The order card states that the subscriber may cancel the subscription immediately after receiving the free issues.) There is, after that, a postscript, reminding the reader once again of the many benefits, and the text of these explanations is quite effective, in my opinion.

In many other cases, such letters are characterized by many marks and comments made most boldly with a marker pen. Words and phrases are circled and comments are scrawled in longhand in margins and between lines. This has the effect of high-pressure selling, and obviously must work effectively for some. However, no single approach is universally the right answer; what works very well in one situation does not work at all well in another. Marketing in general and direct-mail marketing in particular are not sciences; they are arts. And in this case, underlines and capitalization are used to emphasize the points the writer wants to stress, rather than the more popular bold marking-pen strokes and flourishes. Which is better? It would be impossible to say without making tests, and even that would not produce immutable truth but only truth of the moment, for there are many variables that affect the results in each given case.

About Brochures

The very word *brochure* is not an exact or definitive term. (My own rather large dictionary defines it with a swift dismissal as a "pamphlet.") But in fact a great many different kinds of documents are referred to as brochures, ranging from simple sheets of typed information to quite elaborate and costly bound documents of many pages and multicolored illustrations. And if the sales letter is the centerpiece of the direct-mail package, the brochure is a closely following runner-up in most such packages.

There are many variants. One small business owner, Barbara Brabec, publishes a periodical that is a hybrid newsletter and magazine, and she also publishes a growing line of books, all devoted to helping individuals succeed in homebased businesses, usually craft businesses. A recent piece she mailed out in a dm (direct-mail) package illustrates another approach. It is a four-page letter and brochure, with several illustrations, resulting in a quite attractive presentation. The first page is illustrated in Figure 6-1. Again, and to an even larger degree, the offer is presented immediately, although the proposition—the proffered sale of a book—is only partially described. The full proposition is explained only inside, on a third page. The piece builds further on the opening theme of help (Figure 6-2) and explains the discount in the order form (Figure 6-3), where she also presents other offerings.

One commonly used layout is the 6-panel 4 × 9-inch brochure, made up by printing the copy in six columns on both sides of a 9 × 12-inch sheet and folding it to the 4 × 9-inch size. It then fits into a number 10 regular business size envelope. A variant of this is the 8-1/2 × 11-inch sheet, also folded so that it has six panels and will fit into a common business envelope. Figure 6-4 illustrates this format, showing the exterior panels of the sample brochure. The brochure is folded so that an outer panel serves as the introduction, making the offer (benefits listed in lower half of outer panel) after the proposition is stated as a one-day seminar, with the day and date listed. Figure 6-5 shows the interior panels, where the details are presented and an order form (registration form) is included.

The same seminar, sponsored by another organization, is described in a four-panel 8-1/2 × 11-inch brochure (Figure 6-6), made up by printing the copy on both sides of a sheet that is 11 × 17 inches and folding that. (Some

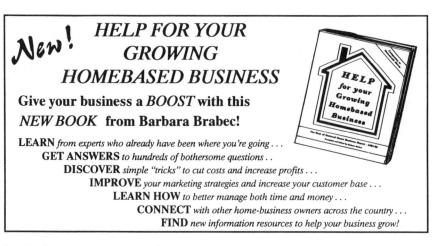

HELP FOR YOUR GROWING HOMEBASED BUSINESS

New!

Give your business a *BOOST* with this

NEW BOOK from Barbara Brabec!

LEARN *from experts who already have been where you're going . . .*
GET ANSWERS *to hundreds of bothersome questions . .*
DISCOVER *simple "tricks" to cut costs and increase profits . . .*
IMPROVE *your marketing strategies and increase your customer base . . .*
LEARN HOW *to better manage both time and money . . .*
CONNECT *with other home-business owners across the country . . .*
FIND *new information resources to help your business grow!*

Dear Reader:

It's easy to **START** a business at home. The **TRICK** is in surviving the first few years. I know. I've been there. Maybe that's where you are now. Or maybe you're still trying to get up the necessary courage to just begin the business you've been dreaming about?

Either way, I know that each day brings new questions or problems that need to be addressed. If you are presently trying to expand an existing business, those questions and problems will only multiply as you probe new markets, consider growth options, and meet daily business challenges.

As you may know, my business is helping others succeed in small businesses based at home. **Through my workshops, my books, and my quarterly periodical, I help individuals like you make business decisions, find new opportunities for growth, and get the answers needed to keep moving in a profitable direction.**

I'm writing now to tell you about my newest book, *Help For Your Growing Homebased Business.* It may be just the boost your homebased business needs right now. See inside for details about how this *companion guide to Homemade Money* will benefit you. (If you're still trying to get your business off the ground and have not yet read *Homemade Money,* I urge you to do so now. You can preview this book in your local library, but do note that a new and enlarged edition was published this year. Some information in older editions is no longer accurate as a result.)

Whether you're just beginning in business, or trying to cope with the unique problems that come with time and growth, I'm sure you'll find one or more of my home-business publications just right for your present needs. *In fact, I could be the best home-business friend you'll ever have.* **To take advantage of the special help I offer, just clip and mail the order form inside.** Before long, I'll bet you'll be thanking me . . . all the way to the bank.

Barbara

P.S. *More than A HUNDRED THOUSAND readers have already benefited from my home-business guides. I'd like YOU to benefit, too.* You risk nothing by ordering now because I offer a **GUARANTEE OF SATISFACTION!** Don't just *dream* about making money at home . . . use my *proven success guides* to turn your dreams into **financial reality!**

FIGURE 6-1   First page of sales letter/brochure: the offer. (Courtesy Barbara Brabec Productions)

$12.95 ppd.

HELP for your Growing Homebased Business

What's in it for you?

 the following and see for yourself.

(Just a sampling of the many topics discussed)

Chapter 6: **MARKETING MAKES THE DIFFERENCE.** ☐ Outline for a simple marketing plan, pg. 76. ☐ **Success Tips:** Why it's important to appear successful, even if you're not; the importance of "positioning" and information about "guerrilla marketing," pg. 81. ☐ **Pricing tips** for home-business owners, pg. 83. ☐ **How to tap new markets,** including the Canadian market, pg. 85; museum shops, pg. 86; the "plush animal industry," pg. 82; and the Christian Gift Store market, pg. 100. ☐ **A no-risk test marketing method,** pg. 89. ☐ Mail order marketing secrets, pg. 90. ☐ Working with sales representatives, pg. 97. ☐ **Publicity Secrets--advice from pros!** How to figure out newsworthy press release hooks and angles that will result in local or national visibility, pg. 102.

Chapter 4: **MONEYTALK:** ☐ Learn about a mistake banks commonly make--one that could have your checks bouncing from here to Kingdom Come! Pg. 41. ☐ **Discover new ways to avoid bad checks or collect bounced checks,** pg. 42. ☐ Should your business have charge card capabilities? More here than meets the eye. Pg. 44. ☐ **How to get a loan when you** have no collateral, pg. 50. ☐ How to create a simple cash flow report, pg. 51...PLUS financial planning and tax tips from experts.

Chapter 5: **AVOIDING LEGAL PIT-FALLS:** ☐ The truth about the Better Business Bureau, pg. 59. ☐ **Ways to cope with restrictive zoning laws,** pg. 62. ☐ Advantages and disadvantages of incorporation, pg. 65. ☐ **Partnership pit-falls,** pg. 66. ☐ Legal guidelines concerning the manufacture and sale of products and services that utilize the name, voice, signature, photograph or likeness of deceased personalities. ☐ Insight into the world of licensing, pg. 68. ☐ **How to avoid lawsuits** by complying with consumer product safety guidelines related to the manufacture of toys,

children's articles and clothing, pg. 69. ☐ Why you may not need to file a formal trademark application and **the power of "common-law trademarks,"** pg. 71. ☐ Special tips on how to fight copyright infringement, plus insight into patents, pg. 72.

Chapter 3: **WORKING SMARTER:** ☐ Learn a simple secret that could enable you to double your income overnight! Pg. 29. ☐ **Ten steps to greater profits** every year, pg. 31. ☐ Why the wrong business name can kill a business, and how to pick the right kind of name for YOUR business, pg. 32. ☐ Insurance pitfalls home-business owners must avoid, pg. 35. ☐ Character traits that spell SUCCESS in business, pg. 39.

Chapter 1: **HOME-BUSINESS PERSPEC-TIVE**--A report on conferences, trends and surveys that emphasize the importance of homebased businesses to the nation's economy. PLUS **the agony and ecstasy of self-employment--what it's** *really* like to run a business at home. Barbara's readers have shared their private thoughts on this topic, and you're sure to find yourself mirrored somewhere on these pages.

NOTE: This is an intensely *personal* business book. All the information in it is based on someone's actual experience. YOU GET SPECIFIC HOW-TO INFORMATION AND GUIDELINES, NOT THEORY. Here you learn what has worked for many, what hasn't...and why. It's like sitting down with a group of special business friends to discuss the new problems that have arisen since your business began to roll.

This is networking at its best...in printed form!

Barbara Brabec Productions   •   P.O. Box 2137   •   Naperville, IL 60566

FIGURE 6-2 Second page of sales letter/brochure: the follow-up. (Courtesy Barbara Brabec Productions)

CLIP AND MAIL THIS ORDER FORM TODAY. ⟶

Barbara's books are recognized "bibles" of the make-money-at-home industry. Her magazine columns have helped thousands of creative individuals to greater success. Her newsletter is a leader in its field--and her **HOME BUSINESS NETWORK** is without equal. Take advantage of the help she offers by ordering these publications today!

GUARANTEE: If for any reason you are not completely satisfied with your purchase of one of Barbara's books, simply return the undamaged book within ten days to receive a complete refund. And, if you are not delighted with your first issue of National Home Business Report, *the balance of your subscription will be refunded on request.*

Yes!   PLEASE ENTER MY ORDER FOR:

☐ *National Home Business Report,* $18/year, 4 issues. ($9 with purchase of any book listed below.) $_____

☐ *Homemade Money,* $16.45 ppd. $_____

☐ *Help For Your Growing Homebased Business,* $12.95 ppd. $_____

☐ *Creative Cash,* $11.95 ppd. $_____

☐ *Crafts Marketing Success Secrets,* $10.95 ppd. $_____

Note: Illinois residents, add 6 3/4% sales tax to book orders.

PAYMENT ENCLOSED: $_____

Name: _____

Business name: _____

Address: _____

City: _____ State: _____ Zip: _____

☞ MAIL TO: Barbara Brabec Productions, P.O. Box 2137, Naperville, IL 60566

Keep the HELP Coming . . .

...with a subscription to *National Home Business Report,* the **quarterly dedicated to helping small businesses grow.** Stay informed and up to date on the home business industry--what's happening where, who's doing what, and how it affects YOU.

"Worth Getting," says *Changing Times* magazine! "...contains a smorgasbord of information for homebased businesspeople. Written in a breezy, informal tone, it includes cottage-industry news and legislative updates, write-ups of useful organizations for networking, profiles of successful home businesses, columns on marketing and computers, book reviews...and plenty of off-the-cuff advice from the editor."

Special Offer ➤

Now, with your purchase of one or more of Barbara's books, **get four issues of** *NHBR* **for just $9** – regularly $18/year! The current issue of *NHBR* will accompany your book order, and you will receive three additional issues thereafter in regular subscriber mailings.

KEEP THE HOME-BUSINESS HELP COMING by subscribing NOW! Remember...your satisfaction is *GUARANTEED!*

6 x 9 in., 28 pg. Quarterly.

Just getting started?

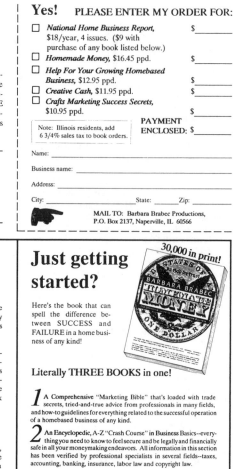

30,000 in print!

Here's the book that can spell the difference between SUCCESS and FAILURE in a home business of any kind!

Literally THREE BOOKS in one!

1 A Comprehensive "Marketing Bible" that's loaded with trade secrets, tried-and-true advice from professionals in many fields, and how-to guidelines for everything related to the successful operation of a homebased business of any kind.

2 An Encyclopedic, A-Z "Crash Course" in Business Basics--everything you need to know to feel secure and be legally and financially safe in all your moneymaking endeavors. All information in this section has been verified by professional specialists in several fields--taxes, accounting, banking, insurance, labor law and copyright law.

3 A Mind-Boggling, 500-Listing RESOURCE DIRECTORY that brings together, for the first time, the most important FREE and low-cost resources for homebased workers in all fields--actually a mail-order catalog of information! Books, periodicals, how-to guides, business suppliers, marketing and planning guides, publicity aids, supplier directories, trade information, government resources . . . and MORE!

✿ NEW in the 1987 edition: A 24-page chapter, "Computers in Homebased Businesses," which emphasizes what a computer can do for a small business and how it impacts both the business and personal lives of its users.

". . . one of a select few really good how-to guides . . . superb start-up resource for homebased business enterprises." --Jan A. DeYoung, SMALL BUSINESS DEVELOPMENT CENTER, Iowa State University

---

FIGURE 6-3   Third page of sales letter/brochure: the proposition. (Courtesy Barbara Brabec Productions)

HOW TO SUCCEED AS AN INDEPENDENT CONSULTANT

A ONE DAY MARKETING SEMINAR

Saturday, May 12, 1984
9:00 A.M. – 5:00 P.M.

Sponsored by:
University of Miami
School of Continuing Studies
Department of Conference Services

Among the topics to be covered:
- How to successfully market your skills
- How to expand the Profit Centers of your consulting services
- "...how to assess your own resources, analyze the needs of the marketplace, and design your consulting product to satisfy those needs."
- FREE BOOK by Herman Holtz

James L. Knight International Center
400 Southeast Second Avenue
Miami, Florida 33131

University of Miami
Conference Services
400 S.E. 2nd Avenue
Miami, FL 33131

A private, independent international university
An equal opportunity/affirmative action employer

Dated Information
Please Post or Forward
to Interested Parties

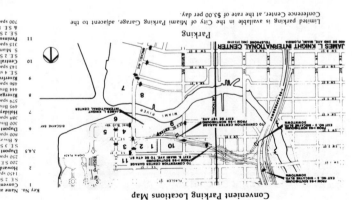

Convenient Parking Locations Map

JAMES L. KNIGHT INTERNATIONAL CENTER
400 SE 2ND AVE, MIAMI, FLORIDA
TELEPHONE (305) 372-0277

Parking

Limited parking is available in the City of Miami Parking Garage, adjacent to the Conference Center, at the rate of $3.00 per day.

Key No.	Name and Location
1	Convention Center Garage S.E. 2 St to SE 1 Ave 1150 spaces
2	Howard Johnson's Garage 200 S.E. 2 St 250 spaces
3,4,5	Dupont Plaza Lots S.E. 3 St. between SE 2 Ave 800 spaces
6	Dupont Plaza Hotel Garage 300 Biscayne Blvd Way & Biscayne Blvd 389 spaces
7	Holiday Inn Garage 495 Brickell Ave 486 spaces
8	Rivergate Plaza Garage 444 Brickell Ave 579 spaces
9	Riverfront Lot SE 4 st @ S Miami Ave 143 spaces
10	Central Lot SE 1 2 St between S Miami Ave & SE 1 Ave 315 spaces
11	Peninsula Federal Garage SE 2 St between SE 2 Ave & SE 1 Ave 700 spaces

"A large portion of those who enter into consulting services as a profession do not survive the first year, the chief reason being the failure to market their services effectively."

FIGURE 6-4 Exterior panels of small brochure

155

If you have the technical skills and even sales ability — it isn't enough to become a successful consultant. This one day seminar focuses on the marketing of your skills and developing other Profit Centers to keep your business growing.

Learn how to not only market your consulting services generally, but how to tap into the public sector markets on the federal, state and local levels. Learn first-hand how to create proposals, successful bids and contracts. Let Mr. Holtz show you how to expand your business into the profitable areas of WRITING, PUBLISHING, PUBLIC SPEAKING and other FREELANCE PROJECTS.

For the man or woman who's considering consulting professionally, or who's starting a practice and wants to develop it, HOW TO SUCCEED AS AN INDEPENDENT CONSULTANT is an A-Z seminar that will guide you to success.

Each participant in the seminar will receive a copy of Mr. Holtz's book: HOW TO SUCCEED AS AN INDEPENDENT CONSULTANT.

Instructor
HERMAN HOLTZ
- Consultant
- Lecturer
- Author
- Engineer
- Seminar Leader
- Winner of over $125 million in government contracts

Herman Holtz is an independent consultant in Washington, D.C. and the author of several books including:

- HOW TO SUCCEED AS AN INDEPENDENT CONSULTANT
- PROFIT FROM YOUR MONEY-MAKING IDEAS: How to build a new business or expand an existing one.
- DIRECTORY OF FEDERAL PURCHASING OFFICES: Where, What, How to Sell to the U.S. Government.
- GOVERNMENT CONTRACTS: Proposalmanship and Winning Strategies.
- THE WINNING PROPOSAL: How To Write It.

Mr. Holtz has been Director of Marketing at Volt Information Sciences, Inc. and Applied Science Associates, and has worked in various capacities as Editorial Director of the Educational Science Division, U.S. Industries. He has been a successful seminar leader in the marketing field in Washington, D.C.

SEMINAR OUTLINE

I. Introduction
A. What Is a Consultant Today? Which Type of Consultant Are You?
   The Essential Elements of Consulting Services.
B. Marketing as the Key to Consulting Success.
   Are Technical Skills Enough?
   Mastering Sales and Marketing Skills.

II. Understanding the Marketing Process
A. The Three Elements of Marketing Successfully.
B. The Elements of Selling: Promise and Proof.

III. Marketing Your Consulting Services Generally
A. The Basic Need to Instill Confidence.
B. How to Gain Prestige and Build a Professional Image.
C. Developing the All-Important Leads.
D. Following Up Leads Correctly.

IV. Marketing To The Public Sector
A. Understanding Public Sector Markets.
B. The Skill of Proposal Writing.

V. Broadening The Base of Your Consulting Practice.
A. Expand Your Profit Centers.
B. Writing: How To Write and Sell Successfully.
C. Publishing: Including newsletters, reports, books, tapes.
D. Public Speaking For Profit.

VI. Open Discussion.

REGISTRATION

The registration fee of $195.00 per person includes all workshop materials, morning and afternoon breaks, luncheon and certificate of attendance. Refunds will be made until April 27, 1984, subject to a $25.00 administrative fee. **No refunds after April 27th.** Registration limited.

TAX DEDUCTION for all expenses of continuing management education (including registration fees, travel, meals and lodging) undertaken to maintain and improve professional skills (Treas. Reg. 1-62-5 Coughlin vs. Commissioner, 203724307).

FOR MORE INFORMATION contact Brenda Mayer, Department of Conference Services, at (305) 372-0140, or register in person at the Knight Center, 400 S.E. 2nd Avenue.

REGISTRATION FORM
(Please print or type)

HOW TO SUCCEED AS AN INDEPENDENT CONSULTANT
MAY 12, 1984

Name
Company
Address
City   State   Zip
Telephone (   )

Registration Fee: $195.00   **Amount Enclosed:**
☐ **VISA**   **Card Number:**
☐ **MasterCard**   **Expiration Date:**
Signature:

Make checks payable to: UNIVERSITY OF MIAMI

Detach and send to: Independent Consultant Seminar
University of Miami
Conference Services
400 S.E. 2nd Avenue
Miami, Florida 33131

FIGURE 6-5 Interior panels of small brochure

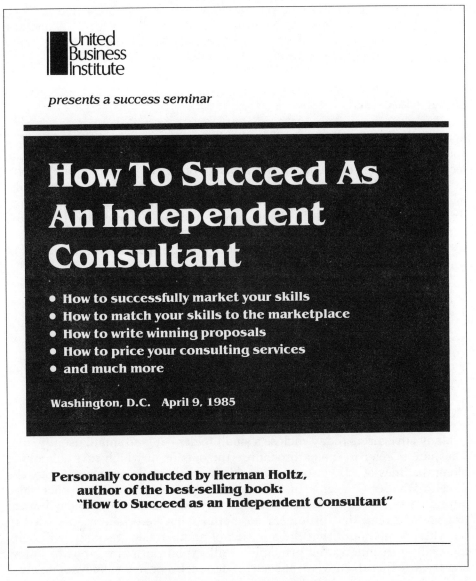

▌▌United
▌▌Business
▌▌Institute

presents a success seminar

How To Succeed As An Independent Consultant

- How to successfully market your skills
- How to match your skills to the marketplace
- How to write winning proposals
- How to price your consulting services
- and much more

Washington, D.C.   April 9, 1985

Personally conducted by Herman Holtz,
author of the best-selling book:
"How to Succeed as an Independent Consultant"

FIGURE 6-6 First panel of larger brochure

use an 11 × 24-1/2-inch sheet and then fold that down into an 8-1/2 × 11-inch six-panel brochure.) Of course, the larger format, especially the six-panel format, allows much more space for copy, and advertisers sending out the large brochures often mail the brochure alone—i.e., without cover letters and separate order forms—believing that such large brochures are sufficient to deliver the entire presentation without the support of other elements.

Notice once again that the offer—set of benefits—is presented at once in the introductory copy of the front panel. The proposition—a one-day seminar—is also made clear, although details are reserved to the order form—a registration form, in this case—which is inside.

Other Materials

My own experience indicates that the cliche "The more you tell the more you sell" is a truism, at least within some reasonable limits, and so the inclusion of other elements in the package often prove to be quite helpful in supporting the presentation overall. Those additional materials may take many forms and be used to serve more than one purpose. For example, some dm packages include a little plastic card, resembling a credit card, with the addressee's name inscribed on it. This device is a bit expensive, but where its use is appropriate, it offers support for the dm package in a number of ways:

1. It impresses—has a certain perceived value for—some people because it does resemble a credit card.
2. It tends to flatter the recipient because his or her name is inscribed on the card.
3. It helps support the advertiser's credibility, making his or her offer appear more bona fide.
4. It helps command attention, by virtue of these attributes.

Many advertisers today enclose a small folder—it is so small, usually, that I hesitate to refer to it as a brochure—the outside of which says something along the lines of, "Don't open this unless you have decided not to buy the Excello Wonder Gadget." Inside this little pamphlet is still another sales argument, of course. And the advertiser fully expects that everyone will want to open and read that little gem no matter what he or she has decided to do. There is no doubt that the addition of another sales message will help, especially if it follows the principle I will explain in paragraphs to follow shortly, whether the novelty of such an item helps or not. (I know of no clear evidence one way or the other as to this.)

In my own experience, I have found it quite helpful to use more than one brochure in a mailing. In fact, I personally prefer several small brochures to one large one. However, you should be at pains to avoid the common mistake many make when they include several separate sales presentations, which is to say essentially the same thing in each sales presentation, as though iteration and reiteration—sheer insistence on repeated urgings—make for a more powerful presentation; they do not. But before explaining what I have found to be the most powerful way to use multiple brochures (and I use the word *brochure* rather loosely here, for it may refer to several sales letters, circulars, and/or other elements), let us consider another common and concomitant mistake in writing sales copy: that is, the mistake of trying to be or promise to be all things to all people in a single presentation. It is just not effective, usually, to introduce excessive numbers of arguments, promises, benefits, or anything else in a single presentation. Focus is important, and it is lost when you present too many ideas at once. You get, instead, either distraction of the reader from your main point or you create confusion—the reader is not sure what your point is.

The way to use multiple brochures in a single dm package, then, is to create a separate focus for each. Here are a couple of examples from dm campaigns of my own.

In one case I was selling a set of materials—an instruction booklet, samples, and forms—to train and equip respondents to conduct a resume-writing service. I had made up a general brochure and salesletter describing the package and sent it out to a list of people who had responded to my inquiry advertising. The results were somewhat disappointing, not a loss, but not what I had hoped for and thought the mailing would bring.

I did some research and thinking and revised my original brochure, while I developed two more little brochures to include in the mailing. One was based on information that had been published to describe a peer group of job seekers who met to help each other in their quest. I extrapolated from that to suggest how the respondent might organize such a group to promote his or her own resume-writing service. The other suggested some other ideas I developed for promoting resume-writing services and diversifying them into related fields. In fact, I had hinted broadly at these things in my original brochure but, I decided, had been too general to be effective. Instead of one general brochure, I now had three that were specialized and focused sharply on different aspects of the reader's interests, on various ways to benefit from my package. I left it to the cover letter to make the general presentation and introduce the three specialized brochures, with ample reasons given for reading them with care.

The increase in orders was apparent immediately—not merely because there was more copy, but because there was more useful information—clearer and more detailed information on benefits to be derived from the package I was selling.

The point is not to keep urging the respondent to buy, but to keep urging the respondent to do what is in his or her own direct interest. To do this, you must focus your attention on what *is*, in fact, in your reader's own direct interest. Think hard about this and how you can help the reader get what he or she wants. Do that effectively—and sincerely, for insincerity has a way of shining through the most eloquent phrasing—and you need never urge the reader to buy from you; wild horses couldn't hold him or her back!

There is an excellent platitude that is appropriate here, the origin of which I do not know, but it has been expressed by many writers, especially writers on selling and influencing others in general, in many ways. It is this: the way to get what you want is to help the other person get what he or she wants.

My offer, in another case, was not paper and ink, nor even information. They are the means, not the benefit. The offer—the real benefit I promised— was help in winning government contracts. It was only when I learned to make that offer explicit that I began to experience real success in this venture. And eventually I learned how to construct my package of materials to support this offer.

There was a two-page cover letter that made the basic offer of help in winning government contracts, with an explanation of my credentials as an expert and with a basic sales argument for my approach to the problem. Each of the other four sheets—two pages each—was devoted to some closely related matter. One included a questionnaire—"test your government-marketing and proposal-writing I.Q."—pointing out that the materials I sold answered all the provocative questions listed—and they were provocative. One asked the reader, for example, if he or she knew how to *appear* to be the low bidder, whether he or she was or was not, in fact, the low bidder. Another discussed proposal writing in some depth and explained its importance. Another probed various aspects of government procurement regulations that marketers to government agencies should know, along with some useful and informative statistical information. And a final one described the materials, explained the money-saving aspects of buying the entire package, and provided an order form with all the possible options.

Certainly, the success of that truly simple package ("simple" in that all the copy was on plain white paper and except for the headlines was "typeset" by electric typewriter) illustrated one important fact quite clearly: the cosmetic aspects of a package—costly type, paper, color, and other such flourishes— may be helpful in many ways, but they are by no means essential to success nor of nearly as much importance as the *content* of the package. That simple dm package drew orders from some of the leading corporations in the United States.

One might well assume that had the package been a bit slicker—a colored brochure with eye-catching illustrations, an order form on colored card stock, and other such refinements—it would have worked even better. On the other hand, perhaps the "poor but honest" appearance of the simple, straightforward presentation helped persuade respondents that the offer was a worthy one. (There are prospects who are suspicious of too slick a presentation and are "turned off" by obviously costly brochures and other materials.) There is only one way to find out, and that would be to test. But it would have been very costly to have made up that slick package. And if the test had resulted in evidence that the simple package outpulled the more ornate one, that expense would have represented a dead loss and a drag on the campaign. It was not a good gamble for a small campaign, although it would have made sense for a large one. But let us discuss testing in general, for it is an important part of the process of conceiving, planning, and conducting direct mail campaigns.

■ Testing

It is considerably easier to test direct mail solicitations than it is to test media advertising. There are, in fact, at least three major advantages:

1. You can conduct the tests and evaluate the results much more quickly in dm because you have total control. In advertising, you are restricted by deadlines, so there can easily be two or three months of delay before your advertising runs. With direct mail you can make up the mailing package quickly, send it out, and be monitoring and evaluating the first results within a couple of weeks.
2. It is much easier to key your mailers so that you get an accurate measure of response. There is usually a fairly large uncertainty factor in tests of advertising copy.
3. It is ordinarily much less costly to test a direct-mail program than to test media advertising. (For one thing, you can make the test as large or as small as you like, something not as easy to do with media advertising.)

The concept is generally simple enough. You make two or more mailings, varying only one factor in each. That is important, of course; for the tests to have any significance, you must test only one thing at a time. Obviously, if you change more than one thing, you will have no reliable way of judging what change was responsible for the difference in results. And equally obvious, the mailings must be as similar to each other as possible in other respects. That is, you must not introduce uncertainty factors by mailing to different lists or at different times.

The Factors to Change

A great many dm people test their prices, first of all, generally trying out three different prices—one they consider the "right" price, another one a low price, and a third one a high price. Others test their headlines, their body copy, the terms they offer, different colors of ink, and other factors, most of which are not of primary importance.

It has been my experience that price and/or other factors relating to the proposition are secondary factors to test—not unimportant, but secondary. In my opinion, and based on my own experience, the offer is the first thing to test.

Testing the Offer

The rationale for this is simple enough: unless your prospect has or develops an interest in what you want to sell—is attracted by the promised benefit and thus finds your offer an attractive one, it is absolutely futile to test price or anything else. No price will attract a buyer who doesn't want what you are selling or doesn't have faith in your offer, and no price will discourage the buyer who does want urgently enough what you offer.

This is not to say that there is not a middle group, a group that is fence-sitting and may be toppled to one side or the other by another factor, such as the price or the impact of the presentation. But even for those the first need is for an offer that causes them to sit on the fence indecisively, waiting to be persuaded to buy.

I have found it possible to test offers with small mailings, as small as 500 pieces to each group. Divide a mailing list into two, three, or more segments of equal sizes, one for each version you wish to test, using as random a method as possible, make your mailing, and measure the results.

The heart of the offer is the promise, as you have read repeatedly. And it was through testing that I became convinced that subtlety has no place in direct mail; it is necessary to express the promise of benefits in the most basic and direct way, appealing to the prospect's emotional wants, not to his or her reason. I was truly amazed at the great difference in response to an appeal that promised prospects guidance in writing winning proposals and another that promised help in winning contracts.

Try to understand that emotional appeal and its importance. Here are a few simple examples of what most people do and do not want. (These ideas were inspired by actual copy that crossed my desk.)

1. They do not want to find the healthful and intelligent way to diet; they want to find the easy, fast, painless way to lose weight.
2. They do not want to learn karate; they want to be safe from attackers and able to strike back effectively.
3. They do not want to subscribe to the *Money Maker's Digest*; they want to make money at home and make it easily.

Both kinds of information are needed in your presentation; the question is which kind should be in the headline, representing the offer. Let's consider these three examples.

The first one is quite simple. The question here is whether the offer should promise all three benefits—easy, fast, and painless—or focus on one and perhaps add the other two. I would test each, and I suspect that the "fast" way would be the most attractive—and quite possibly the most credible — one to prospects. Prospects may well be somewhat skeptical of "easy" and "painless" allegations from prior experiences, but they are likely to want to believe in "fast," and that alone helps make it more credible a promise.

The second example offers two alternatives, in my opinion. Everyone, and women especially, has some fear of being on the streets alone at night these days, and being safe is an appealing idea. However, I suspect that knowing how to strike back would be even more appealing, and I would test both. Again, many people like the idea of revenge and "just desserts" for wrongdoers, and may find the prospect of striking back effectively every bit as attractive as the notion of being more secure.

The third example is a bit more complex, but a great many people want to earn money, and many of those would love to earn money in their own homes. That appeal never wears out, no matter how often it appears in advertising literature. "Insider" and "expert" information is also an intriguing idea for a great many people, so it can be part of the promise or part of the proof. But there are other emotional factors that may enter into this. Even those who do not have a need for more money, such as an individual with a highly satisfactory job or the wife of a prosperous and generous husband, are often attracted by the notion of becoming more independent, making a contribution to the family income, or other emotional satisfaction.

In short, it is important to identify the principal or most influential emotional motivator, and you can rarely estimate or predict it as accurately as you can identify or measure it through actual testing.

Secondary Test Factors

The secondary factors to test are those which are most likely to sway the "undecideds" among your prospects. Low price is not always the key, however, for there are many people who judge quality and validity of offers by price, so that low prices make them suspicious. (Don't forget that important matter of credibility.) If you do want to offer a price that appears to be far below the market for similar items, rationalize it. Explain why your price is so low, why and how you are able to beat the competition so effectively, while maintaining at least equal quality. However, there is another side to the price question. It is this: the "best" sales piece is not necessarily that one (i.e., price, in this case) that produces the greatest number of orders, but that which produces the best return on investment. Let's consider the case of an item that costs you $10 to buy and $2 to "fulfill"—pick, pack, and ship. Now let us consider three prices at which you test it and three rates of response and assume that this is the result of a small test mailing of 1,000 pieces:

Selling Price	Gross Profit	Rate of Response	Total Gross
$42	$30	1.5%	$450
34	22	3 %	660
28	16	4 %	640

You can see in this simple example that the $34 price produces the best results, if you are after sales alone. Of course, if your main objective is to create new customers (assuming, of course, that this mailing is to new prospects, rather than an existing customer list), with immediate sales only a secondary objective, you will do best with the $28 price, since that produces the largest number of customers. Even so, never assume that the lowest price always produces the largest number of customers, for that is not true, either. Surprisingly often the lowest price is regarded by many prospects with enough skepticism to affect the response rate strongly. (Again, here is that important credibility factor.)

You can test many less important factors, if you wish, such as the difference in response rates resulting from the use of two- or three-color printing versus black-ink-only printing, slicker-looking packages, novelty inserts, and sundry other such refinements. It is my opinion that these things are rarely worth testing for small mailings of a few thousand pieces because their effect is usually in fractions of a point—e.g., 0.005 percent. This may amount to a significant amount of money in a mailing of millions of pieces or even of hundreds of thousands, but even a half dozen such tiny increments rarely mean enough in dollars to be worth the trouble of testing them in a mailing of perhaps 50,000 pieces. That is, you might get 2,005 orders instead of 2,000 orders as a reward for all the cost and trouble of testing those smaller items.

Bounceback Orders

The matter of what the industry refers to generally as "bounceback orders" is a separate issue, although it is not entirely unrelated to testing, either. Bounceback orders are those orders you get resulting from enclosing additional sales literature with the merchandise when you ship the original order, and they can represent a significant amount of additional business. They are, moreover, a factor to consider when deciding whether to opt for the greatest number of new customers for most profitable operation. Since you get these orders at virtually no additional cost, they are usually highly profitable, and may be even more profitable than the original orders were.

And, in fact, those orders coming from people who buy loss leaders, such as the name-and-address labels described earlier as the sales leader of a large mail order firm, are really bounceback orders themselves, although that is not the strategy underlying the use of loss leaders.

■ Exercises

Once again, a set of exercises is offered to help you review the ideas that were offered in this chapter and do some thinking about them. You can thus determine for yourself how well you understand and can apply these to various situations. Again, there are no target scores, and often no absolute right or wrong answers, for we are studying a subject that is more art than science. And, again, don't hesitate to write in answers of your independent construction where you think it necessary.

Mail Order versus Direct Mail

While names and terms are not of themselves especially important and many are ambiguous, what they denote can be important. Hence, see whether you can recall the major point or points that distinguish or at least justify distinguishing one from the other. Decide which of the following statements accurately describes the significant difference between the two methods of marketing merchandise and services. (That is, check off one statement only or, if you think none are adequate, write in one of your own.)

☐ **1.** Mail order depends on some form of media advertising, while direct mail seeks customers by sending sales literature directly to prospects.

☐ **2.** Mail order is not confined to advertising by mail alone, while direct mail is so confined.

☐ **3.** Direct mail is much easier to test than mail order is.

☐ **4.** _____

   _____

Mailing Lists

Discover how much you know about mailing lists by checking off choices for each of the following statements:

1. The lists you rent from those who deal in such services are usually lists the renters (check one)
    - ☐ own themselves
    - ☐ compile themselves
    - ☐ manage for others
    - ☐ rent from others
    - ☐ _____

2. The valid measures of mailing-list quality include the following items (check off all appropriate items):
    - ☐ demographic characteristics
    - ☐ percentage of nixies
    - ☐ whether names of buyers or inquirers
    - ☐ recency
    - ☐ match with needs
    - ☐ _____

3. The alternative methods of acquiring mailing lists include the following:
    - ☐ borrowing
    - ☐ compiling
    - ☐ buying
    - ☐ advertising
    - ☐ _____

4. Some kinds of mailing lists are more valuable than others. Study the following descriptors and decide which are the most valuable lists, then place numbers in the boxes to indicate the priority, starting with number 1 for the most valuable.
    - ☐ your recent inquirers
    - ☐ someone else's recent inquirers
    - ☐ your customers
    - ☐ somebody else's customers
    - ☐ high-priced rented list

5. Decide which are the essential criteria to have in mind when choosing a list or pursuing candidates for a list you are building and indicate those by checking off choices or writing in your own below:
    - ☐ the match of those on the list with your offer
    - ☐ the freshness or recency of the list
    - ☐ the buying history of those on the list
    - ☐ the professions of those on the list
    - ☐ the match of those on the list with your proposition
    - ☐ _____

The Offer

The offer, rarely defined or even discussed in direct marketing literature, except obliquely, has been given special meaning in this chapter and the overall approach to marketing in this book. The offer is, in fact, the heart of marketing generally, and merits some thought.

The meaning used here to define an offer is not the conventional one that many apply to the term, and that makes this review especially important. Check the statement that you believe most accurately states that definition or, if you are not satisfied with the statements offered, write in one of your own.

☐ An offer is what you claim the item of sale is in terms of its beneficial characteristics.

☐ An offer is what you promise will be the direct beneficial results of buying or using the item you are selling.

☐ An offer is the item, its price, and the set of terms you will extend to a prospect who agrees to buy.

☐ An offer is _____
_____

The Proposition

Defining an offer in the special meaning given it here required that we also define something we decided must be called a *proposition*. We must therefore consider again just what we mean by that term by once again choosing the best definition or creating one.

☐ A proposition is what you claim the item of sale is in terms of its beneficial characteristics.

☐ A proposition is what you promise will be the direct beneficial results of buying or using the item you are selling.

☐ A proposition is the item, its price, and the set of terms you will extend to a prospect who agrees to buy.

☐ A proposition is _____
_____

Identifying Motivators and Clinchers

Everyone in marketing accepts the notion that customers buy benefits. However, we do not always translate that notion into practice effectively. For there are those qualities that whet a prospect's appetite for what you promise—motivators—and those qualities that help the prospect believe in your promise—clinchers or convincers. Write in, beside each item M or C to identify it as a motivator or clincher.

1. High quality   _____
2. Convenience   _____
3. Low price   _____
4. High speed   _____
5. Available   _____
6. Prestigious   _____
7. Enhances self image   _____
8. Easy to use   _____
9. Easy to learn   _____
10. Endorsed by stars   _____
11. Famous brand   _____
12. Glittery appearance   _____

The Direct-Mail Package

Although a mailing of a single salesletter or a postcard to a list of names is direct-mail marketing, it is not typical direct mail. Typically, direct mail involves the mailing of a package of materials, with a usual minimum of three or four items. Check off the four items in the following list that are those usually considered to be the obligatory minimum.

☐ Broadside
☐ Circular
☐ Letter
☐ Brochure
☐ Flyer
☐ Return envelope
☐ Order form
☐ Advertising novelty
☐ Business card

Closing in Direct Mail

In face-to-face selling, the close is the peak of the art of selling. The best— most effective—salespeople are invariably good closers. But closing in direct mail is another proposition, a far different one, one many consider not possible. But it is possible to simulate the face-to-face situation to a degree in direct-mail presentations. Check off among the following items those which help produce in a direct-mail presentation at least some simulation of the close in face-to-face selling.

- ☐ a discount offer
- ☐ a rebate coupon
- ☐ a "free" offer
- ☐ a set of options
- ☐ a plastic card
- ☐ an "in case you decided not to buy" pamphlet
- ☐ an option of requesting more information

Testing

Testing is a most important activity in direct mail, and there are a number of items you can test. Assign priorities by writing in numbers in the boxes for the tests you think most important, starting with the number 1 for the most important of these.

- ☐ black-ink printing versus 2- or 3-color printing
- ☐ the most attractive price
- ☐ the most attractive promise
- ☐ the most motivating name
- ☐ the return envelope versus no return envelope
- ☐ _____

There are three kinds of prices to consider in testing, the highest price, the lowest price, and the right price. But "right" is not an absolute term; what is the right price in one case is not necessarily the right price in another case. Choose, from among the following items, the factor(s) to consider in deciding what is the right price.

- ☐ what others are charging for similar items
- ☐ what customers are willing to pay
- ☐ what brings in the largest number of orders
- ☐ what brings in the greatest profit
- ☐ what your main objective is
- ☐ _____

Loss Leaders

Direct marketers use loss leaders, just as supermarkets and department stores do and for similar reasons, despite the difference of the way in which each does business. Select the best reason for using loss leaders from among the following:

☐   to make your name well known
☐   to collect a list of prospects
☐   to get the bounceback orders
☐   to check your mailing lists
☐   to build customer lists
☐   _____

CHAPTER SEVEN

Examples and Exercises: Newsletters

The newsletter, properly conceived and used judiciously, can be the most potent PR and marketing-promotional tool in your kit. In fact, it may thus make most of your other PR/promotional tools superfluous and even irrelevant.

■ The Newsletter as a Modern PR Tool

The newsletter is probably the most widely used tool of PR and marketing promotion, after the news release. It is, in fact, such a popular tool (there are an estimated 100,000 newsletters published in the United States) that it is the chief use cited by computer manufacturers for the new desktop publishing systems they have introduced recently. Figure 7-1 is one advertisement the Aldus Corporation has used to promote its PageMaker® software, one of the leading programs of its kind. Note that it stresses newsletter production with the PageMaker software, as do most other producers of desktop publishing software.

The newsletter industry—and it has become important enough and pervasive enough to merit that term—spans the extremes of the business world. As a for-profit venture, it includes large, multi-newsletter publishers with hundreds of thousands of subscribers and multi-million-dollar budgets, while it also includes the mini-small publisher laboriously turning out a two- or four-page typewritten sheet with a few hundred subscribers, at most. But even as a PR venture, newsletter publishing exhibits such a profile. Tiny businesses turn out their little newsletters to promote their fledgling ventures, but thousands of newsletters are produced by supercorporations, nonprofit organizations, and even governments to help them promote their own activities and carry out their missions.

There are several reasons for the growth of the newsletter as a PR tool. Not the least of the reasons is its versatility in this role. It offers many advantages.

The new PageMaker Portfolio gives you the ability to create professional looking newsletters on your Macintosh™ with PageMaker® desktop publishing software. Even if you've never designed anything in your life.

You'll get disks containing seven collections of professionally designed newsletter templates, 21 in all, that need only your masthead, copy and graphics to be complete. Plus a 114-page workbook that teaches the basics of graphic design and gives you a set of tips for working with PageMaker, all for just $79.

Call toll free 1-800-33-ALDUS for order information, or see PageMaker Portfolio at your local Aldus dealer today.

And start making your newsletters look more newsworthy.

Aldus Corporation, 411 First Ave. S., Suite 200, Seattle, WA 98104.

PageMaker Portfolio: Designs for Newsletters will be available soon for PC AT™ and compatible computers.

PageMaker is a registered trademark of Aldus Corporation. Macintosh is a trademark of Apple Computer, Inc. AT™ is a trademark of International Business Machines Corporation.

999-375

FIGURE 7-1   Newsletters and desktop publishers. (Courtesy Aldus Corporation)

It is highly "respectable." That is, it does not appear to be advertising matter, if properly designed, and so is immediately assumed to have some value. It is therefore not easily discarded after a mere glance—again, *if properly designed.*

It is easily mailed. Most are mailed folded to fit into a number 10 envelope, so that (again) it does not appear to be advertising matter or "junk mail."

A supply is easily carried in a briefcase, readily available to hand out to others.

It is easily distributed at meetings, conventions, and other such gatherings.

It is a good general mailing piece.

In short, a well designed newsletter can be used as a brochure, circular, and general information piece, and it gains entry where ordinary advertising matter may not. Moreover, it can be far more effective in its overall impact and effect than typical advertising matter is. Therefore, it is time to discuss, briefly at least, what "well designed" means.

◼ Newsletter Design

Bear in mind that we are discussing here the newsletter as a promotional piece to be given away freely, not as the base of a for-profit venture. "Well designed" must therefore mean, in this case, designed to maximize its usefulness in PR and marketing promotion. And yet there are some desirable qualities both must have in common with each other. (If necessary, you may review the earlier discussions in Chapter 3.) The design objective in creating a newsletter useful for PR and sales promotion is to provide enough news material in the product to induce the prospect to read it and, if possible, to file it for future reference, and yet incorporate enough advertising and sales material in it to generate sales or, at least, good leads for sales.

Figure 7-2 illustrates an approach to this. It reproduces the front page of a newsletter published by J.F. Straw, whose own bank gets prominent mention, as he himself does, in a box on the front page. Bank advertising is always relatively sedate and dignified, as necessary for a business that must inspire and sustain public trust. A newsletter is almost ideal for this situation. The mere fact of a newsletter bearing information about the bank is itself an asset. And, of course, you can see the quiet and modest tone of the nameplate and typeface of the *Offshore Banking News*, as compared with the more "commercial" look of some of the newsletters illustrated in the previous figure.

The second page of this newsletter is shown as Figure 7-3. In this figure you can see the masthead, that column of type that reveals the ownership

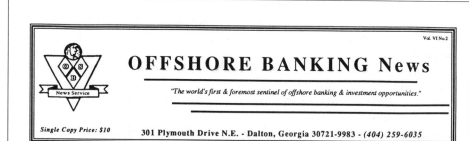

Vol. VI No.2

OFFSHORE BANKING News

"The world's first & foremost sentinel of offshore banking & investment opportunities."

Single Copy Price: $10   **301 Plymouth Drive N.E. - Dalton, Georgia 30721-9983 - (404) 259-6035**

ROH PROMISES BRIGHT FUTURE TO ORDINARY PEOPLE

Roh Tae-Woo came out as the winner in South Korea's first direct presidential election in 16 years. As the standard bearer for the ruling Democratic Justice Party, Roh garnered a plurality of the ballots. The election fever which had disrupted the country for the last few months has now abated. Roh pledged during the campaign to create "a new era for ordinary people." Now the people are anxiously awaiting on what he will do with the national economy.

Roh is a firm believer in the Capitalist system and is proud that South Korea has grown by leaps and bounds. He is looking to solve the labor and management problems, and the differences between social classes and different interest groups, in order to maintain the country's extraordinary growth. Mr. Roh has already unveiled an economic package supporting free business and fair taxation.

J.F. Goes To Washington.

J.F. (Jim) Straw, Editor & Publisher of Offshore Banking News, will be the keynote speaker at the upcoming "Symposium 88 on International Banking," to be held in Washington, D.C., February 27, 1988.

Principal stockholder and Chairman of the Board of the First American Bank Ltd., in Saipan, Mr. Straw spent 20 years in the business world before becoming a writer and publisher. He has written over 200 books, booklets, reports and articles on the subjects of money-making opportunities, investments, finance, advertising and business management. He is one of the highest paid business consultants in the country today.

The Symposium will also feature Jonathon Rose, Vice-President of Capital Bank N.A.; Don Moss, former I.R.S. training officer; Arthur Zdobysz, C.P.A. and partner in a Washington investment planning firm; and various other acclaimed speakers.

Focusing on international investing, the Symposium is especially geared to the self-employed business person or entrepreneur. In a one-day intensive symposium, investors will learn how to open an offshore bank account; write checks that will never bounce; secure letters of credit for unlimited amounts; write checks that bypass the Federal Reserve System; and how to shield their assets or even own their own offshore bank.

For more information on the Symposium, or to register, write: Market Development Symposium, Grove Corporate Plaza, 555 Grove Street, Herndon, VA 22070. Or call; 1-703-478-9303

FEBRUARY 1988

NOT ALL INVESTMENT MARKETS BLEAK!

Few in 1988 will have the first-hand recollections of what it was like to own investments in late 1929. Not that we are suggesting that the world is on the verge of repeating the terrible times of the 1930's. Nevertheless, the present is being compared with that earlier era, with some justification — not since that fateful day in 1929 have the stock markets crashed as they did last October. Even more unnerving, many markets dropped by larger percentages than on the infamous "Black Tuesday", sixty years ago.

How bad has it been? No stock exchange has been spared, although some have lost less than others. So far, Japan's market has held up relatively well (down 13% since October) and in December was still 22% higher than a year ago. At the other extreme, the Australian All Ordinary Index lost more than 44% of its value between October and December. However, over the past year the index declined by only 16%. The Swiss stock market, by comparison, lost twice that percentage during 1987, and Frankfurt's loss was even greater; more than a third of its value was erased last year, most of it in the last few months.

Neither was 1987 a banner year for bonds, although those denominated in marks, yen, pounds or Swiss francs saw small price gains. In U.S. dollar terms, bond gains have been greater. This is because those currencies continued to climb through the stock crash against the dollar.

In fact, dollar-based investors who held foreign currency bonds and gold in 1987 did very well. These investments continued the bull markets they have been in since early 1985. (In dollar terms gold rose almost 25% last year).

So investment markets have not been uniformly bleak. And even for the admittedly hard-hit stock markets, the past few months' actions do not necessarily mean economic catastrophe. And clearly, there are still signs of the continued economic health of the industrial nations. Britain's economy in particular is booming, and as yet there are no distinct signs of slowdown in others.

Another reason for hope that we are not on the brink of depression, is that unlike 1929, relatively few people today have their entire future tied to the stock market. Now real estate is the more universal investment. Until and unless real estate values plunge, most people who were well-off before the crash will still see themselves as prosperous.

What will 1988 bring? We are skeptical of any forecast for the next 12 months. After all, who, even five months ago, successfully predicted the October crash?? — IF the October massacre was just a correction, we will have a rebound. And even assuming the worst, that October 1987 proves to be the watershed October 1929 was, remember that by April 1930, stock prices had recovered most of the ground lost that previous October. In other words, prices rose smartly enough that those not fortunate to take their profits earlier were given a second chance!

FIGURE 7-2 *Offshore Banking News,* front page. (Courtesy J. F. Straw)

of interest.....

HELPING THE REDS.........The Soviet Union, short of cash because of declining oil prices, has borrowed US$6 billion from Western banks in the past two years, according to CIA studies and other documents. The information was included in two volumes of documents published by the joint economic committee of Congress that told of strains on the Soviet economy. (No wonder they're dining at the White House...the cupboards at home are bare)

NZI Buys Stake in FOCO BANK.......NZI Corporation, the New Zealand banking and insurance group, has purchased 35% of the Zurich-based Foreign Commerce Bank (FOCO) for 150 million Swiss Francs. The purchase is subject to the approval of the Swiss Banking Commission. Although NZI will have representatives on the FOCO bank board, they do not envision any major changes, and expect to keep the current executives and staff.

MEXICAN INTEREST rates as high as 137% for 3 month Treasury Bill.....but, before you get excited.....you must convert your dollars to the Mexican peso which lost almost 50% of its value in 1 day recently. That, added to a 144% a year inflation rate should discourage any sane investor. Currently the Peso is 2,600 to the dollar. At the beginning of 1987 it was 927 to the dollar! — (Rumors abound that the Mexican government will soon impose an economic "shock" package - perhaps even freezing bank accounts! If you're not already out of Mexican investments, times-a-wasting!)

Says Richard Stricof, a tax expert with Manhattan's Seidman & Seidman accounting firm: "If I were doing something that I didn't want federal authorities to know about, I would pick a place that was inconspicuous. Switzerland isn't." — (*Time magazine/ 12-7-87*)

FDIC WOE$.....The Federal Deposit Insurance Corp. (FDIC) which insures deposits up to $100,000 in many U.S. banks, is facing its first loss in its 54-years history. Because of almost 200 bank failures last year, the federal agency may lose $200 million to $300 million of its $18 billion fund, which insures about $2 trillion in deposits. (In others words, if push comes to shove, the agency only has enough funds to cover less than 9% of deposits) William Seidman, Chairman of the FDIC, is expecting the same number of failures again this year.

MEXICO.....The good news....& the bad news... The good news for Mexican laborers is an immediate two-stage wage package raising salaries by 15%......meanwhile, the bad news....Mexico devalued it's currency by 17.4%. Threatening a general strike if not granted a raise, Mexico's Confederation of Mexican Workers union, in essence has just won a 2.4% reduction in <u>real wages</u>. With Labor Leaders like these, Mexican workers need no enemies! It now takes 2,600 Mexican pesos to buy a green-back U.S. dollar.....

569 U.S. Bank Failures! Since OSBN started publishing in January of 1983, 569 U.S. banks have failed. Almost 200 just last year (1987). Worst hit have been Texas (97), Oklahoma (66), & Louisiana (23). No improvement in the number of bank failures is expected this year, with most economists and banking officials predicting another 200 or more failures.

CHILE — The Shell-Chile consortium will begin large-scale gold and silver production in an open-pit mining operation located at Choquelimpe this July. They expect an annual production of 1.7 tons of gold and 28 tons of silver. The same consortium, in conjunction with Chevron, expects to put copper mining operations into production later this year.

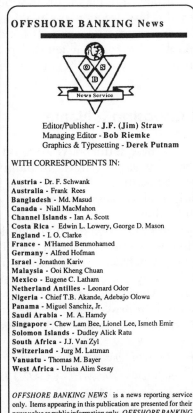

OFFSHORE BANKING News

Editor/Publisher - **J.F. (Jim) Straw**
Managing Editor - **Bob Riemke**
Graphics & Typesetting - **Derek Putnam**

WITH CORRESPONDENTS IN:

Austria - Dr. F. Schwank
Australia - Frank Rees
Bangladesh - Md. Masud
Canada - Niall MacMahon
Channel Islands - Ian A. Scott
Costa Rica - Edwin L. Lowery, George D. Mason
England - I. O. Clarke
France - M'Hamed Benmohamed
Germany - Alfred Hofman
Israel - Jonathon Kariv
Malaysia - Ooi Kheng Chuan
Mexico - Eugene C. Latham
Netherland Antilles - Leonard Odor
Nigeria - Chief T.B. Akande, Adebajo Olowu
Panama - Miguel Sanchiz, Jr.
Saudi Arabia - M. A. Hamdy
Singapore - Chew Lam Bee, Lionel Lee, Ismeth Emir
Solomon Islands - Dudley Alick Ratu
South Africa - J.J. Van Zyl
Switzerland - Jurg M. Lattman
Vanuatu - Thomas M. Bayer
West Africa - Unisa Alim Sesay

FIGURE 7-3 *Offshore Banking News*, second page and masthead. (Courtesy J. F. Straw)

and principal functionaries of the publication. (In this case the newsletter is operated as a business venture of its own, although the publisher is the Chairman of the Board of his own offshore bank. This is an ideal arrangement, if it can be arrived at.)

This is also a monthly publication. When a newsletter is used primarily as a promotional piece, it is a good idea to seriously consider less frequent publication, such as bimonthly or even quarterly. The benefits to be derived from a newsletter as a promotional piece are generally every bit as great with the less frequent publishing schedule, and the burdens of time and costs are greatly lessened. It is not at all difficult to increase the frequency of publication if and when that proves advisable, but it is difficult to reduce that frequency if you begin with frequent publication.

◼ Choosing a Name

Name a newsletter as you would an advertisement. That is, use approximately the same criteria in naming a newsletter as you would in devising a good headline. As in the case of advertising, it is no time or place for subtlety, cleverness, or "artiness." It is a time and place for clarity and communication.

When I launched my first newsletter, my company was Government Marketing News, Inc., acronym GMNI, and so my newsletter became *The GMNI Report*, which was not my first (nor last) mistake. A bit later, wiser as a result of my struggles to make this newsletter a success, I renamed it *Government Marketing News*. That was no stroke of brilliance either, but it was a definite improvement; it at least said something.

Consider the names of the newsletters illustrated in Figure 7-1:

Pacific Nursery Retailers Association News
Mega Views, the MEGA CADD Dealer Newsletter
Investment Options
Madison General's Health File
Construction Materials
The South Sarasota Yacht Club Windjammer
Legal Line

Except for the second one, there is little doubt about what any of these newsletters is about; the title tells the tale. And even that second one is revealed as the newsletter of some kind of association, as is the first newsletter. Another is published by a hospital, evidently, and another by a yacht club. Even in the case of those newsletters where the name is of relatively little importance because the circulation is to members of an organization, the titles are indicative of the subject and content. But this is far more important when you wish to use a newsletter as a promotional tool.

Bear in mind that you wish those seeing your newsletter for the first time to become interested enough to at least begin reading it. That means, usually, that the title of the newsletter must "grab" them at one, preferably by appealing immediately to their direct interests.

Of course, that means that you must know what those interests are. That is, you must know just whom you are addressing or trying to reach. The newsletter *Construction Materials* is fairly broad in the implications of the title, as far as revealing the kinds of readers the publisher hopes to reach and interest. The first class that comes to mind is that of builders in general. But it will probably also appeal to architects, who specify materials, and it might appeal to manufacturers of construction materials. All these people must keep up with what is happening in their fields, and the title is broad enough to cover a wide range of interests, while still being quite specific in identifying its content and subject matter.

On the other hand, if the publisher wished to make the appeal somewhat narrower, he or she might have narrowed the title to something such as *Builders' News*. It is possible to do either—broaden or narrow the appeal— of course, and each has its advantages and disadvantages. Even today, years after I published a newsletter I created and sold to an association, I am still getting occasional inquiries about subscriptions to *Contracting Opportunities Digest*. The title still appeals to those seeking leads for contracts of any kind, and without ever seeing an issue—on the basis of hearing the title alone— people track me down to find out where and how they can get copies. Such is the power of the right title.

Not for Profit

Note that four of the seven newsletters shown in Figure 7-1 are not-for-profit newsletters. Nor is that at all unusual; quite a large portion of all the newsletters throughout the United States are published for reasons other than profit. Their existence and great numbers illustrate the power and the popularity of the newsletter.

Ironically enough, more than a few of today's successful for-profit newsletters began life as free newsletters, created to support PR and promote sales. One well-known example was the *Gallagher Report*, created a number of years ago by Bernard Gallagher to support his small business as a seller of securities. It became so successful that he abandoned his original venture in favor of the newsletter business. But there have been many other such cases.

In today's increasingly technological world newsletters are becoming increasingly more "cosmetic." Earlier, two influences acted to keep the typical newsletter extremely simple and informal in its appearance. Because of limited budgets and small circulation figures—often only a few hundred subscribers—most newsletters were composed by typewriter, even in the days of the clumsy manual machines. However, even when larger circulation and larger budgets would have financed formal typesetting, many newsletter publishers opted for the effect of spontaneity and clung to the simpler composition by typewriter, deliberately shunning the more polished appearance of formal typesetting.

With the emergence of electric typewriters, the quality of typewriter composition improved greatly, but soon inexpensive "cold type" machines began to appear, and it became possible to achieve a typeset appearance without going to great expense. But even then many newsletter publishers preferred the less-formal look of typewriter composition on the supposition that the latter appearance was more indicative of last-minute, up-to-date information, and would be more appealing to readers as a result.

Today, the desktop computer and desktop publishing systems are steering newsletter composition more and more to the typeset appearance, as the Aldus advertising of Figure 7-1 reveals. All those newsletter front pages shown in that figure were created on desktop computers by the Aldus Page-Maker software, with a laser printer to translate the electronic data into printed characters on paper. You can, of course, use such software and hardware to create typewriterlike composition, but it is just as easy to compose newsletters with much more professional looking typefaces and fonts. Desktop publishing is making available to even the smallest office staff typesetting of a quality that is beginning to rival that of the professional typographers, and layout of a skill rivaling that of publications production specialists. Certainly the days of typewriter composition and improvised layouts and makeup appear to be growing shorter and shorter.

■ Editorial Policy

Editorial style is an important matter to consider, but before getting to that matter it is necessary to discuss the closely related matter of editorial policy. And you should develop a specific editorial policy—e.g., decide what kinds of coverage you will include and what kinds you will not include, what features you will carry, and a few related matters. It is important that readers come to understand and be able to anticipate what they will find in your newsletter, and you must therefore have a set of standards and adhere to them. However, in this special case—special because the newsletter is to be a promotional tool, rather than a product sold for profit—there is an editorial question that must take precedence. It is this: How much of the newsletter will be unadulterated advertising or PR and how much will be pure newsletter editorial matter?

Now the fact that your real objective is PR and promotion should not blind you to the need for this to be a legitimate newsletter. That is, you cannot make the vehicle 100 percent PR and advertising and make a success of it. Your readers will soon enough perceive that your alleged newsletter is simply a thinly disguised brochure, and that will be the end of it.

On the other hand, you must include a reasonable amount of promotional copy, if you are to gain benefits from the effort. So the question comes down to, first, how much of each kind of coverage should you have, and, second, will your promotion be blatant advertising or will it be more subtle?

My suggested answers to the two questions are these:

On the matter of the division of material into true newsletter editorial matter and promotional copy, I would not make more than one-half the coverage self-serving promotion, perhaps even less, depending on the circumstances I will discuss next.

On the matter of subtlety versus blatancy of promotional coverage, I would suggest a division, including both extremes. That is, I would include at least one or two unabashed advertisements for whatever my organization sells or does for customers, but I would also include a great deal of much more subtle promotion, some of which would be subtle enough to actually serve as straight editorial content, thereby permitting you to make that suggested 50-50 split between editorial and promotional coverage without taking undue exploitative advantage of the newsletter vehicle. And to illustrate that idea, here are a few examples of coverage that would be of direct interest and use to your readers while also serving as promotion for you:

☑ Ideas and application notes for using your products in various situations and to satisfy various needs.
☑ Useful information on manufacturing processes in your company.
☑ Case histories regarding your products and their uses.
☑ Developmental history of some of your products.
☑ Profiles of leaders in your organization.
☑ Your organization's activities with regard to community affairs.

■ Editorial Style

Editorial style in newsletters tends to be informal—even intimate—as compared with a newspaper. Certainly, your role as publisher of a newsletter is not that of a great policy maker or molder of public opinion. You must remember always at least these truths about newsletters in general and especially newsletters published for promotional purposes:

☑ Your appeal is or should be to a rather narrowly defined readership, in this case to those who are customers or good prospects.

☑ Your end-goal is promotion; that is the only reason for the existence of the newsletter.

☑ All content of your newsletter that is not aimed directly or indirectly at promoting your product, service, or cause is aimed at inducing the reader to read on and to keep your newsletter.

If you keep these facts always in mind they should enable you to avoid making some of the mistakes that overtake those who forget exactly what they are about and why they are about it in turning out a newsletter as a promotional tool. For example, exploiting controversial issues would almost surely alienate some of your readers—who are customers and customer-prospects. Don't be a crusader. You are not truly a journalist and should not try to be; you are a marketer and PR specialist, and it is important that you do not lose sight of that.

In the same vein, work at keeping the content of your newsletter always in good taste. It is surprisingly easy to give offense to someone, no matter how innocent your intent. "When in doubt, leave it out" is an old platitude, but still a valid one. Use it as a guideline. (A simple line drawing of a cocktail waitress in a typically skimpy costume, used as one of several illustrations in a mailing piece of mine, drew an angry letter from an executive who accused me of exploiting women and using bad taste in my advertising.)

Be very cautious in using humor. It can be deadly in its effects. The most good-humored jest at some minority, people with some peculiarity, or even individuals who think mistakenly that you are having fun at their expense can result in their becoming quite irate.

Perhaps it is not possible to avoid offending some overly sensitive person now and then. However, if you wish to absolutely minimize the number of such events, here are a few guidelines:

☑ Never make anyone but yourself the butt of a humorous story. Better yet, tell funny stories about a pet or an occasion that exposes no individual to possible ridicule. Or, if you cannot resist telling a funny story about some person, make the subject a completely anonymous "anyperson," one that is hard for anyone to identify with.

☑ Avoid—scrupulously—jesting or even discussing religion, politics, sex, disarmament, world conflicts, and any issue which is controversial at the moment.

☑ When you mention a specific individual, be sure to get his or her name spelled correctly and title accurately identified. Individuals can be quite sensitive about these matters, and it is worth checking carefully to be sure that you get these right.

☑ An excellent idea, also, is to involve readers as much as possible. Invite readers to write with news items, comments and questions, reporting these, along with names, and publishing answers. Guest editorials are also a good way to involve readers. Information about things is rarely quite as interesting as information about people. Seek to get some of that latter kind of information into your newsletter.

■ Exercises

Complete the following sentences by checking off the correct choice or writing in one of your own:

1. The content of your newsletter should be
   - ☐ 100 percent PR/advertising
   - ☐ 100 percent straight editorial matter
   - ☐ 100 percent PR/advertising disguised as straight editorial matter
   - ☐ _____

2. The title of your newsletter should be
   - ☐ as simple as possible
   - ☐ definitive of its objective and content
   - ☐ one that includes the name of your organization
   - ☐ _____

3. Editorial policy of your newsletter should be
   - ☐ Specific and firmly established
   - ☐ Flexible to accommodate new ideas
   - ☐ Reviewed every month
   - ☐ _____

4. The advertising and promotional matter in your newsletter should be
   - ☐ Always very subtle and low key
   - ☐ Honestly blatant and unabashed
   - ☐ A mix of subtle material and frank advertising
   - ☐ _____

5. To keep readers interested and pleased with your newsletter the copy should be
   - ☐ Rigorous and highly controversial
   - ☐ Primarily about things, rather than people
   - ☐ Primarily about people, rather than things
   - ☐ _____

Following is a True/False series to help you judge how well you have digested and understood a few key points made in this chapter:

		True	False
1.	Humorous material of any kind ensures satisfied readers.	☐	☐
2.	The sole objective of your newsletter is promotion.	☐	☐
3.	All advertising in your newsletter should be disguised.	☐	☐
4.	Editorial style should be highly structured and formal.	☐	☐
5.	The reader should never be allowed to forget who the publisher of the newsletter is and why it is published.	☐	☐
6.	Readers usually enjoy having fun poked at them.	☐	☐
7.	Readers are often offended if their names are not spelled correctly.	☐	☐
8.	Readers should not be allowed to suspect that your real purpose is promotion.	☐	☐
9.	The best publishing frequency for this type of newsletter is monthly.	☐	☐
10.	Newsletters should always be composed by typewriter.	☐	☐

CHAPTER EIGHT

Illustrations

Good illustrations are integral, not an afterthought, and they are often easier to acquire or create than you might imagine.

■ The Basic Role of Illustrations in Writing

One of the most serious errors some writers make is basing their efforts on the supposition that writing is primarily the use of language—words—to organize appropriate structures to communicate information, ideas, arguments, emotions, and whatever else a writer wishes to express. To writers who subscribe to that notion, an "illustration" is an example, an analogy, or a metaphor—a language device, that is. And as a result of that premise, such writers tend to resort to graphic illustrations—photographs, drawings, charts, and other such devices—only as an afterthought, using such devices either because it seems to them that it is time for the litany of words alone to be broken and the monotony relieved, or because occasionally the words need to be supplemented or supported by something more—when words seem to fail.

The latter is often the case: frequently, words alone are simply not enough to do the job well or, at least, to do the job efficiently. It would be difficult, if not impossible, for example, to explain many geometric figures and their mathematical relationships by words alone. And a thick tome would not enable the average reader to envision many objects as clearly as would one good drawing or photograph. Try, for example, to convey in language alone an accurate image of the Apollo moon rocket standing on its pad, breathing clouds of vapor, ready to launch, or even of the full color, shape, and detail of a carved ivory figure or some classic piece of furniture.

However, this is not an argument for turning to graphic aids only when words fail. Quite the opposite; it is an argument for a different premise, the premise that the mission of a writer is the conveyance of information and images via the most effective means, whether that is by words or by something else. That is, the judicious use of graphics to carry out the writing mission is as much a part of writing as is the use of language. Writers ought to be able to detect the need for and find or conceive proper graphic illustrations as a necessary part of their writing responsibility. While critics may judge the work of novelists, playwrights, and some other writers by their skill in using words, the work of those of us who are less celebrated writers—copywriters, for example—can be judged only by its effectiveness in achieving its intended purpose.

■ The Cost Consideration

In technical publications many of the illustrations tend to be quite costly to create, since they often must be highly accurate, detailed drawings of complex equipment. Because of that, some engineering project managers whose contracts require them to produce technical manuals for the equipment they develop try to skimp as much as possible on illustrations. They have been heard to complain, for example, that a single one-page illustration may cost as much as 10 pages of text. That may well be true, and it may even be a conservative estimate of cost, but it overlooks a salient fact: one good illustration, properly conceived and strategically employed, should do more than 10 pages of text—should *displace* at least its cost in text—so that there is no overall cost penalty. (And it also overlooks the fact that, regardless of cost, there is often no adequate substitute for a graphic illustration, and the lack of one may lead to a far greater cost of another kind, when the customer finds the manual unacceptable, a not unprecedented occurrence!)

■ Judging the Quality of an Illustration

In fact, that (the text-displacement idea) turns out to be a good measure of an illustration. It is a good measure of both the illustration itself—its intrinsic worth as a medium for conveying information—and of the effectiveness of its use under such circumstances that it does replace a great deal of text that would otherwise be required—the strategy of its use.

Of course, not every illustration imposes additional cost on the writing project. In many cases, illustrations are already in existence and available, so that no cost of creation is involved. And in many cases an illustration is available that is not exactly right for the need but can be easily adapted to the need.

Actually, every candidate illustration, whether it already exists in finished form or is only a rough sketch, ought to be reviewed in that light and tested immediately with the following two questions:

1. How does it compare with some set of words for effectiveness and efficiency in conveying what you wish to convey?
2. How much language is required to support and explain the illustration?

Of course, a good illustration ought to require very little explanation. If a drawing or photograph requires a great deal of explanation it is either not well-conceived or it is not used wisely. This is not to say that there may not be extended discussion of that which the illustration depicts, but the illustration itself ought not to require much more than a title and a legend, since it is itself the medium of communication and presentation. (Consider such famous illustrations as the painting of Washington crossing the Delaware and the photograph of the Marines raising the flag at Mount Suribachi on Iwo Jima, two illustrations that speak quite well for themselves with nothing more than a caption.)

■ Illustrations in PR and Advertising

The question of illustrations and their use is quite germane to advertising and promotion. Let's consider a few occasions and kinds of material that are likely to involve the need for illustrations of one kind or another:

Press events and press kits. There arise occasions when you must prepare to receive the press and supply press representatives with a package of PR materials. That may be at a convention, when some official of your organization is delivering a speech, when you are announcing a new product or a merger, or on any of many such occasions. This set of materials is generally known as a *press kit*, and usually includes both text and graphic materials, such as photographs—8 × 10-inch black-and-white glossies, traditionally, although smaller prints are usually also acceptable today—brochures, transcripts, and other materials, often illustrated freely.

Product releases. A product release is similar to a press release, but offers an editor information on a new product that is of interest to his or her readers—e.g., a new computer item for a computer magazine or a new cosmetic item for a woman's magazine. In almost all cases, an illustration or two is a must. In most cases, probably, a photograph is the right illustration, but there are occasions when a drawing or chart of some sort is more appropriate.

Articles. In many cases an article in a trade journal is a most effective PR effort, and many of the articles in those trade papers were written and contributed by PR specialists. The inclusion of several good illustrations greatly increases the probability of acceptance of the article. Periodical editors—at least, in most cases—are traditionally fond of illustrations, especially photographs, and will often accept an article primarily because it includes several good illustrations. That is, you can greatly improve your chances for having your PR-oriented article accepted by including a few good photographs with it.

Releases in general. Even the average press or publicity release can be greatly improved, as far as acceptance and use of it is concerned, by including a good photograph or two with it. Again, the fondness of most editors for graphic material can be turned to advantage in this manner.

Print advertising. You pay for space *per se* when you buy advertising in print media, and the temptation to make maximum use of that space to print words is understandable. You may tend to resist using some of that costly space for mere graphic illustration. But in many cases that is a more effective use of the space. Remember that the most effective sales message is usually the one with the greatest emotional appeal, and graphic illustrations can be effective in making that kind of appeal. Give that some serious thought.

Other advertising media. Of course it is a *non-sequitur* to consider graphics in connection with radio, but it is unavoidable when considering TV as an advertising medium. Here, the words are incidental, and the visual image is dominant. To create effective TV commercials, you must learn to *think* graphically, and that is probably the chief "secret" of TV writers: they have trained themselves to think in sequences of graphic images, rather than in assemblages of words, while they have also mastered the production techniques of close-ups, two-shots, zooming, panning, and other methodology of the trade.

Direct presentations. Marketing people are often called on to present what is often referred to casually as their "dog and pony show." This jocular reference is to whatever the marketers offer in a formal presentation to the prospective customer. Typically, this is in a board room, if proffered to a single corporate or government client, or in an auditorium or meeting room of some sort, if offered to an assembled group of prospects. The presentation is usually verbal, accompanied by an extensive set of transparencies, slides, or posters, and sometimes also with a blackboard. But it may include a movie and/or prerecorded tape. In almost all cases, it is a highly visual presentation.

■ Types of Illustrations

Graphic illustrations fall into several specific categories. For convenience of reference, let us consider the following designators and descriptions as indicative of those classes and categories:

Photographs
Sketches
Outline drawings
Renderings and wash drawings
Detail drawings
Charts, plots, and graphs

Photographs really require no elaboration, except to remark that they may be of several varieties, from black-and-white to color and from candid or snapshot-quality to studio quality.

Sketches likewise require little discussion, except to point out that I refer here to artist's sketches, not writer's sketches. The difference? This: with perhaps rare exception, writer's sketches are quite crude and intended primarily to act as a note and jog the writer's memory or as a cue for a better illustration to be found or created. On the other hand, a true artist's sketch may easily be good enough to use as part of your copy, and may, in fact, be the effect you specifically want.

An outline drawing is generally to scale but contains little or no detail other than the outline of the item depicted. Again, it may represent a special effect you want.

Renderings and wash drawings are an artist's attempt to create something approaching the photographic effect, although the artist may very well not be attempting to achieve anything resembling photographic detail.

A detail drawing is a line drawing, but one that provides a detailed presentation of the subject. An engineering drawing, for example, would generally be a detailed line drawing of some object.

Plots, graphs, and charts are among the most useful illustrations, and they do not necessarily require the services of a professional artist or illustrator. There are some expedients that can enable you to produce plots, graphs, and charts of reasonably professional quality yourself. But, for that matter, there are some devices and methods that can enable you to create even more complex illustrations yourself.

■ Artist's Aids for the Lay Person

Art supply stores and even well-stocked stationers, in many cases, offer a variety of aids that anyone can use to create many kinds of illustrations. For one thing, there are a great many plastic templates that enable you to draw boxes, lines, arrows, and other shapes by simply running a pencil or pen around the openings provided in the template. Figure 8-1 illustrates

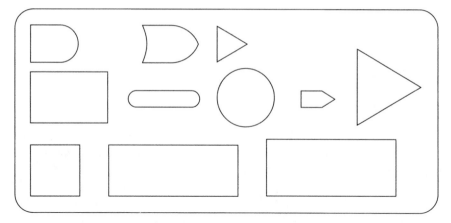

FIGURE 8-1 A typical drawing template

one such template. This one is used for drawing "logic symbols," used in computer engineering drawings and charts, but there are dozens of others available for other kinds of drawings, including many that simply provide shapes—circles, ovals, angles, triangles, rectangles, arcs, and lines.

But templates are only one aid you can use. There are also decals for lettering, pasting up technical symbols, drawing plain and fancy lines, and constructing various other shapes on paper.

Today there is an even easier avenue in the form of desktop computers—and there is hardly an office today, large or small, that does not boast at least one modern desktop computer. (More on that in a later chapter.)

Figures 8-2 thru 8-8 illustrate just a few of the kinds of charts and diagrams you can easily construct in your own office with simple tools, such as templates or with a desktop computer and some proper software programs. In fact, these are all simple charts, and far more complex charts are easily possible.

Clip art is another easily available resource. Clip art is art supplied in clean printed form as camera-ready art that you may cut and paste to illustrate a variety of items. (It is usually heavy with cartoons.) If you think you recognize certain art as illustrations you have seen before, you are probably right. Such art is sold by the creator with a blanket permission to reproduce it as you please; that is the entire concept in selling it.

FIGURE 8-2 Simple block diagram

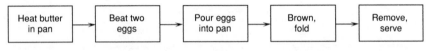

FIGURE 8-3   Diagram slightly more detailed

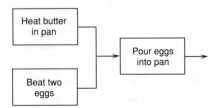

FIGURE 8-4   Diagram arranged to show time relationships

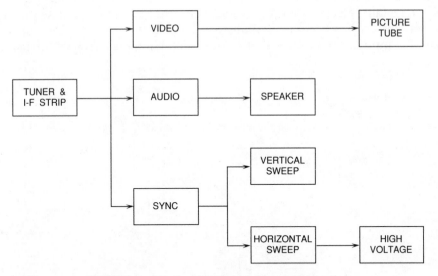

FIGURE 8-5   Complex block diagram of major TV functions

PROJECT SCHEDULE

Time in Months	0	1	2	3	4	5	6	7	8	9	10
Task Analysis . . .	▬▬	"	"	"	"	"	"	"	"	"
Preliminary Plan	▬▬	"	"	"	"	"	"	"	"	"
Review	▬	"	"	"	"	"	"	"	"
Revision	▬	"	"	"	"	"	"	"	"
Field research	▬▬	"	"	"	"	"	"	"
Interviews	▬	"	"	"	"	"	"	"
Draft lesson plans	▬▬	"	"	"	"	"
Tryouts	▬▬	"	"	"
Analysis of tryout results	▬▬	"	"
Final revisions and turnover	▬▬

FIGURE 8-6 Schedule chart

Traditionally, clip art has been sold in booklets by category, so that you can order the selection you believe will be most useful for your own purposes. Since the arrival of the desktop computer and its rapid proliferation—its almost instant success took everyone in the industry by surprise—a new kind of clip art has become available: it is computer clip art. That special area of computer technology that has become known as *desktop publishing*

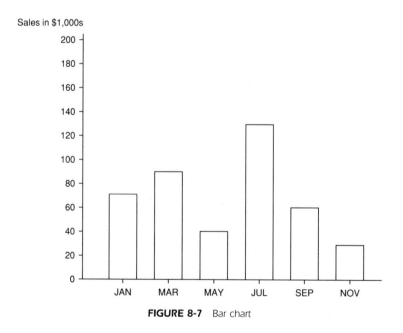

FIGURE 8-7 Bar chart

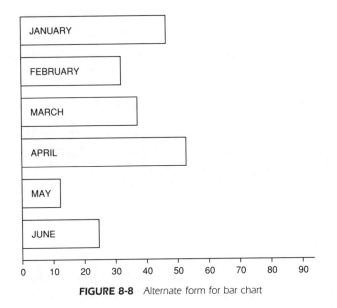

FIGURE 8-8 Alternate form for bar chart

has resulted in an offering of many special software programs, a number of which include figures of various kinds, with the proviso that, while the software program itself is protected by copyright, the art included is clip art in the traditional sense and may be used and reproduced freely by the owner of the software.

■ Other Resources

Actually, before turning to such sources as these, you should have investigated whatever may be available as in-house resources. Many organizations have extensive files of materials that can be pressed into service. Depending on the type of organization you are, there are other departments to check into—engineering, production, drafting, marketing, etc. These departments may have photographs and/or other kinds of illustrations in their files as residue from earlier uses—conventions, trade shows, or other special events. All too often we wind up "reinventing the wheel"—creating new materials that are no better than readily available old materials.

Sometimes there are in existence useful materials that are your property although not on your premises. Printers, graphic arts shops, advertising agencies, consultants, or others who have done work in the past for your organization may have in their files materials that are, in fact, the property of your organization and are available to you on demand. (Unfortunately, vendors are not always as scrupulous as they ought to be about returning to the client all "residue" of completed assignments.)

■ Vendor Services

The alternative to all of this is the vendor—the professional illustrator and/or photographer who can and will provide such services as you need to illustrate your texts or flesh out your storyboards. In some cases this may be the most practical approach for you, and should be considered when evaluating your needs and options for satisfying them.

Ordinarily, the professional illustrator and the professional photographer are two different individuals; each performs a highly specialized service, and rarely does any individual provide both services. However, there are graphic arts shops—organizations, rather than free-lancing individuals— who can provide both services.

■ Exercises

Once again, bear in mind that the choices offered are not always absolutely wrong or absolutely right. The point is to select or construct the best choice, even though another choice may be right also. Check off or write in your choices for the following items:

1. Use drawings or photographs when
   - ☐ You can't find the words to express what you want to say
   - ☐ You haven't used a drawing or photograph for a long time
   - ☐ The concept requires creating an image difficult to verbalize
   - ☐ _____
2. The writer's prime responsibility is to
   - ☐ Use language well
   - ☐ Get the message across
   - ☐ Create an image
   - ☐ _____
3. One effective test of an illustration is
   - ☐ Its cost
   - ☐ Its effectiveness in presenting an image
   - ☐ Its independence of supporting explanations
   - ☐ _____
4. An illustration is a virtual must in the case of
   - ☐ Print advertisements
   - ☐ Posters
   - ☐ Signs at trade shows
   - ☐ _____

CHAPTER NINE

Editorial and Production Functions

There is such a thing as natural writing talent, but even that is rarely of much use without experience, method, and rationale. Not everyone can be a great novelist or playwright, but every literate person can learn to write effective prose.

■ On Brevity

If brevity is the soul of wit, as the Bard wrote, it is even more the essence of effective and efficient writing. Blaise Pascal has been quoted so often as apologetically explaining in a letter that the letter was lengthy because he had not had the time to write a short one. An anomaly? Not really, for it does take time and patience to create a brief and efficient message in which you manage to say exactly what you wish to say and achieve exactly the effect you wish to achieve. You will certainly find, through probably painful experience, that this is true, unless you have the good fortune to be an unusually gifted "natural" writer—and such geniuses are in exceedingly short supply.

As one professional writer put it rather succinctly, all good writing is rewriting. And an experienced editor has suggested that effective editing probably reduces most first-draft manuscripts by about one-third. And in the cases we are considering, even that is conservative, and the reduction of verbiage is often much greater, especially in the case of creating an effective print advertisement, which taxes writing skill.

The simple fact is that most writers, experienced professionals as well as others, tend strongly to overwrite in first drafts. But the experienced professional is well aware that he or she has done so, and after finishing a draft embarks routinely on self-editing and rewriting to improve it, by cutting as well as by rephrasing. It is only the neophyte who thinks that his or her first draft is deathless prose and who cannot bear to see those precious words go to a discard pile and has yet to learn—and ultimately to appreciate—the improvements that are achieved by cutting and rewording. In fact, one of the greatest advantages of the modern word processor (*the* greatest advantage, as far as I am concerned) is the facility it has brought to self-editing and rewriting. That immeasurably greater ease of editing and rewriting ought to encourage a maximum degree of editing and revision (it has for me), and thus bring about improvements in the quality of writing, as well as in the ease of creating written materials.

■ Recommended Writing Practices

Every writer develops his or her own work practices, generally those with which he or she is most comfortable and believes are most productive. Organizations also develop certain practices and procedures, usually requiring writers to conform, although these ought to be broad and flexible enough to permit each writer to adapt his or her own working style to the standard procedure. The practices I will recommend here are offered with full recognition that each writer must have his or her own preferences, and so I shall try to make these recommendations general but also explain the rationale underlying each.

Writers and WPOs

Unfortunately, in too many offices today writers are still scrawling their words in longhand on lined yellow paper, which is then handed over to a typist (now, euphemistically, a "word processor operator" or "wpo") to be "keyboarded"—entered into the computer via the word processing program and printed out as a first-draft manuscript, known in computer parlance as the "hard copy," to distinguish it from the digital data on the disk and the text it represents on the screen, which are the "soft copy."

Subsequently, editor and writer pore over the hard copy, mark it up for revisions, and return it to the wpo for correction and another hard copy printout—a second draft—for further review.

This iteration may be repeated several times, until there seems to be nothing further to change or the schedule mandates an end to processing and a designation of the latest draft as final copy. A great deal of time has been wasted, and—much worse—the chief advantage of word processing technology (what it can do for the quality of one's writing) has been lost.

The answer lies in writing at the keyboard. Aside from the greater efficiency, itself no mean consideration, there is the contribution to creativity that word processing makes when the writer can see the words forming on the screen and change them so readily, reviewing continually, experimenting with alternative constructions, reorganizing, and generally polishing and improving the copy in ways that are simply not possible by older means. Writing is a flow process, and the inevitable iteration is immeasurably more effective when it is continuous, as in writing with a word processor, than when it is continual or sporadic, as in the case of writing and revising on paper.

Planning and Preparation

Writing, even the prosaic writing of advertising and marketing, is largely a creative art, dependent on human resourcefulness, imagination, and even inspiration. Yet, it is also partly science and methodology, and that means that it ought to be planned. It is rare that any writing effort turns out well, at least not without enormous waste of effort expended in trial and error approaches, without being planned adequately in advance. Once again, this—careful planning and preparation—is one of the hallmarks of the professional.

The general planning tool for a writer is the outline. The outline is a tool of logic. A proper outline organizes information for the contemplated presentation in synoptic form and telegraphic expression, with a logical progression that reveals the interrelationships of various ideas and concepts. However, that is getting ahead a bit, for the first item that must be identified before even considering the presentation itself is the primary and immediate objective.

Setting objectives

In the case of any sales/advertising/promotional piece (as, for that matter, in the case of any presentation) the first question you must ask yourself is this: what do you wish the reader to do as a result of the presentation? (Remember that "reader," as used here is a generic term, and stands also for "listener" or "viewer.") Of course, the long-term objective is always to persuade the reader to buy something, but that is not always the immediate objective. That is usually one of the following:

1. To order the advertised item by visiting a retail outlet, calling, writing, or placing a direct order. (To become a customer.)
2. To make a inquiry by visiting, calling, writing, etc. (To become a sales lead.)
3. To become familiar with the product or organization, learn to recognize the name, and otherwise be conditioned properly for future sales efforts. ("Institutional" advertising.)

That settled, the next step is to decide on a basic offer strategy. You may appeal to either of the two basic motivators: greed and fear.

"Greed" is not a flattering term, but I use it here for impact, and not to suggest that people are generally avaricious and selfish to some excessive degree. I use it to represent a perfectly normal desire for gain—to be more secure, to have more money, to win greater recognition, to be more attractive, and other such desires that most of us have.

Fear is another matter, and is quite real. I suspect that in general it is a more powerful motivator than is the desire for gain. All of us have fears of some sort; any normal person must inevitably become aware of the many hazards of life and the potential disasters that can overtake us.

Outlining

The preliminary planning must proceed logically to the next step: what is it that the reader is to be promised as a gain or warned against as a fear? Let us outline this a bit, to illustrate the outline method, as well as the process:

I. Immediate objective
  A. Gain
    1. Money
    2. Weight loss
    3. Attractiveness
    4. Prestige
    5. Convenience
  B. Fear
    1. Fire
    2. Accident
    3. Job loss
    4. Illness
    5. Burglary

These lists can be expanded, of course, according to the nature and characteristics of what you are selling and the policy of your management in presenting your products or services. The efficient way to do this outlining is to make the lists as long as possible, in a kind of brainstorming, even by yourself. (But it is better if you have others to work with and can compile the ideas of many.)

At this point you are ready, presumably, to begin making choices by weighing each item and, finally, choosing the ones you will use and which will be the basis for your presentation. You then develop the outline further to summarize what you will say—what information and arguments you will use.

Here, again, technology has something to offer. As an analog to word processing, there is a software concept referred to as "idea processing" or "thought processing." This is an outlining tool with a great capability for spontaneous expansion and contraction to suit the writer's needs. You might create an outline that presents information at, say, five levels. (The sample outline shown here is at three levels.) Moreover, at one or more levels you can have "leaves." These are expansions into whole paragraphs of information and ideas. You can display all levels or only some of them, and you can display or suppress the leaves. You can move information around readily, change the level of some material, and generally maneuver the outline at will. Some people find this kind of program a great aid in analyzing a need for written material and planning a presentation that will satisfy that need. It should be especially useful to the writer who is not familiar with outlining as a method for organizing ideas and information in advance.

Alternatives

The time and effort needed for the development of a formal outline in preparation for writing short copy, such as a print advertisement of a few column inches, is probably unjustified overkill. Still, if the full-blown, formal method is not justified, the concept is. But, as a practical matter, it can be carried forward in a very much simplified manner, and many experienced professionals do handle it in this manner as a practical alternative to the more formal outlining process:

1. Decide what the immediate objective is to be.
2. Begin writing, not even as draft, but as a set of notes or raw data, everything you can think of in connection with the item—its qualities and characteristics, what it can do for the user, etc.
3. Keep writing, adding items (alone, if necessary, with others, if possible) until you run out of ideas.
4. Cull and trim, weighing each item for merit, discarding as necessary, until you have reduced the collection to one clear idea (offer) and tightly organized supporting information.
5. Polish and repolish that final, surviving material, until it shines as the information and presentation you want.

It is not an easy task to do this. It takes a great deal of effort to compile that data to begin with, and a great deal of intestinal fortitude to slash and discard most of it. But that is the process necessary to do the job right. You cannot select the whitest or largest egg in a dozen unless you examine the entire dozen and discard all the second-class contenders.

■ Preparing Copy for Print Media

It is possible to send simple manuscript and camera-ready artwork (if your copy is to include artwork) to a print medium—periodical, that is—and have the periodical's production people handle all the details. That is, the periodical will set type and lay out your copy as "pubset" advertising. You may be disappointed with the results, however; the periodical production staff is trying to anticipate your desires.

Layouts

It is probably better—most advertisers find it so—to have your copy typeset and laid out yourself, furnishing the periodical camera-ready art. Years ago, in the days of metal type, you would usually have furnished a matrix, but in today's environment of offset printing, you usually need furnish only a clean original that can be photographed. Hence, the term *camera-ready*.

To plan properly you need to prepare at least a rough layout, such as that of Figure 9-1. This indicates approximately how text and illustrations will be placed, and is generally prepared as a rough pencil sketch. It becomes a bit more refined as copy and other details are finalized and firm commitments can be made, as shown in Figure 9-2, where heads and other details have become firm commitments so that type can be set and art sized. Whereas the first layout is a rough layout, known in the trade as a "rough" (a term

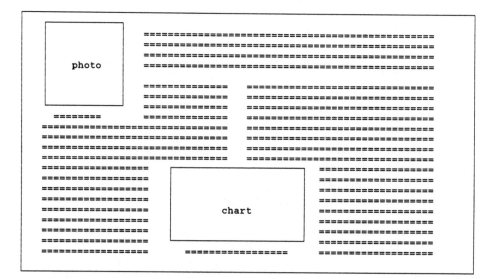

FIGURE 9-1   Rough layout

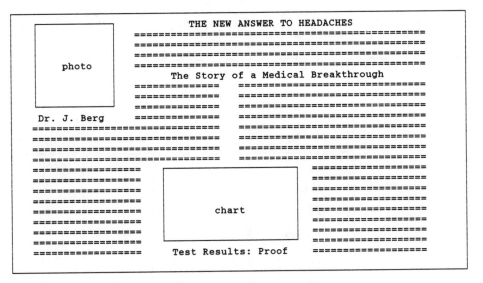

FIGURE 9-2   Comprehensive layout

also used to describe a rough sketch), the more finished layout is a "comprehensive" layout, often referred to by the shorter term "comprehensive."

Art Sizing

Artwork—photographs, drawings, charts, and other such matter—must be sized to fit the space allotted in the layout. These can be enlarged or reduced—they usually require reduction—in the photo lab. But photographs generally require cropping first. That's because most photographs contain distracting details that are not germane to the main theme. Cropping is a procedure that advises the printer of which portions of the photograph are to be used. The method is illustrated in Figure 9-3. The photograph is mounted on stiff backing—"art board"—and lines are drawn on the backing. The imaginary extension of the lines onto the photograph indicates the area that is to be reproduced in the printed material. (The lines actually drawn on the art board appear as solid lines in the figure; the imaginary lines appear as broken lines.) In this manner, a small portion of a photograph—perhaps a single figure in a group—may be selected without destroying the rest of the photograph.

Reproduction Form

Copy may be typed or typeset on plain white paper, of course, and often is. If clean and sharp, it is perfectly suitable as camera-ready copy, copy

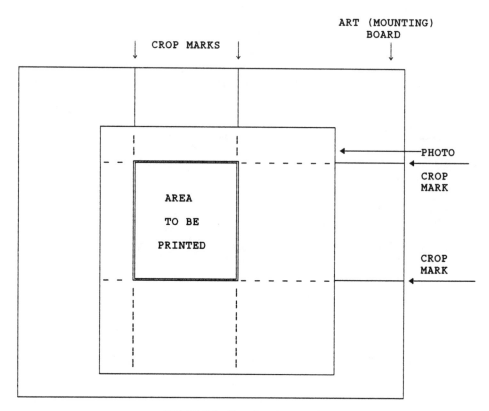

FIGURE 9-3 Cropping photographs

from which printing plates may be prepared. However, many organizations use special forms for typing or composing their text pages. One such form, typical of those used, is shown in Figure 9-4. In practice, the form is printed in a pale blue ink because that color will not reproduce: the camera will see it as white, hence invisible. The numbers are a convenience in identifying and referring to specific items during editorial processes, as well as a guide to the compositor or typist in preparing the copy, and the guide lines help in positioning copy as desired. The vertical lines in the center are a guide for setting copy in two columns, if desired, providing the necessary "gutter" between the two columns of type, and the box at the bottom is for the page number. The form can, of course, be modified to tailor it to your own special needs, and many variants of this general format are found. Moreover, some organizations design and use special paper or forms for each kind of special document—proposals, bids, quotations, etc. The purpose is to make each document distinctive, of course.

If you are unused to computers and word processors, the use of the term *column* may seem a bit strange. In traditional typewriter usage we always

Column 1   Column 38   Column 76

```
 1 ─────────────────────────────── │  │ │ ─────────────────────────── │
 2                                  │  │ │                             │
 3                                  │  │ │                             │
 4                                  │  │ │                             │
 5                                  │  │ │                             │
 6                                  │  │ │                             │
 7                                  │  │ │                             │
 8                                  │  │ │                             │
 9                                  │  │ │                             │
10                                  │  │ │                             │
11                                  │  │ │                             │
12                                  │  │ │                             │
13                                  │  │ │                             │
14                                  │  │ │                             │
15                                  │  │ │                             │
16                                  │  │ │                             │
17                                  │  │ │                             │
18                                  │  │ │                             │
19                                  │  │ │                             │
20                                  │  │ │                             │
21                                  │  │ │                             │
22                                  │  │ │                             │
23 ─────────────────────────────── │──│─│ ─────────────────────────── │
24                                  │  │ │                             │
25                                  │  │ │                             │
26                                  │  │ │                             │
28                                  │  │ │                             │
29                                  │  │ │                             │
30                                  │  │ │                             │
31                                  │  │ │                             │
32                                  │  │ │                             │
33                                  │  │ │                             │
34                                  │  │ │                             │
35                                  │  │ │                             │
36                                  │  │ │                             │
37                                  │  │ │                             │
38                                  │  │ │                             │
39                                  │  │ │                             │
40                                  │  │ │                             │
41                                  │  │ │                             │
42                                  │  │ │                             │
43                                  │  │ │                             │
44                                  │  │ │                             │
45                                  │  │ │                             │
46 ─────────────────────────────── │──│─│ ─────────────────────────── │
47                                  │  │ │                             │
48                                  │  │ │                             │
49                                  │  │ │                             │
50 ─────────────────────────────── │──│─│ ─────────────────────────── │
```

FIGURE 9-4   Reproduction form

referred to *spaces*, and generally allocated an "image area"—that portion of the page in which typing appeared—of approximately 6.5 × 9 inches, leaving margins of one inch each for the top, bottom, and sides of the page. With elite or 12 pitch (10 point) type that meant 12 characters or spaces per inch or a line of 78 characters/spaces. Of course, with pica or 10 pitch (12 point) type there were only 10 characters or spaces per inch so the line was 65 characters/spaces wide. In computer usage we no longer speak of spaces, but of columns. The de facto standard for screen display is thus a presentation that is 80 columns wide by 24 lines deep, or slightly less than a half-page. (There are six lines to the inch, vertically, so a 9-inch image area provides space for 54 lines, and the full page, including margins, is 66 lines deep.) We will be discussing computer usage in this work in the next chapter, however, and so will not discuss relevant details here.

■ Contracting Out

The entire process of developing all those sophisticated advertising and sales materials calls for a wide variety of skills. And even if you fully understand all the functions, as you should, it is not likely that you or any other individual can perform all those skills with equal competence. It is possible that your own organization will have a great many in-house resources to turn out copy—perhaps even printing, binding, stuffing, and mailing facilities, as well as a full complement of staff specialists for all the functions. However, in the typical case (and also with the exception of those organizations who now have some of those most modern computer-based facilities that we will discuss in the next chapter) you are likely to find it expedient and even necessary to vend out much of the preparatory work to specialists whose business it is to provide such services. You should therefore know what kinds of services are available and how to find them. (A starter list is also supplied in an appendix.)

Most metropolitan areas afford access to a number of supporting services. One of these resources is referred to as a "letter shop." The very term, *letter shop*, has been with us or a long time, although the relevant functions have changed over the years. The modern letter shop offers a variety of direct-mail services, which may include planning, writing, labeling, printing, mailing-list rental, and mailing itself, among other things. In fact, the Yellow Pages directory for this area (the District of Columbia and environs) suggests that those looking under letter shop services review also firms listed and advertising under "Copying and Duplicating" and "Photo Copying" categories.

That itself—identifying and defining desired services—is something of a problem, and you will find many individuals and firms advertising their services under more than one descriptor, as witness some of the following examples.

Artists and commercial illustrators may be found under "Graphic Designers" in our local Yellow Pages. Checking into the firms thus listed we find a wide variety of advertising support services offered, many of which overlap those of the letter shops. In fact, many letter shops are also found here, advertising their services.

You may also try "Editorial Services," and you will find help with writing and editing. But you will also be advised to seek help under "Typing Services" and "Word Processing Services."

"Writers—Business" is a category all its own. Again, you can find a variety of editorial services, and the names of firms already listed under some of those other categories.

"Printers" is an exceptionally extensive category, at least in this area, and—again—includes many of the services already described. The large print shops do a great deal more than printing; they do art work, typesetting, copy preparation, and lithography, among other things, and many of them are listed under those other categories.

Of course, "Advertising" is a large category too, and again you will find many of those letter shops, lithographers, writers, consultants, and other specialists listed here.

In short, there is abundant help, and you have many options. You can, in fact, go to the largest firms in your area and get "complete, one-stop service" supplied by a single firm. That has some advantages of convenience, but it has some disadvantages too. A given supplier may be an excellent typographer but a poor printer or mediocre illustrator. For that reason alone many seek out a complement of individual support persons, patiently discovering the best individual or organization for each function or set of functions.

In general, you are likely to do the creative work in-house and vend out the work that is more or less mechanical—the typesetting, the layouts, the printing, and the mailing. This is not to say that you must not be "on top" of everything—monitoring, evaluating, and verifying that all is done in a manner that satisfies you and your standards. Even with the best of vendors you must do this. Use vendors to provide services, but never delegate the decision-making itself to the vendors; that is your province and your responsibility.

■ Exercises

There are just a few important principles that must be mastered here, and the few exercises offered here will help you verify your mastery of these principles or guide you in review.

The Essence of Good Writing

Check off True or False for the following statements.

		True	False
1.	"Good" writing is writing that includes all details, even the smallest ones.	☐	☐
2.	"Good" writing gets to the point quickly and includes all pertinent detail but excludes trivia.	☐	☐
3.	The best writers never have to rewrite.	☐	☐
4.	Almost all good writers rewrite.	☐	☐
5.	Good editing means polishing the copy.	☐	☐
6.	Good editing means reducing the total verbiage.	☐	☐
7.	Most writers tend not to provide enough detail in their first drafts.	☐	☐
8.	Advertising copy should be written by gradually adding detail to the first draft.	☐	☐
9.	Writers should work on lined yellow paper and have a word processor operator then keyboard their copy.	☐	☐
10.	Writers should work at the keyboard.	☐	☐

Planning and Preparation

Choose the best completion phrase for each of the following sentences or write in one of your own.

1. The first step in planning and preparation of advertising or other written material is
   - ☐ setting an objective
   - ☐ writing out the offer
   - ☐ deciding what the proof is to be
   - ☐ _____

2. The main purpose of any advertisement or promotional copy is making sales, developing sales leads, or
   - ☐ building a mailing list
   - ☐ finding the most persuasive words
   - ☐ helping your distributors
   - ☐ _____

3. The two most basic motivators are
   - ☐ convenience and greed

☐ security and greed
☐ fear and greed
☐ _____

4. Outlining, formal or informal, is necessary for
    ☐ all writers
    ☐ neophyte writers
    ☐ only lengthy pieces
    ☐ _____

5. The most effective approach to writing good copy is usually
    ☐ constant revision
    ☐ continuous embellishment
    ☐ continuous tightening
    ☐ _____

CHAPTER TEN

Modern Technological Methods

Technology proceeds ever faster, and already it is easily possible to be independent of outside experts and yet turn out highly professional results. The expert skills are, to a large degree, built into the technology and the equipment.

■ Technology and Its Impact Here

The work we are discussing in these pages is very much affected by modern technology. In fact, the development and production of written materials is at the very heart of a great deal of the most recent technological developments, especially the technology of modern, desktop computers and their related hardware and software. However, there are two distinct aspects to what this technology means to us and how it affects us. On the one hand, the technology is a boon to the production functions, and this is probably the most readily recognized application. Less well recognized and less well understood is the contribution of technology to the creative functions—the creative skills that are built into the software and hardware. Yet, this is probably the more significant and more important function of the technology. But let's review the hardware briefly first, in terms of its contribution to production functions. Then we can consider the other aspects.

■ Technology and Production

It was not very long ago—three or four decades ago—that the modern technology of photolithographic offset printing began to push letterpress technology into history. And only about two decades ago "cold type" devices and methods began to do the same for the hoary California cases (wooden cases used to set metal type by hand), linotypes, monotypes, and the other trappings of raised-type printing, replaced by electric typewriters, other "strike on" typesetting devices, and phototypesetters of various kinds. But the technological revolution continued, and electric typewriters have been all but disappearing under the onslaught of desktop computers, with word processor software and inexpensive printers. But it hasn't stopped yet; the latest technological outburst has been something known as *desktop publishing*, a development based heavily on what is called the *laser printer* and on the newest developments in software designed for the graphic arts.

There is no useful purpose to be served by an extensive technical discourse here, but it is probably useful and perhaps even necessary to have a general understanding of what this technology is all about. Don't worry overmuch if you do not fully grasp all the technical detail of the following simplified discussions. In fact, you may skip them without losing much, if you wish.

■ Laser Printers

The laser printer is an outgrowth of the xerographic technology, that produced the Xerox® office copier and the many others that are now available, married to modern computer technology, especially that of word processing. In the office copier, a camera photographs the page to be copied and deposits a corresponding electrostatic pattern (pattern of electrical charges) on a metal drum or master. (The coating of the drum is sensitive to light, and the pattern of light and shadow from the camera lens is deposited as an analogous pattern of static electrical charges.) A black powder (toner) is then applied to the drum, clinging where the electrical charges have been created. The toner is then transferred to a sheet of paper, and is fused to the paper by heat. However, in the laser printer, instead of a camera presenting the pattern of light and shadow to be translated into a corresponding pattern of electrical charges representing the characters, a laser beam translates the digital pulses to light and shadow to represent the characters. That is, the laser provides the light and "paints" those characters as static electricity on the drum or master. The rest of the process is similar to that of the copier. With good equipment and good software, the quality of the final, printed impression is quite excellent.

■ Pixels, DPI, and Quality

If you look closely at a photograph in the newspaper you can see that it is made up of a pattern of dots, and the shades are not truly shades; all the dots are of the same shade, and what appears to be the photograph's shade is an illusion, an effect of the number of dots per unit of area. If you look closely at a photograph printed on the smooth paper of a magazine you will note that the photograph has much better clarity—"resolution," in the jargon of the trade—but you will have some difficulty in distinguishing the dots because they are much smaller than those used in newspapers. This is due to the difference in paper; it is not possible to get as fine a set of dots on the coarse newsprint used for newspapers. And the finer the dots, the more dots per unit of space, and therefore the greater the resolution or "definition," if you prefer that term.

The presentation on the computer screen is also made up of dots, but they are called *pixels*, an acronym for "picture elements." As in the case of the printed photographs in newspapers and magazines, the smaller the pixels, the greater their number in a given area, and the greater the resolution.

An analogous situation exists with respect to computer printers. Early *dot matrix* printers offered rather coarse patterns, with printheads of only 7 pins and capabilities of depicting characters in matrices of only 5 × 7 dots—i.e., a small number of dots per inch (dpi). As they were improved, they began to offer "near letter quality" results, with 9-pin heads becoming something of a standard for some time. At present, the latest dot matrix printers, with 24 pins instead of nine making the dots, offer true letter quality. However, laser printers generally offer a greater number of dots per inch (dpi) than do dot matrix printers. Hence, their better quality. While you can use a good, 24-pin dot matrix printer to produce camera-ready copy, most desktop publishing programs are written to be printed out by laser printers, and laser printing is generally considered to be a necessity for effective desktop publishing operations.

Apple Computer, Inc., with their Macintosh computer line, has been a pioneer in the development of computer capabilities for graphic art applications, and the Macintosh computers are heavily favored by many for desktop publishing, especially for the development of drawings via the computer screen. On the other hand, most other producers of desktop publishing programs tend to stress the capabilities of desktop publishing for creating newsletters and other such materials. Whereas traditional publication processes of recent decades depended heavily on physically cutting and pasting many text and graphic elements to make up pages, with suitable hardware and software, it is possible to do all the cutting, pasting, layout, and makeup on the screen and print out the final page as a single entity, ready for the print shop. One does not have to be an experienced editorial specialist because most of the skills required are built into the software and hardware, and the many manipulations of the copy—cutting, pasting, and layout—are performed electronically and even displayed on screen for approval and final touches before anything is printed out.

There are no boundaries defining what is and what is not desktop publishing software. Many programs offer some of the desktop publishing capabilities, if not all of them. The program FormWorx, for example, a product of Analytix International, Inc., is designed to produce forms of various kinds but is actually quite useful for producing many kinds of charts and graphs. It provides all the desktop publishing functions necessary to producing forms and simple charts and graphs, that is, and they prove to be quite useful. Some of the illustrations presented in earlier chapters were produced by that program, as were the following.

Figures 10-1 and 10-2 are two bar charts created by Formworx. They illustrate different techniques for bar charts. The program offers a variety of "fill" patterns (see Figure 10-3), and a number of these were used here to demonstrate just a little of the variety available. Figures 10-4 thru 10-6 are self-explanatory, and are offered here merely to illustrate some of the versatility of these programs.

■ Computer Clip Art

Many desktop publishing programs today offer computer clip art—illustrations that you can use in your presentations. Figure 10-7 illustrates just a few of these from the Fontasy® program, while Figure 10-8 illustrates a few samples of clip art from the The Newsroom Pro™ desktop publishing software.

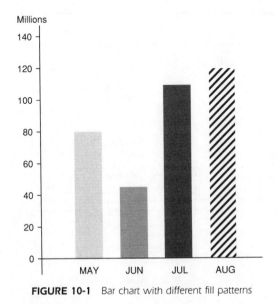

FIGURE 10-1   Bar chart with different fill patterns

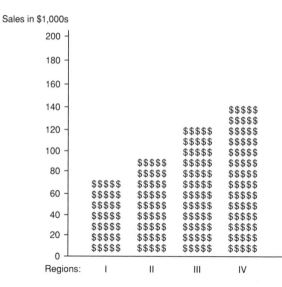

FIGURE 10-2 Another bar chart with a different kind of fill pattern

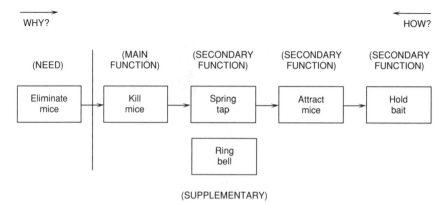

FIGURE 10-3 Some of the available fill patterns

WHY? →

← HOW?

| (NEED) | (MAIN FUNCTION) | (SECONDARY FUNCTION) | (SECONDARY FUNCTION) | (SECONDARY FUNCTION) |

| Eliminate mice | Kill mice | Spring tap | Attract mice | Hold bait |

Ring bell

(SUPPLEMENTARY)

FIGURE 10-4 Special diagram used by value engineers

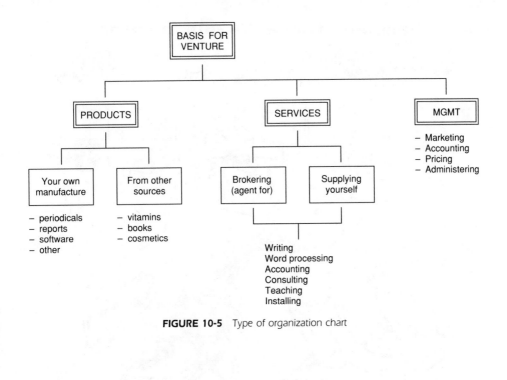

FIGURE 10-5   Type of organization chart

PHASE II OF MAGOG PROJECT

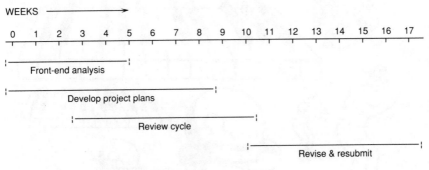

FIGURE 10-6   Milestone chart

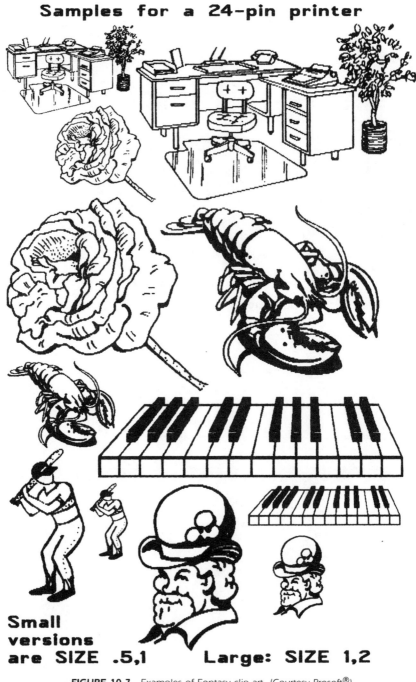

FIGURE 10-7 Examples of Fontasy clip art. (Courtesy Prosoft®)

FIGURE 10-8   Examples of The Newsroom Pro clip art. (Courtesy Springboard Software, Inc.)

A word of caution is not amiss here. These desktop publishing programs, like the modern desktop computers, are technological marvels; they make many things possible that were not possible before they arrived on the scene. Yet, there are limitations, and we must be aware of them. For one, neither the software nor the hardware are adequate substitutes for human imagination and resourcefulness; don't expect the machines to solve all your problems. Nor can the best software program substitute for human judgment and decision-making; in the end, the decisions are still yours to make. Nor are all the benefits to be had in only the most advanced and most recent kinds of software and hardware; many of the greatest benefits are in systems, that have been with us almost since the appearance of the modern desktop computers. Among the most useful such programs are those that you can use to create and manage your mailing lists.

■ Shareware Programs

A great deal of the software sold through typical commercial channels has tended to be relatively expensive. Many word processors, for example, run to $500 and more, and there are many programs that are even more costly. Partially, this cost reflects large amounts of expensive labor that must go into the development of such programs—most require extensive testing and "debugging" (refinement to detect and eliminate errors and shore up unexpected and unanticipated weaknesses). Partially, too, this is a reflection of conservative estimates of the number of copies that can be sold—i.e., the basis for amortization of the development and marketing costs. Too, I refer here to "cover" or "list" prices, those prices the retail customer is expected to pay; many copies of such programs are given away to reviewers, many are sold through dealers who pay wholesale prices for their copies, and many copies are sold at greatly reduced prices to hardware manufacturers who include free programs with the machines they sell.

Steadily increasing competition has forced software prices down. However, the practice of selling programs as "shareware" has sprung up. These are programs developed by independent software developers—often individuals operating from their homes on a part-time or "moonlight" basis—at greatly reduced prices with "try before you buy" privileges. The reason for this is simply that these independent software entrepreneurs can't or choose not to (usually can't!) afford the great expense of distributing their programs through conventional commercial sources. Instead, they offer their programs through distribution schemes that cost them little or nothing, other than telephone tolls. They use various channels through which they can invite users to try out their programs without cost, and appeal to their honesty and sense of fairness to pay a usually quite modest sum if they (the user) find the program useful and decide to keep it and use it regularly. And to encourage the user to pay the fee and become a registered user, the entrepreneur usually offers certain inducements, such as these:

☑ A printed manual (user instructions in the original version are in a form that requires the user to read them on-screen or print them out).

☑ Free or low-cost updates whenever the program is revised and improved (most successful programs are revised periodically in this manner).

☑ "Support" services, meaning that the user may write or call for help if he or she encounters problems with the program.

☑ A disk with the complete program. (In some cases, the "try before you buy" version lacks all the features of the program.)

There is quite an enormous number of such programs offered, ranging from simple little routines to change the size or shape of a cursor or count the number of words in a manuscript to complete word processing or spreadsheet programs. And there is an equally enormous range in the quality and usefulness of such programs. Many of them are highly specialized and useful to only a computer technician, and many of them are not very well designed or free of "bugs." However, many of them are as good as the best programs offered by the leading software development firms. Using shareware does not have to mean sacrificing or compromising quality.

In terms of cost, shareware usually costs only a fraction of what the equivalent program would cost in conventional channels. For example, word processors that are the equal of $500 commercial word processors are likely to sell for well under $100.

◼ Mailing List Managers

As in the case of other kinds of software, mailing list managers are available as "shareware" programs. I have been reviewing one such program called *Mass Appeal*, and I think it is reasonably typical of other such programs, and certainly useful enough. Figure 10-9 presents a message the author of *Mass Appeal* presents to new users who review his program. Note the inducements to remit the modest price of this program and the encouragement to pass copies on to friends.

Figure 10-10 shows the opening menu of the program. The first item produces a menu suitable for adding new names to the list. That menu is illustrated in Figure 10-11. Note that it provides for up to five lines in the name and address, plus telephone numbers and special coding via the *Category* and *Comments* blocks provided. Figure 10-12 illustrates the menu change when the entries are completed and the bottom line changes to offer

```
Thank You Very Much  For Using Mass Appeal. This Version (Ver. 2.40)
Of Mass Appeal Is The Initial ShareWare Release. If You Use This
Program Frequently, Please Register  Your Copy  Of Mass Appeal.  For
A  Registration Fee Of Only $35.00,  You Will Receive:  The  Latest
And  Greatest Version Of Mass Appeal That Has Additional Features Not
Implemented In This Version,  Complete Doc, Free  Updates For One Year,
And Support From  The Author. Feel Free To Share This Program  With
Friends  (If You Like The Program), Or  Enemies  (If You Don't Like
The Program). To Register Your Copy, Simply Send $35.00 To:

Steve Hughes            NOTE: Mass Appeal Is NOT A  Public Domain
1422 Applegate Drive    Program. It Is  Distributed  Under The
Alabaster, AL  35007    Shareware Concept. Please Support!
```

FIGURE 10-9 Message from the author of the Mass Appeal program

```
********** Mass Appeal Mailing Program -- Main Menu **********

            Please Enter Your Choice Here:

            Y o u r   P o s s i b l e   C h o i c e s   A r e

                 1) Add Entries
                 2) Edit/View Entries
                 3) Pack The Data Base
                 4) Generate Some Output
                 5) Group Delete Or Recovery
                 6) Change Active Data Base File
                 7) Access The Maintenance Routines
                 8) Exit This Program, Return To DOS....

      The Currently Active Data Base File Is As Follows: MAILER.DBF
```

FIGURE 10-10 Opening menu of Mass Appeal program

```
Rec #: 0,000,133 | Record Marked For Deletion:  No    | Date:  03/09/88

        ******* Adding / Editing -- Mass Appeal Program *******

Last Name:              First Name:              Salutation:

Company:

Address 1:

Address 2:

City:                         State:      Zip Code:

Home Phone: (  )  -     Work Phone: (  )  -          Date:  03/09/88

Category:     -  -  -  -  -  -  -  -     Comments:

Press <Ctrl-W> For Menu          * Duplicates Previous Entry For That Field
```

FIGURE 10-11 Form for entering names and addresses

```
┌──────────────────────────────────────────────────────────────────┐
│  Rec #: 0,000,133  │  Record Marked For Deletion:  No  │ Date:  03/09/88 │
│                                                                    │
│       ****** Adding / Editing -- Mass Appeal Program ******        │
│                                                                    │
│  Last Name:              First Name:           Salutation:         │
│  Company:                                                          │
│  Address 1:                                                        │
│  Address 2:                                                        │
│  City:                       State:       Zip Code:               │
│  Home Phone: (   )   -    Work Phone: (   )   -    Date:  03/09/88 │
│  Category:    - - - - - - -    Comments:                           │
│                                                                    │
│  ADD:   More  Re-Edit  Help  Return                                │
└──────────────────────────────────────────────────────────────────┘
                            295
```

FIGURE 10-12 *Options listed when entry is complete*

several options: *More* cycles to the next number, which would be 134, in this case. (See upper left corner of the form.) *Re-Edit* permits you to go back and make corrections or changes. *Help* provides a menu of instructions. And *Return* takes you back to the opening menu, where you can review the new entries, order printing or a report, make changes to accommodate your needs, or exit the program.

To print out names, you have a number of options. You can print envelopes, labels, rotary file cards, or a paper report. Or you can simply review them on-screen. And you can do so selectively. As Figure 10-13 reveals,

```
┌──────────────────────────────────────────────────────────────────┐
│  1) Narrow Report Down By City                                     │
│  2) Narrow Report Down By State                                    │
│  3) Narrow Report Down By Salutation                               │
│  4) Narrow Report Down By Zip Code Range                           │
│  5) Narrow Report Down By Category Field                           │
│  6) Narrow Report Down By Date Field Range                         │
│  7) Narrow Report Down By Home Phone Area Code                     │
│  8) Narrow Report Down By Work Phone Area Code                     │
│  9) Narrow Report Down By Company Name Keyword                     │
│ 10) Narrow Report Down By Comment Field Keyword                    │
│                                                                    │
│  CRITERIA:  All Entries.                                           │
│                                                                    │
│  REPORT: More-Criteria  Save-Criteria  Retrieve-Criteria  Finished │
└──────────────────────────────────────────────────────────────────┘
```

FIGURE 10-13 *Options for retrieval and/or printing*

you have at least 10 search terms by which to select names. You can sort by zip codes, cities, states, dates, telephone area codes, names, or by special keywords you have inserted in the category and comment fields to code your list. You can, for example, mix all the names and addresses that are your own house lists, and yet keep them separate by coding them for retrieval as customer lists, prospect lists, walk-in customers, mail-order customers, and by hundreds of other codes you might devise to suit your needs. Even the relatively small desktop computer can handle a sizable number of names and classifications.

Such a program is used also to *maintain* your mailing lists—to delete names you don't want or which are no longer useful for any reason, to enter changes of address, to revise codes, and otherwise to keep your lists up to date for maximum effectiveness. But even that is not all of it; there are other uses as well.

■ Mail-Merge Applications

You have probably received in the mail salesletters that you knew were form letters, although they were addressed to you by name. Of course, it is computers that do this kind of work, but it is not necessary to turn to the multi-million-dollar mainframe computers to do this today. Ordinary desktop computers and printers are capable of doing this kind of work for you.

The kinds of programs that address a copy of a form letter personally to each name on your mailing list is referred to generally as *mail-merge* software. It simply types the form letter out, over and over, addressing each copy to another name from the mailing list you designate for this, merging the file containing the form letter with the file containing the mailing list; hence the name. In fact, you do not necessarily have to have special software for this; many modern word processors include the capability as one of the regular functions, for modern word processors are almost all multi-functional.

■ Other Useful Word Processor Functions

There are a great many ways in which computers generally, and word processors especially, can save you much time and labor. One of these is by the use of "swipe files." As the term suggests, these are merely standard files of material that can be used gainfully again and again, sometimes with minor changes and often with no changes at all. In my own work, for example, I send out a great many letters for various reasons, often to enlist the help of companies to permit me to use their materials and products as illustrations. I keep a file of such letters, but all are based on a more or less standard form that I evolved through experience. However, each time I modify an old letter to create a new one, I save the modified letter in a special archive file, adding it to the growing list. Then, when I need a new letter, I review those on file to select the one that is closest to my new need. I modify it as necessary and then print it out. I can thus create a new letter in minutes.

I do the same thing with the many charts, graphs, plots, and forms I generate. I retain all of these in archive files that I research when I need something new for an illustration. Again, it is usually a simple matter of selecting the material closest to my new need and modifying it so that it is exactly right for the new need.

On the other hand, many of the functions modern word processors offer are designed to be useful in preparing lengthy documents. They include such aids as spelling checkers, thesauri, and capabilities for indexing, footnoting, and preparing bibliographies. They are of rather little use in creating advertisements, salesletters, and other brief or relatively brief papers. However, when and if the occasion arises to create lengthier sales documents, such as formal proposals, some of those other functions become most useful.

■ Hardware Tips and Suggestions

Early on, the most common advice given those considering the purchase of a computer was to identify the software programs the prospective buyer would want to use first, and then seek out the machine that would run that software. It was probably good enough advice then, for several reasons that should be clear in a moment, but conditions are far different today. For one thing, there is now a superabundance of software, and for another the bulk of it will run on most of the machines being offered today. Consequently, we do not hear such counsel being given anymore.

A Brief History

Before IBM produced and marketed the first IBM PC (personal computer), most of the personal computers being marketed (with the principal exception of those manufactured by the Apple Computer Company) were of a general species known as CP/M (Control Program/Monitor, also believed by some to stand for Control Program/Microcomputer). However, every manufacturer had his own version of the CP/M operating system, so there was relatively little standardization. The IBM PC, which used an operating system known

as PC DOS, changed all that. Many manufacturers, here and in Asia, manufactured computers that were virtual clones of IBM's machines and operated
under MS DOS, a virtual clone of PC DOS. In very short order, the industry
(again with the notable exception of Apple computers) achieved a de facto
standardization: most of the clones are highly compatible with each other
in both the software—which will run on most of the clones—and the hardware—which is largely interchangeable.

The March of the Clones

The rate of change was phenomenal. Anything in computers a year old
was almost certainly obsolescent. For a long time, the future was only six
months away, in fact. But eventually, once the influence of the IBM PC and
its many clones imposed a kind of standardization on the industry, the rate
of technological growth began to subside until it reached a more stable rate,
while millions of clones were sold. Many came from Japan, Taiwan, and
Korea. And even those that were assembled here—and many were and still
are—were done so largely with parts coming here from Asia. But there are
some exceptions to the de facto standardization. The "true" clones achieve
nearly 100 percent compatibility; some of the others are considerably less
compatible, especially in that many of the components are peculiar to the
machine and cannot be replaced by generic types. If you are about to buy
a computer, therefore, it is probably wise to take whatever measures are
necessary to satisfy yourself about the degree of compatibility.

Probably the most popular clone is the XT (for extended technology),
although the later IBM model, an AT (for advanced technology) is considerably faster in operation as a result of using a faster chip (the 80386). And
IBM announced an entire new line, a series of several new computers, some
time ago. These newest computers are still compatible and operate with the
PC DOS system, but an entirely new operating system is planned for them
eventually. Nevertheless, there is such a large established base of the earlier
PC DOS/MS DOS machines—millions of machines and users—that it will be
a long time before they can be considered obsolete. Moreover, the cost of the
clones, especially the XT models, has dropped to a point where a reasonably
good desktop computer and printer can now be had for about the price of
a good electric typewriter—perhaps even less than that, in fact. There is,
therefore, relatively little risk in buying a clone XT or AT even now. Parts
and programs for these machines will be available here for a very long time.

Configurations

For a long time, the principal means of storage in desktop computers was on
floppy disks. Typically, these disks were 5-1/4 inches in diameter and could

hold 360K (360 kilobytes or 360,000 bytes) of data. A byte is the equivalent of one alphabetical or numerical character, and 360K represents, roughly, 150-175 double-spaced pages of text. Later models offered floppy disks that could hold 760K or 1.2M (1.2 megabytes, or 1,200,000 bytes); floppy disk drives of even higher capacities are now being developed and marketed.

Eventually, hard disks, disks of much greater storage capacity than floppy disks, were manufactured for desktop computers. These ranged, at first, from about 5M up, but were quite expensive. (Few people today buy hard disks smaller than 20M.) Eventually, the price of these hard disks (also referred to as fixed disks because the disk cannot be removed from the drive, as a floppy disk is) began to fall, and today it is an increasingly rare desktop computer used for "serious" purposes (e.g., for business) that does not have a fixed disk of 20 or 30 megabyte capacity. A 20M fixed disk is equal to approximately 55 360K floppy disks, for example, and today is offered in the marketplace at well under $300.

Many machines today are offered with either two floppy disk drives or one floppy disk drive and a fixed disk. However, I personally use a machine with two floppy disk drives and a 20M fixed disk. I find this a much more convenient arrangement than having only one floppy disk drive, and I recommend this configuration enthusiastically.

Monitors

The monitor or screen is, of course, an important part of the system. The basic choices are monochrome and color, although there are choices within each of these options, which are too technical to discuss here. Color is not the best choice for computers used primarily for word processing and related functions because the resolution on color monitors is usually not as good as on monochrome monitors. (There are exceptions to this, with the latest in color graphic cards, but that imposes a large and unnecessary extra expense.) It is possible to find some monitors using a white phosphor, but green is probably the most popular monochrome color, although many people profess a preference for amber screens.

Printers

Printer technology has kept pace with computer technology, evolving rapidly from the early 7-pin dot matrix machines to the latest 24-pin dot matrix machines. Early on, the daisywheel printer was preferable as the type of printer that produced true "letter quality," which meant, in practical terms, quality equal to that of a good electric typewriter. The chief difference among the daisywheel machines was speed. The most expensive ones were the fastest ones, while the dot matrix machines were usually considered to be a cheaper alternative, suitable only for rough drafts.

Unfortunately, the daisywheel machines could do little but straight text. They were not suitable for graphics, and could not produce type larger than that which would be available from any good typewriter. On the other hand, the dot matrix machines were capable of turning out graphics and large typefaces, but at a considerable sacrifice in quality.

Today, most users of desktop computers for "serious" work use either good-quality dot matrix printers or laser printers. The latter, still relatively expensive, are gaining in popularity quite rapidly, despite the good quality of the latest and best dot matrix printers. Figure 10-14 illustrates some of the range of type sizes available in the WordStar Professional Release 4 word processor, using a 24-pin NEC P6 dot matrix printer. (Much larger sizes of type are possible with other programs, designed for the purpose.) And, as simple examples of the graphic capabilities of the printer, a number of the earlier figures presented in this and preceding chapter were produced on that same printer, albeit with other software, the FormWorx program in most cases. However, desktop publishing software, even when used with a good dot matrix printer (remember that desktop publishing software is designed to be run with laser printers for best results), can produce pleasing results. As an example of that, see Figure 10-15, in which a complex and detailed line drawing of a fire hose nozzle is presented, as sketched by the NEC P6 24-pin dot matrix printer, using the Xerox Ventura Publisher desktop publishing software.

Still another example of what can be done with this kind of printer is shown in Figure 10-16, which is a reproduced line drawing of the space

```
4 characters/inch       (.CW 36)
5 characters/inch.    (.CW 24)
6 characters/inch.   (.CW 20)
8.6 characters/inch.  (.CW 14)
10 characters/inch.  (.CW 12)
12 characters/inch.  (.CW 10)
17.1 characters/inch.  (.CW 7)
```

```
4 CHARACTERS/INCH       (.CW 36)
5 CHARACTERS/INCH.    (.CW 24)
6 CHARACTERS/INCH.   (.CW 20)
8.6 CHARACTERS/INCH.  (.CW 14)
10 CHARACTERS/INCH.  (.CW 12)
12 CHARACTERS/INCH.  (.CW 10)
17.1 CHARACTERS/INCH.  (.CW 7)
```

FIGURE 10-14 Examples of type sizes available with dot matrix printers

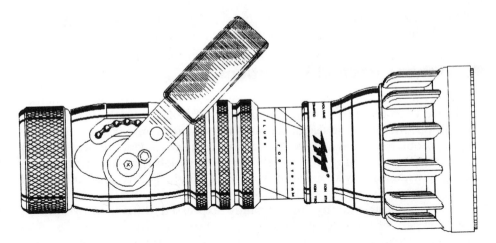

FIGURE 10-15 A fire hose nozzle sketched by a 24-pin dot matrix printer using Ventura Publisher software. (Courtesy Xerox Corp.)

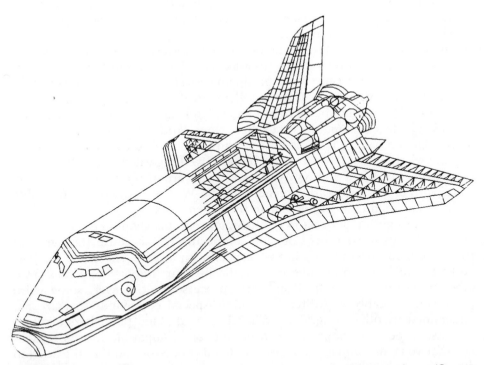

FIGURE 10-16 Space shuttle *Columbia* sketched by printer using Ventura Publisher software. (Courtesy Xerox Corp.)

shuttle *Columbia*. This is also from one of the Ventura software program files and sketched by that program.

◼ Software Tips and Suggestions

Controversy sometimes rages among computer enthusiasts as to whether hardware or software is more important. Obviously, neither is of much use without the other, so the question is of only academic importance. The biggest problem with software has changed greatly. Once it was finding the right software; today it is largely deciding which is most suitable from among a wide variety of programs, most of high quality and undoubted usefulness.

There is a long-running and strongly expressed difference of opinion among owners of the most popular type of software, word processors. The first major word processor to appear was the WordStar program. It had an impact on its market not unlike that of the IBM PC on its market: it became a de facto standard as the best selling word processor by far, and held that position for a long time. In so doing, WordStar greatly influenced many other types of software, and the command structure of many other programs, both word processors and other types of software, still reflect that influence in their command structures.

Unfortunately, MicroPro,® who developed WordStar, rested on their laurels too long, stubbornly refusing to make significant improvements to their product, while competitors were producing constantly improving word processors. Today, MicroPro has an excellent word processor in the latest versions of WordStar, but MicroPro lost its lead during its period of somnolence, and WordPerfect became the best seller. Now WordPerfect has its own huge following who believe it is the best word processor offered today.

Somewhat behind these in sales, but also well regarded as excellent word processors, are Word and XyWrite. And there are also a number of shareware word processors available, including PC-Write and Galaxy, as probably the best known and most popular in their own class.

One shortcoming of desktop publishing programs should be noted. Most are inferior to word processors for composing text because they are not truly designed for efficiency in that aspect of the work. Therefore, the best desktop publishing programs permit the user to "import" text files from other programs, especially from word processors. However, some word processors—notably WordStar—use many special commands that are not understood by other programs. When buying desktop publishers or word processors, be sure that the two programs are compatible in this sense— i.e., that you can compose your text via word processor and that the desktop publisher can read your word processor copy without difficulty.

There are many ancillary programs, software that provides labor-saving aid and affords convenience in handling a myriad of smaller tasks. A list of just a few of these types of programs is offered in a table that appears as Figure 10-17.

Type program	Explanation
Word counter	Counts the words in a text file (and often the number of lines and bytes also)
Find	Searches all the directories of the disks designated to find files and report their location
Global commands	Executes a command on all directories
Sort	Sorts items in a list, alphabetically and/or by other parameters, as designed
Macros	Sets up one- or two-key combinations to execute frequently used long series of commands or text sequences, even entire paragraphs of boilerplate information, standard statements, etc.
Forms	Collections of commonly used forms—e.g., expense reports and travel requests—for ready reproduction, with or without modification to your own special needs
Browse	Programs that enable you to browse through text files, going backward or forward, skipping to beginning or end, printing out portions, etc
Fonts	Programs that set your printer to print in various fonts, many special ones; some permit you to design your own fonts
Readability	Programs to measure the readability—e.g., "fog count" and/or grade level—of your text; some also offer direct help in improving readability
Typewriter programs	Programs that enable you to use your computer and printer like a typewriter, a line at a time; useful for tasks such as addressing envelopes and labels, writing memos, and other minor chores that do not justify using a full word processor
Notepads	Programs that enable you to jot brief notes in a special file without leaving the program you are working on at the moment
General aids	Programs that furnish such available functions as typewriter and notepad software, plus an on-screen calculator, telephone dialer (if you have a modem), and sundry other such aids
Mailing list managers	Software to compile, maintain, sort, and print out names and addresses

FIGURE 10-17   Useful ancillary software types.

■ Exercises

This will be the last set of exercises. Once again, use this as a means of evaluating your own progress, and reread the text, as necessary.

The Significance of Technology

Try your hand at a general review first via the following True-False exercise.

		True	False
1.	Technology can solve all our problems in this work.	☐	☐
2.	The latest technology is word processing.	☐	☐
3.	Desktop publishing is another name for word processing.	☐	☐
4.	Resolution on screen depends on the number of pixels per unit of area.	☐	☐
5.	Resolution in a printout depends on the number of dpi.	☐	☐

Desktop Publishing

Complete the following statements, using your own write-in statement if you do not agree with any of the supplied completion items.

1. The chief difference between daisywheel printers and dot matrix printers is
   ☐ dot matrix printers are less expensive
   ☐ dot matrix printers are more expensive
   ☐ dot matrix printers are more accurate
   ☐ dot matrix printers are less accurate
   ☐ _____

2. As compared with laser printers, good 24-pin dot matrix printers
   ☐ print with about equal resolution
   ☐ print with somewhat less resolution
   ☐ print with better resolution
   ☐ print with much less resolution
   ☐ _____

3. Clip art is art that you
   ☐ clip out of newspapers and magazines
   ☐ art that you can buy with permission to use it

□ art that you draw on the screen with computer help

□ art that you hire a part-time or moonlight illustrator to draw

□ _____

4. Probably the most dominant feature advertised by sellers of desktop publishing software is its usefulness for

□ creating illustrations of various kinds

□ supplying the user with clip art

□ handling all kinds of editorial/publications functions

□ creating newsletters

□ _____

5. Aside from its usefulness for creating graphic illustrations, the chief advantage of desktop publishing over word processing is that desktop publishing software

□ is faster at composing copy

□ handles mailing lists

□ handles all the functions in the computer

□ is cheaper than word processors

□ _____

Hardware

Write in a word or phrase to complete each of the following statements correctly.

1. Except for _____computers, almost all computers today use PC DOS or MS DOS.

2. Most computers using MS DOS and PC DOS are _____with each other.

3. _____computers were the pioneers in desktop publishing and are still leading players in that field.

4. In today's market it does not make sense to use a desktop computer without a _____.

5. For word processing, it is usually most practical to use a _____monitor.

Appendix

The journey is far from over; you have yet many miles to go. Here I offer you a road map to guide you on your way.

This book represents an ambitious undertaking, in that I have essayed here to cover the vast field of developing sales and promotional materials of all kinds for all situations, using both conventional or traditional methods and the most modern technology. I do not represent that everything known or worth knowing is contained between these covers. Quite the contrary, this is just the beginning of your journey through this field. I therefore offer here, in this final section, a diverse array of what I hope will be valuable reference materials. Included here are bibliographic listings of books, periodicals, and computer programs; lists of consultants and mailing-list brokers; and other such resources. Of course, these are mere starter listings, a small fraction of all the resources available to you as help; you will undoubtedly discover many more as you proceed to master the art of developing sales and promotional materials.

■ A Few Useful Books

Arth, Marvin and Ashmore, Helen, *The Newsletter Editor's Desk Book*, Shawnee Mission: Parkway Press, 1980.

Bly, Robert W., *Create the Perfect Sales Piece*, New York: John Wiley, 1985.

Caples, John, *How to Make Your Advertising Make Money*, Englewood Cliffs: Prentice-Hall, Inc., 1983.

Gosden, Freeman F., Jr., *Direct Marketing Success*, New York: John Wiley, 1985.

Hoge, Cecil C., Sr., *Mail Order Moonlighting*, Berkeley: Ten Speed Press, 1976.

Holtz, Herman, *The Direct Marketer's Workbook*, New York: John Wiley, 1986.

Holtz, Herman, *Marketing with Seminars and Newsletters*, Westport: Quorum Books, 1986.

Kuswa, Webster, *Sell Copy*, Cincinnati: Writer's Digest Books, 1979.

Lewis, Herschell Gordon, *Direct Mail Copy that Sells!*, Englewood Cliffs: Prentice-Hall, Inc., 1984.

■ Relevant Periodicals

DM News, Mill Hollow Corporation, W. 21st Street, New York, NY 10010. Trade journal of direct marketing; semi-monthly tabloid; free to "qualified" individuals and organizations.

Target Marketing, North American Publishing Co., 401 N. Broad Street, Philadelphia, PA. Monthly trade journal—smooth-paper magazine format; free to "qualified" individuals and organizations.

Direct Response Letter, Galen Stilson, P.O. Box 1075, Tarpon Springs, FL 34286. Monthly newsletter of Stilson, a copy consultant.

■ Computer Software

Macros or Key Redefiners

SmartKey,™ Software Research Technologies

ProKey,™ RoseSoft, Inc.

Word Processors

WordStar,® MicroPro® International Corporation

WordPerfect,™ Satellite Software International

MS Word,™ Microsoft® Corporation

PC-Write, Buttonware, P.O. Box 5786, Bellevue, WA 98006 (shareware)

Galaxy, OmniVerse, P.O. Box 2974, Renton, WA 98056 (shareware)

Desktop Publishing Programs

The Newsroom Pro,™ Springboard Software, Inc.

ClickArt Personal Publisher,™ Software Publishing Corporation

Fontasy,™ ProSoft®

FormWorx,™ Analytx International, Inc.

PageMaker,® Aldus Corporation

Harvard™ *Presentation Graphics*, Software Publishing Corporation

Idea/Outline Processors

Ready,™ Living Videotext, Inc.

PC-Outline, Softwork Development, 750 Stierlin Road, Suite 142, Mountain View, CA 94043 (shareware)

Readability Measurement

Maxi-Read, RWS & Associates, 132 Alpine Terrace, San Francisco, CA 94117 (shareware)

PC-Read, Joey Robichaux, Wash 'n' Ware Software Products, P.O. Box 91016-199, Baton Rouge, LA 70821 (shareware)

Read, A Program to Calculate Flesch Readability Scores, Glenn Spiegel, 4821 Morgan Drive, Chevy Chase, MD 20815 (shareware)

Fog Finder, Joey Robichaux, 1036 Brookhollow Drive, Baton Rouge, LA 70810 (shareware)

Mailing List Processor

Mass Appeal, Steve Hughes, 1422 Applegate Drive, Alabaster, AL 35007 (shareware)

■ A Few Mailing-List Brokers

American List Counsel, Inc.
88 Orchard Road
Princeton, NJ 08540
(201) 874-4300
800-526-3973

Association for Computing
Machinery
11 West 42nd Street
New York, NY 10036
(212) 869-7440

Boardroom Lists
330 West 42nd Street
New York, NY 10036
(212) 239-9000

Cahners Direct Marketing Service
1350 East Touhy Avenue
Des Plaines, IL 60018
(312) 635-8800

Compilers Plus
2 Penn Place
Pelham Manor, NY 10803
(914) 738-1520
800-431-2914

Dependable List Management
33 Irving Place, NY 10003
(212) 677-6760

1825 K Street, NW
Washington, DC 20006
(202) 452-1092

Direct Media List Management
Group, Inc.
70 Riverdale Avenue
Greenwich, CT 06830
(203) 531-1091

D-J Associates
Box 2048
445 Main Street
Ridgefield, CT 06877
(203) 431-0452

Ed Burnett Consultants, Inc.
2 Park Avenue
New York, NY 10016
(212) 679-0630
800-223-7777

Hayden Direct Marketing Services
10 Mulholland Drive
Hasbrouck Heights, NJ 07604
(201) 393-6384

ICO List Rental Services
9000 Keystone Crossing
P.O. Box 40946
Indianapolis, IN 46240
(317) 844-7461

The Kleid Company, Inc.
200 Park Avenue
New York, NY 10166
(212) 599-4140

List Services Corporation
890 Ethan Allen Hwy
P.O. Box 2014
Ridgefield, CT 06877
(203) 436-0327

Phillips List Management
7315 Wisconsin Avenue,
   Suite 1200N
Bethesda, MD 20814
(301) 986-0666

PCS Mailing List Company
125 Main Street
Peabody, MA 01960
(617) 532-1600

Qualified Lists Corp.
135 Bedford Road
Armonk, NY 10504
(212) 409-6200
(914) 273-6700

Roman Managed Lists, Inc.
101 West 31st Street
New York, NY 10001
(212) 695-3838
800-223-2195

Steve Millard, Inc.
Spring Hill Road
Peterborough, NH 03458
(603) 924-9421

Woodruff-Stevens & Associates,
   Inc.
345 Park Avenue South
New York, NY 10010
(212) 685-4600

■ Advertising Services and Mailers

DialAmerica Marketing, Inc.
125 Galway Place
Teaneck, NJ 07666
(201) 837-7800
Telemarketing

Fala Direct Marketing, Inc.
70 Marcus Drive
Melville, NY 11747
(516) 694-1919
Mailing, fulfillment, printing,
data processing, telemarketing

Hahn, Crane, Inc., Advertising
114 West Illinois
Chicago, IL 60610
(312) 787-8435
Advertising, consulting

Hughes Communications, Inc.
211 West State Street
P.O. Box 197
Rockford, IL 61105
(815) 963-7771
800-435-2937
Card deck mailings

Solar Press
5 South 550 Frontenac
Naperville, IL 60566
(312) 357-0100
Card deck mailings

Index